New Directions in
Professional Higher Education

SRHE and Open University Press Imprint
General Editor: Heather Eggins

Current titles include:

Catherine Bargh *et al.*: *Governing Universities*
Ronald Barnett: *The Idea of Higher Education*
Ronald Barnett: *The Limits of Competence*
Ronald Barnett: *Higher Education*
Ronald Barnett: *Realizing the University in an age of supercomplexity*
Neville Bennett *et al.*: *Skills Development in Higher Education and Employment*
John Biggs: *Teaching for Quality Learning at University*
David Boud *et al.* (eds): *Using Experience for Learning*
Etienne Bourgeois *et al.*: *The Adult University*
Tom Bourner *et al.*(eds): *New Directions in Professional Higher Education*
John Brennan *et al.* (eds): *What Kind of University?*
Anne Brockbank and Ian McGill: *Facilitating Reflective Learning in Higher Education*
Stephen Brookfield and Stephen Preskill: *Discussion as a Way of Teaching*
Ann Brooks: *Academic Women*
Sally Brown and Angela Glasner (eds): *Assessment Matters in Higher Education*
John Cowan: *On Becoming an Innovative University Teacher*
Heather Eggins (ed.): *Women as Leaders and Managers in Higher Education*
Gillian Evans: *Calling Academia to Account*
David Farnham (ed.): *Managing Academic Staff in Changing University Systems*
Sinclair Goodlad: *The Quest of Quality*
Harry Gray (ed.): *Universities and the Creation of Wealth*
Norman Jackson and Helen Lund (eds): *Benchmarking for Higher Education*
Merle Jacob and Tomas Hellström (eds): *The Future of Knowledge Production in the Academy*
Mary Lea and Barry Stierer (eds): *Student Writing in Higher Education*
Elaine Martin: *Changing Academic Work*
David Palfreyman and David Warner (eds): *Higher Education and the Law*
John Pratt: *The Polytechnic Experiment*
Craig Prichard: *Making Managers in Universities and Colleges*
Michael Prosser and Keith Trigwell: *Understanding Learning and Teaching*
John Richardson: *Researching Student Learning*
Stephen Rowland: *The Enquiring University Teacher*
Yoni Ryan and Ortrun Zuber-Skerritt (eds): *Supervising Postgraduates from Non-English
    Speaking Backgrounds*
Maggi Savin-Baden: *Problem-based Learning in Higher Education*
Peter Scott (ed.): *The Globalization of Higher Education*
Peter Scott: *The Meanings of Mass Higher Education*
Anthony Smith and Frank Webster (eds): *The Postmodern University?*
Imogen Taylor: *Developing Learning in Professional Education*
Peter G. Taylor: *Making Sense of Academic Life*
Susan Toohey: *Designing Courses for Higher Education*
Paul R. Trowler: *Academics Responding to Change*
David Warner and Elaine Crosthwaite (eds): *Human Resource Management in Higher and
    Further Education*
David Warner and Charles Leonard: *The Income Generation Handbook* (2nd edn)
David Warner and David Palfreyman (eds): *Higher Education Management*
Diana Woodward and Karen Ross: *Managing Equal Opportunities in Higher Education*

New Directions in Professional Higher Education

Edited by
Tom Bourner, Tim Katz
and David Watson

The Society for Research into Higher Education
& Open University Press

Published by SRHE and
Open University Press
Celtic Court
22 Ballmoor
Buckingham
MK18 1XW

email: enquiries@openup.co.uk
world wide web: http://www.openup.co.uk

and 325 Chestnut Street
Philadelphia, PA 19106, USA

First published 2000

A catalogue record of this book is available from the British Library

ISBN 0 335 20614 X (pbk)   0 335 20615 8 (hbk)

Library of Congress Cataloging-in-Publication Data
New directions in professional higher education / edited by Tom Bourner,
Tim Katz, and David Watson.
     p.   cm.
   Includes bibliographical references and index.
   ISBN 0-335-20615-8 (hb)—ISBN 0-335-20614-X (pb)
   1. Professional education—Great Britain—Case studies.   2. Continuing
education—Great Britain—Case studies.   3. Education, Higher—Great
Britain—Case studies.   4. University of Brighton.   I. Bourner, Tom, 1955–
II. Katz, Tim, 1952–   III. Watson, David, 1949–

   LC1072.C56 N49   2000
   374'.973—dc21   99–050129

Typeset by Graphicraft Limited, Hong Kong
Printed in Great Britain by St Edmundsbury Press, Bury St Edmunds, Suffolk

Contents

Contributors

University of Brighton contributors

Linda Ball is Senior Lecturer and Area Leader for Business and Professional Practice in the School of Architecture and Design.

Ivan Birch teaches in the Department of Podiatry.

Maggie Blake is the Coordinator of the Centre for Learning and Teaching.

Tom Bourner is Professor of Personal and Professional Development in the Faculty of Business.

Rachel Bowden is Senior Research Project Assistant in the Education Research Centre, Faculty of Education and Sport.

Gordon Bull is Professor of Information Technology and Dean of the Faculty of Information Technology.

Lynne Caladine is Head of Division of Physiotherapy, School of Healthcare Professions, Faculty of Health.

Maggie Carroll is Head of the School of Education.

Duncan Cullimore is a senior lecturer in business education.

Martin Daniels is European Director of Studies in the Faculty of Information Technology.

Steve Flowers is a principal lecturer and programme manager in the School of Business.

Linda France is Research Projects Assistant in the Centre for Learning and Teaching.

Richard Griffiths is Senior Lecturer in the School of Computing and Mathematical Sciences.

Lorraine Harrison is Course Leader (PGCE Primary Years) in the School of Education.

Tony Hartley is Professor of Language Engineering in the School of Languages and Associate Researcher at the Information Technology Research Institute.

Katie Herson is the School of Pharmacy and Biomolecular Sciences IT Support Officer.

Robert Hughes teaches software project management on a number of courses at both undergraduate and postgraduate level.

Colin Jackson is a principal lecturer in the School of Computing and Mathematical Sciences and course leader for the undergraduate degrees in computer science and software engineering.

Tim Katz is a principal lecturer in engineering as well as a member of the Centre for Learning and Teaching.

Stuart Laing is Assistant Director (Academic Affairs).

Jackie Langley is a social worker and a senior lecturer in social work.

Andrew Lloyd is Reader in Pharmaceutical and Biomedical Sciences.

Avril Loveless is a senior lecturer in IT in education.

Marion Martin is an occupational therapist, and is a senior lecturer on the postgraduate diploma in occupational therapy.

Katharine Martyn is a senior lecturer in applied life sciences, module leader and personal tutor.

Ann Moore is Professor of Physiotherapy and Head of the Clinical Research Unit for Healthcare Professions in the Faculty of Health.

Jane Morris is Clinical Education tutor for the School of Healthcare Professions (Physiotherapy).

Becci Newton is a programme administrator for postgraduate programmes within the School of Business.

Suzanne O'Hara is a senior lecturer in the Faculty of Business and is also a member of the Management Development Research Unit.

Cameron Paine is a senior technician in the School of Business.

Patrick Palmer lectures in civil engineering.

Lyn Pemberton is Principal Lecturer in the School of Information Management.

Angela Pickering is a senior lecturer in TESOL (teaching English to speakers of other languages) in the School of Languages.

Raf Salkie is Principal Lecturer in the School of Languages.

Daniel Simpson is Head of the School of Computing and Mathematical Sciences.

Jenny Smith is a senior lecturer in occupational therapy within the School of Healthcare Professions.

Mike Smith is a senior lecturer in the School of Computing and Mathematical Sciences.

Michael Hal Sosabowski is a lecturer in chemistry in the School of Pharmacy and Biomolecular Sciences.

Graham Stew is a principal lecturer in nursing.

David Watson is Director of the University of Brighton.

Catherine Watts is a senior lecturer in the School of Languages.

In addition, the following authors have contributed to the book; they are not members of the University of Brighton:

Jacques Meyranx, Pantxika Dagorret and *Thierry Nodemot* are from the team from the Institut Universitaire de Technologie IUT of Bayonne.

Javier Torrealdea and *Endika Bengoetxea* represent the Department of Computer Science of the University of the Basque Country (UPV/EHU), San Sebastián, Spain.

Frank Giannasi is Senior Lecturer in Computing at the University of Coventry.

Carlos Navarra and *Fernando Almaraz* teach in the Department of Business Studies, University of Salamanca, Spain.

Foreword

By Sir William Stubbs
Chairman of the Qualifications and Curriculum Authority

The case in the UK for lifelong learning is now widely accepted. However, if it is to become reality for new generations of adult learners, two prerequisites are necessary in our national arrangements: the construction of a comprehensible framework of qualifications and improvements in the ease of access to learning opportunities that lead to these qualifications.

Since it was established two years ago, the Qualifications and Curriculum Authority has made it a priority to put in place a framework of qualifications. Inevitably there have been obstacles to overcome. The traditional British distinction between academic and vocational qualifications has meant that they have tended to be regarded as separate from, rather than complementary to, one another. However, as we enter the new millennium, a new framework should be well on the way to becoming a reality.

At the same time, the Quality Assurance Agency for Higher Education is developing the qualifications framework for higher education, giving particular consideration to the importance of lifelong learning and employability.

As all this work progresses, it seems inevitable that both full- and part-time students who are preparing for work, in work or out of work, will expect to see more opportunities to find a place within a coherent system of qualifications: a system that avoids typecasting the participants according to their educational past or their intended employment futures. Consequently, there is pressure on higher education institutions, collectively as well as individually, to make the arrangements for learning opportunities leading to professional qualifications more transparent and flexible.

Against this background, this volume of critical commentary and analytical material is very relevant. It comes from the University of Brighton, which is one of the more professionally oriented British universities, as measured by the proportion of its courses leading to professionally and vocationally recognized qualifications. Moreover, its reputation for teaching in support of professional preparation and development is supported by a dedication to the effective transfer and application of research findings in a professional setting. The University has been active in developing new forms of partnership in higher education (local, national and international), new priorities for pedagogy (such as work-based learning) and new applications of technology (especially communications technology). The editors and authors of this collection have provided a valuable lesson in capturing both the dimensions and trajectory of this increasingly important part of a diverse higher education sector.

Preface and Acknowledgements

The material in this volume is of three types.

The three 'introductory' chapters attempt to place professional higher education in a context of government policy, social and economic demands, changing roles within work (including working in higher education itself) and pedagogical theory and practice. An overarching theme is the increasing engagement of higher education practice with an external world, at all levels of significance and complexity from the local to the global.

The heart of the book is then in the twenty-one case studies that comprise the next seven chapters. As in a preceding SRHE/Open University Press volume on *Developing Professional Education* (Bines and Watson 1992), an attempt has been made to ally overall developments within the field of professional higher education with immediate, tangible assessment of their impact on practice. At the beginning of the 1990s the hard questions were about modularity in course design, the relationship of traditional disciplines to vocational practice and the assessment of skills and competence. As we enter the first decade of the new millennium, several of these issues seem somewhat dated. Their place has been taken by new dilemmas about partnership, independent learning, the rapid spread of communications and information technology in the workplace (and especially the availability of the Internet), the globalization of the higher education enterprise and much more pervasive and intense expectations of the 'work-readiness' of graduates. Meanwhile, the expansion and democratization of UK higher education has meant that traditional questions about the maintenance and benchmarking of standards persist.

Each of the authors of these sections has been asked to perform an evaluative as well as a descriptive task. This 'book within a book' is intended to provide a compendium of cutting-edge practice – in areas ranging from art and design, through business, computing, education, science, engineering and languages to the most recent additions to the higher education family in nursing, midwifery and the professions allied to medicine. Some such practice is now well-embedded; some is in response to challenges of which the full impact has yet to be felt (for example, the case of teacher accreditation in higher education). In all cases, however, the authors present an honest, well-researched account of what has worked, what seems to be working and the reciprocal.

Finally, three chapters look forward to generic questions about the future of professional higher education. What will be the framework in which both individuals and other interested parties (such as sponsors and employers) conceptualize and record the progress of lifelong learning? What will be the role within this framework of new qualifications at the very highest (doctoral) level? And what will be the implications for research into professional practice? The concluding chapter juxtaposes a new species of research (practitioner-centred research) to sit alongside the traditional assumptions about research in science and in the humanities.

A collaborative enterprise like this aims at an outcome where the sum is more than that of the parts. Many members of the extended community of this highly professionally orientated university – students, staff and external partners and supporters – have made hugely significant contributions to the work of the authors and the editors. To name names would add the equivalent of at least another chapter to what is already a substantial volume. The team would, however, like to record their immense gratitude to and admiration of the project manager for the publication. Linda France of the University of Brighton's Centre for Learning and Teaching assisted in the conception of the book and, when it was conceived, put tireless effort and professional skill into ensuring its birth.

Tom Bourner, Tim Katz and David Watson
Brighton, March 2000

Acronyms and Abbreviations

ABRC	Advisory Board for Research Councils
AEL	accreditation of experiential learning
APEL	accreditation of prior experiential learning
APM	Association for Project Management
ASSET	Accrediting Social Services Experience and Training
ASW	Approved Social Worker
AUT	Association of University Teachers
BCS	British Computer Society
BDA	British Dyslexia Association
BMS	Biomedical Science
BSI	Business School Intranet
CAIPE	Centre for the Advancement of Inter-Professional Education
CAL	computer-assisted learning
CAPAM	Credit Accumulation for the Professions Allied to Medicine
CATS	credit accumulation and transfer
CCETSW	Central Council for Education and Training in Social Work
CCTA	Central Computing and Telecommunications Agency
CDP	career development plan
CHEAD	Committee for Higher Education in Art and Design
CIT	communications information technology
CLT	Centre for Learning and Teaching
CNAA	Council for National Academic Awards
COT	College of Occupational Therapists
CPA	critical path analysis
CPD	continuing professional development
CPSM	Council for Professions Supplementary to Medicine
CSP	Chartered Society of Physiotherapy
CTI–AFM	Computers in Teaching Initiative – Accounting, Finance and Management

CVCP	Committee of Vice-chancellors and Principals
DBA	Doctor of Business Administration
DES	Department of Education and Science
DfEE	Department for Education and Employment
DHSS	Department of Health and Social Security
DoH	Department of Health
EAL	enquiry and action learning
EdD	Doctor of Education
EFL	English as a foreign language
ENB	English National Board
EngD	Engineering Doctorate
EPSRC	Engineering and Physical Sciences Research Council
GCSE	General Certificate in Secondary Education
GNVQ	General National Vocational Qualification
GUI	graphical user interface
HCA	healthcare assistant
HCI	human–computer interaction
HEFCE	Higher Education Funding Council for England
HESA	Higher Education Statistics Agency
HMSO	Her Majesty's Stationery Office
HTML	hypertext mark-up language
ICT	information and communications technology
IFAL	International Foundation for Action Learning
ILA	Individual Learning Accounts
ILT	Institute for Learning and Teaching in Higher Education
InCCA	Inter-Consortium Credit Agreement
INAM	Institute of Nursing and Midwifery
IP	intensive programme
IS	information system
ISDN	Integrated Services Digital Network
ISEB	Information Systems Examination Board
ISM	Industry Structure Model
ISO	International Organization for Standardization
IS/IT	information systems/information technology
IT	information technology
ITT	initial teacher training
IUT	Institut Universitaire de Technologie
MBA	Masters in Business Administration
NACETT	National Advisory Council for Education and Training Targets
NATFHE	National Association for Teachers in Further and Higher Education
NCIHE	National Committee of Inquiry into Higher Education
NCVQ	National Council for Vocational Qualifications
NHS	National Health Service
NIACE	National Institute of Adult Continuing Education

NVQ	National Vocational Qualification
Ofsted	Office for Standards in Education
OHP	overhead projections
OLE	On-line Localization Europe
OST	Office of Science and Technology
PAMs	Professions Allied to Medicine
PBL	problem-based learning
PC	personal computer
PCR	Practitioner-centred Research
PDS	Professional Development Scheme
PhD	Doctor of Philosophy
PiE	Partnerships in Education
PM	project management
PMI	Project Management Institute
PPD	personal and professional development
QAA	Quality Assurance Agency
QTS	Qualified Teacher Status
REs	research engineers
RSA	Royal Society of Arts
SARTOR	Standards and Routes to Registration
SCOP	Standing Conference of Principals
SEDA	Staff and Educational Development Association
SEEC	South East England Consortium
SERC	Science and Engineering Research Council
SME	small and medium sized enterprises
SRHE	Society for Research into Higher Education
SSADM	soft systems analysis and design methodology
TCC	Teaching Company Centre
TESOL	teaching English to speakers of other languages
TTA	Teacher Training Agency
UCAS	Universities and Colleges Admission Service
UCLES DELTA	University of Cambridge Diploma in English Language Teaching to Adults
UK	United Kingdom
UKCC	United Kingdom Central Council
UKERNA	United Kingdom Education and Research Networking Association

Part 1

Setting the Scene

1

Lifelong Learning and Professional Higher Education

David Watson

Professional higher education

Higher education has always been 'for the professions'. Alongside the 'inquiry-based' disciplines of the humanities and the natural sciences, courses of study have prepared students for careers in the church, in law, in medicine, in administration and in the range of technical and professional domains on which society depends.

This historical perspective presents an important corrective to the claims of those who see 'vocational' interest, 'skills' development or even 'outcome'-orientated course design as corrosive of the higher education enterprise itself (Warnock 1996). Often they are making political or status judgements about types of institution as well as types of course, especially when reflecting on the reforms in the UK of the late 1980s and early 1990s, which first gave 'incorporated' independence and then the 'university' title to the former polytechnics (Watson and Bowden 1997).

It was the distinctive strength of the polytechnics that they were able to bring together the 'academic' values associated with subjects and disciplines and the 'professional' values attached to practice and vocation. They did so by engaging in dialogue with employers and professional and statutory bodies regulating recognition and entry into professional practice. They devised new course structures, especially those like 'thin' and 'thick' sandwich courses involving direct work experience. Above all, through the overarching academic authority of the Council for National Academic Awards (CNAA), which 'validated' and then awarded degrees under a central charter, they contributed through peer review, critically involving disciplinary specialists from the 'traditional' university sector as well as 'professional' perspectives from outside of the academy, to the 'enlargement' of the academic enterprise itself (Silver 1990: 90–110). This ensured that diplomas and degrees in so-called 'new' subjects and for professions new to higher education, especially in health and management, joined a single system of higher education with at least formal parity of esteem. The value of this overall development is

Figure 1.1   Number of students by mode of study and level of course, 1979–98

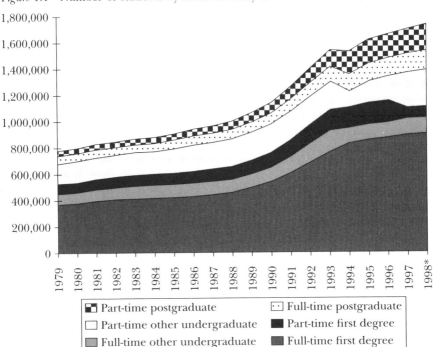

* Provisional data

Sources: DES, 1991, 1992; DfE, 1994; IES, 1996; HESA, 1996, 1997, 1998a, 1999.

clearly shown in research that links work experience within courses, as well as the choice of course, with early success for graduates in finding employment (Harvey and Bowes 1998).

British culture and British public life is, however, profoundly hierarchical, and the advocates of this expansion of professional higher education have had to fight many of the same battles as those concerned to improve the status and recognition of vocational qualifications in the compulsory and '16–19' phases of education. There are now, within the context of the lifelong learning debate, encouraging signs that the key battles are being won.

First there is the demographic data about patterns of participation in higher education. As Figure 1.1 shows, a majority of participants in higher education in the UK are not on full-time first degrees. The 'non-traditional' modes and levels of study – part-time, postgraduate, post-experience, subdegree – are heavily dominated by employment-related aspirations, both for initial employment and mid-career progress. In effect, even before we had the *policies* to underwrite lifelong learning (an equalization of the fee and support structures for full- and part-time students, professional body requirements

Figure 1.2 Home applicants and acceptances through UCAS by subject group, 1997 entry

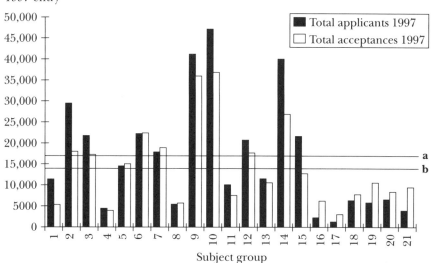

a, average applicants; b, average acceptances.

Subject groups

1. Medicine/dentistry
2. Subjects allied to medicine
3. Biological sciences
4. Agriculture and related subjects
5. Physical sciences
6. Mathematical sciences and informatics
7. Engineering and technology
8. Architecture, building and planning
9. Social studies
10. Business and administrative studies
11. Mass communications and documentation

12. Languages and related disciplines
13. Humanities
14. Creative arts
15. Education
16. Combined sciences
17. Combined social studies
18. Combined arts
19. Science combined with social studies or arts
20. Social studies combined with arts
21. Other general and combined studies

Source: HESA 1998a.

for updating, Individual Learning Accounts [ILAs], etc.), we apparently had already created the *fact* of lifelong learning in the college and university.

Second, this trend is reinforced by student choice, where the general expansion of higher education has been accompanied (in the UK as around the world) with a swing towards professionally and vocationally relevant subjects of study. Figure 1.2 summarizes the data on applications and acceptances processed through the Universities and Colleges Admission Service (UCAS) for 1997–98. This data captures almost the entire set of applications made through the regular cycle of the school and college year and hence provides a snapshot of the preferences of new students. Both the relative volume and the relative demand for practical subjects (medicine, business studies and education) are of interest.

Despite the uncomfortable reactions of the traditionalists, it is hard to evade the conclusion that professional higher education is now in the mainstream. Being there, it has, however, caused some adjustment problems.

Credit and the qualifications jungle

Two such problems relate to credit and the recording of achievement. The government's Green Paper, *The Learning Age*, boldly declares an intention to have a 'national framework for higher education awards as recommended by the Dearing Committee' and an ambitious timetable: 'the main elements should be in place by 2000. We want to see a Credit Accumulation and Transfer System, to underpin the qualifications framework, and more "stopping-off points", separately accredited, during higher education' (DfEE 1998a: 67). As a recent DfEE-supported project demonstrates, this is feasible, but will pose severe challenges to institutions whose commitment to modularity, to credit accumulation and especially to credit recognition for the purposes of internal or inter-institutional transfer, has been more rhetorical than real (Inter-Consortium Credit Agreement [InCCA] 1998).

On the related matter of qualification titles and comparability, there have been two mutually reinforcing attempts to grapple with the situation. In 1996 a working group established by the Committee of Vice-Chancellors and Principals (CVCP), the Higher Education Funding Council for England (HEFCE) and the Standing Conference of Principals (SCOP), chaired by Martin Harris, tackled the specific problems of nomenclature, levels and standards of postgraduate awards (Harris 1996). In 1997, and building on the work of Harris, the Dearing Committee attempted a comprehensive set of proposals, as set out in Figure 1.3 (National Committee of Inquiry into Higher Education [NCIHE] 1997 Summary Report: 18).

Sorting out credit and qualifications, in the interests of flexibility, responsiveness and above all portability of achievement, will require systematic sector-wide commitment. This is an arena where simple 'market' forces cannot be allowed to decide.

'Stakeholders'

Professional higher education builds partnerships and alliances inside and outside of the academy. It is the antithesis of the 'secret' garden image of the curriculum. It requires negotiation, shared purpose and, above all, transparency of aims and outcomes.

The decision by the National Health Service (NHS) to shift the majority of its training for professionals other than doctors into the higher education sector is an excellent test case of these tensions and potential rewards in action. In this new context, the 'service' (represented by health authorities, trusts and purchasing consortia) will want not only value for money and a

Figure 1.3 Dearing qualifications framework

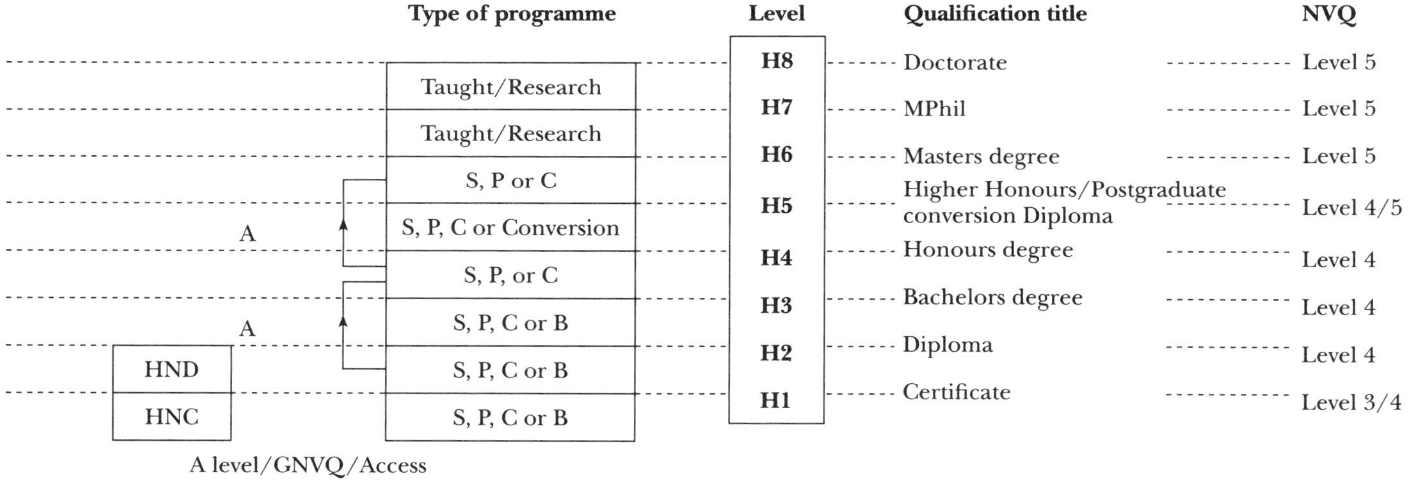

Type of programme	Level	Qualification title	NVQ
Taught/Research	H8	Doctorate	Level 5
	H7	MPhil	Level 5
Taught/Research	H6	Masters degree	Level 5
S, P or C	H5	Higher Honours/Postgraduate conversion Diploma	Level 4/5
S, P, C or Conversion	H4	Honours degree	Level 4
S, P, or C	H3	Bachelors degree	Level 4
S, P, C or B	H2	Diploma	Level 4
S, P, C or B	H1	Certificate	Level 3/4
S, P, C or B			

A level/GNVQ/Access

HND

HNC

Type of programme
A = Accelerated route if correct number of specialist credit points acquired
B = Broad range of subjects
C = Combined subjects
P = Subject leading to professional status
S = Single subject
Conversion = postgraduate conversion course

Notes
1. Each level up to H4 would require at least 120 additional credit points.
2. Students pursuing broad programmes at levels H1, H2 and H3 and securing 360 credit points would be awarded a Bachelors degree.
3. To achieve an Honours degree would require at least 360 specialist credit points. The rate of progress would depend on the amount of previous specialization.
4. It would be for each institution, consulting as appropriate with professinal bodies, to determine the pattern of credits (e.g. how much specialization or how much breadth) required to qualify for an Honours degree.

Source: NCIHE 1997, Summary Report p. 18.

flow of highly competent professionals, but also an enhanced reputation for the various careers involved (leading ideally to higher recruitment and retention). Simultaneously, the students involved now see themselves as not only pre-professional trainees, but also as fully-fledged participants in the culture of higher education. Meanwhile, teachers and mentors combine further complex roles and expectations, including academic and disciplinary commitments as well as the professional values of practice (Watson and Taylor 1998: 68–72).

As the NHS gambled that trusting higher education for a much greater influence over its professional formation would improve practice and service outcomes in the longer term, another agency (also discussed in this volume) has been marching in the other direction. The Teacher Training Agency (TTA) was established by the last Conservative government as a means of wresting responsibility for the professional formation of teachers away from higher education. It has achieved this through a mixture of outsourcing (supporting other providers and new 'routes' to qualification), curricular prescription (there is now a 'national curriculum' for initial teacher training [ITT]) and retention of external quality control (through the Office for Standards in Education [Ofsted]).

It is no accident that a large number of the cases testing new ground for professional formation in this volume come from the areas of health and education.

New Labour

The new Labour government has given no indication that it is at all uncomfortable with these developments. In its combined enthusiasms for 'education, education, education' and 'lifelong learning' the government elected in May 1997 has done much to create the circumstances in which professional higher education should flourish.

The new government received early advice from:

- the Kennedy Report (Kennedy 1997), *Learning Works: widening participation in further education* (June 1997);
- the Dearing Report (NCIHE 1997), *Higher Education in the Learning Society* (July 1997); and
- the Report of the Fryer Committee (Fryer 1997), *Learning for the Twenty-First Century* (November 1997).

They published their response in February 1998 in three papers:

- a Green Paper (DfEE 1998a), *The Learning Age: a renaissance for a new Britain*;
- a response to the Dearing Report (DfEE 1998b), *Higher Education for the 21st Century*; and
- a response to the Kennedy Report (DfEE 1998c), *Further Education for the New Millennium.*

The key ideas in *Learning Works* were as follows:

- equity in access, particularly for those who have so far played no role in the post-compulsory system;
- the need to focus on achievement at Level 3 ('A' Level equivalent) in particular;
- re-prioritization of funding, plus potential use of the Lottery; and
- overcoming inefficiency and waste in administration and funding, as well as the benefits system.

The main arguments in *Higher Education in the Learning Society* were for:

- the contribution of higher education to an integrated system of lifelong learning;
- a new vision for learning and teaching in higher education;
- funding research properly, and according to its intended outcomes; and
- the new compact between students and their sponsors, institutions and government (representing the national interest) (Watson and Taylor 1998: 151–2).

The core argument in *Learning for the Twenty-First Century* was for the establishment of a universal 'learning culture'. The Committee's brief was to clear the way for a White (rather than a Green) Paper on Lifelong Learning, and its main role was to compile lists of initiatives that have worked or could work, with no real prioritization or costings.

In paragraph 4.28 the Green Paper (DfEE 1998a) set out a vision for higher education institutions, as follows:

> We wish universities, higher and further education institutions to be beacons of learning in their local communities. At today's participation rates, 60 per cent of school leavers can expect to enter higher education at some time in their lives. We propose that higher education should play an even bigger part in future by:
> - providing more places to meet demand;
> - offering a wide range of courses up to postgraduate level;
> - ensuring high standards so as to enhance the employability of graduates;
> - improving participation by offering opportunities later in life to those who missed out first time around;
> - contributing more to the economy and being more responsive to the needs of business;
> - collaborating effectively with other institutions, other learning providers and with the world of work; and
> - making itself more accessible by exploiting new technology and flexible delivery with facilities available at times convenient to students.

The government has also continued the role of the National Advisory Council for Education and Training Targets (NACETT). In their latest review, *Fast Forward for Skills*, the targets for 'lifetime achievement' at Levels

3 and 4 have been modified downwards (to 50 per cent from 60 per cent for Level 3 and from 30 per cent to 28 per cent for Level 4, by 2002). The reasons are different. At Level 3 it is claimed that the new target is 'the highest level that we can realistically expect to reach by 2002', but noted that 'we shall need to do much better in the longer term to catch up with our competitors'. At the higher education Level (4), where progress appears to have stuck at just over 25 per cent, 'the big danger we face is complacency: the fact that we are relatively well-placed internationally at present does not mean that we can afford to relax our efforts to raise attainment' (NACETT 1998: 6, 44).

The institutional challenge

As the case studies in this volume graphically illustrate, the 'lifelong learning' agenda poses a complex pattern of challenges to institutions. Some of these are about marketing and promotion: the need to engage with new and prospective markets while maintaining traditional strengths and 'presence' within professional higher education. A second set is about collaboration and partnerships, and a series of 'boundary' questions with which higher education has found it traditionally difficult to deal. The heart of the matter, however, probably lies in the curriculum, its content and its delivery.

On this there are clearly potentially positive and negative outcomes. On the downside there could be pressures to restrict the curricular 'conversation', which is now seen as at the heart of collaborative development (Bocock and Watson 1994: 132–7). These pressures could be compounded by competition between models and frameworks of responsibility for quality assurance, with the net result of a sense of lower status and esteem for whole institutions and individual departments most closely associated with professional higher education. The upside alternative would see institutions seizing the initiative in collaboration with professional and statutory bodies, with a resulting upgrade of both entry-level and continuing professional development (CPD) courses in terms of their attractiveness and the standards achieved. Such courses would maintain the 'added value' of higher education's focus on relevant knowledge as well as practice, and thereby deepen and intensify the tradition of professional higher education. The essays and the case studies in this volume are dedicated to supporting such a worthy outcome.

2

Issues of Professionalism in Higher Education

Catherine Watts

The previous chapter introduced developments in higher education that took place during the 1980s and 1990s. This chapter seeks to explore some of the issues that arise from these changes and affect the lives of those who work and study in higher education today.

As Barnett (1997b) asserts, higher education has become a world of 'supercomplexity' and rapid change. It is, he argues, a world of uncertainty, unpredictability, challengeability and contestability in which our frameworks for understanding ourselves and the circumstances in which we live and work are increasingly complex. If we look at some of the issues facing staff and students in higher education, we can see that it is indeed complicated, even 'supercomplicated'.

From a personal point of view, working as a lecturer for the past 16 years in higher education, the three key changes that have had the greatest impact on my working life have been:

1. I now have to operate within a credit framework that includes the semesterization of the academic year, franchising, modularity and the accreditation of work-based and prior learning.
2. I have had to adapt to working in an environment of increasing student numbers as a result of higher education moving from an élite to a mass system in the 1990s. This has led to larger class sizes and an increase in administration together with a relative decline in resources.
3. I have been increasingly subject to government inspections, including the Research Assessment Exercises. This has led to research, publications and professional development competing for time with the preparation and delivery of quality teaching.

As a consequence of these changes, most academic staff working in higher education today operate within a system that is fundamentally different to the one they themselves experienced as students. It is a system that requires them to constantly balance and re-balance the demands placed upon them in terms of teaching (particularly within new and changing curriculum frameworks), administration, scholarly activity and income generation. This raises important issues for academic staff concerning their professional roles at work, and these issues need to be addressed by the wider academic community.

The nature of the social and cultural changes specifically affecting higher education have been well-documented by McNay (1995), Wagner (1995), Halsall and Hustler (1996) and Middlehurst and Kennie (1997). The last argue that the changes are characterized by incremental shifts in the economic, technological, political and social context. The impact of such changes leads professionals to question all aspects of professionalism, including:

> . . . the value and status to be placed on professional knowledge and competence; the balance between implicit trust and explicit accountability between professionals and clients; the appropriate standards governing professional practice and relationships; the degree of independence and autonomy of professionals; and the means of developing and maintaining appropriate professional attitudes and behaviours.
>
> (Middlehurst and Kennie 1997: 52–3)

Eraut (1994a) notes in particular the shift from a profession-centred concept of service defined by the professional to a client-centred concept of service determined by the clients' needs. He also emphasizes the increasing role of government intervention in the regulation of professional work. These developments raise three particular questions. First, what exactly is meant by the concept 'professional'? Second, how have the working lives of professionals been altered by the social and cultural changes that have occurred in higher education? Third, what issues concerning the nature of professionalism in higher education today do these changes raise? The remainder of this chapter seeks to explore these questions.

The nature of professionalism

Downie (1990) argues that the concept of a profession is, and always has been, a developing one and is therefore subject to change. Broadbent, Dietrich and Roberts (1997) note that professionalism itself comprises a diverse set of practices. However, Eraut (1994a: 223) has identified three core concepts concerning the nature of professionalism which are relevant to this chapter:

> Three central features of the ideology of professionalism are a specialist knowledge base, autonomy and service. Each of these has been significantly affected by social and cultural changes over the last two decades.

These three features raise crucial issues for higher education as a whole and have implications for key aspects of professional practice, which will be addressed later in this chapter.

The notion that a professional has a specialist knowledge base is central to the ideology of professionalism. It is this specialist knowledge base that gives a profession social recognition and forms the basis of the professional skills and expertise that are offered to the client. In terms of higher education, it is this specialist knowledge that underpins the professional judgements and decisions made on behalf of the students. However, the academic staff who make these judgements and decisions are increasingly accountable for them to the students, to the university itself and, it could be argued (as it is, for example, by Barnett 1997a), to the taxpayer and the wider society that sanctions professional authority.

However, there is an important distinction to be made between academic knowledge and expertise on the one hand and the knowledge and expertise of professional educators on the other. It has been argued (for example, Chown 1996; Eraut 1994a) that academics in higher education need both educational expertise and subject expertise if they are to be regarded as 'true' professionals. Thus, it is an academic knowledge of the subject discipline combined with a professional knowledge of teaching and education that are embraced by the term 'professional'. Having an academic knowledge-base alone does not necessarily make an academic a professional and the current emphasis on the accreditation of teaching in higher education could therefore be regarded as a move towards the professionalization of academic staff in higher education.

The second key feature of the ideology of professionalism identified by Eraut (1994a) is that of professional autonomy. Chown (1996) argues that individual practitioners in education, working alone or in a team, make frequent judgements and decisions for which they are ultimately accountable. Consequently they are, as professionals, required to exercise a high degree of autonomy. However, as Chown points out, autonomy is, itself, a complex term, being concerned with responsibility and integrity, reasoned action and principles, self-knowledge and critical reflection (Dworkin 1988; Gillon 1986; Hodkinson 1995; Rawls 1971). Chown argues that the concept of autonomy in the context of professional practice must also take account of the client as well as the practitioner. Hence the notions of service to the client, informed consent and accountability.

Middlehurst and Kennie (1997: 65) similarly argue that: 'professional autonomy is premised on relationships of trust built on mutual respect between clients/sponsors and professionals and belief in the value of professional services'. They, like Eraut (1994a), argue that the increasing distrust of professionals, and of professional autonomy, by society in general during the 1980s and 1990s has led to a far greater emphasis on monitoring, quality and accountability for professional services. As a result, the basis of the professional relationship has changed and this has, in turn, led to changes in the nature of professional autonomy.

Nevertheless, most of the academic staff in the higher education sector do still have a degree of professional autonomy that enables them to conduct their duties in a manner that accords with their professional judgements and decisions. However, as Eraut (1994a: 225) points out, the increasing emphasis on accountability has been presented to those who regard themselves as professional workers: 'more as an external control mechanism than as a strengthening of their moral and professional obligations'. Consequently, it has been perceived by many professional workers as a threat to their professional autonomy rather than as a process of guaranteeing professional autonomy and competence.

The third main aspect of professionalism identified by Eraut (1994a) is the notion of service to the client. Downie (1990) argues that a client–professional relationship is typically based on an inequality of power. Professionals, he suggests, hold the dominant position and, because they must supply a service to a more vulnerable client, they must be governed by ethical principles as well as by a desire to act in the client's interests and thereby win the client's trust. However, when the client's interests, as perceived by the professional, are at odds with the perceptions of the client themselves and the client is encouraged to be more assertive, the traditional nature of the client–professional relationship becomes problematic.

Eraut (1994a) notes the changing attitude of clients towards professionals and points out, like Downie (1990), that the notion of client rights has gained increasing acceptance in recent years. In particular, the free-market, liberal ideology that has shaped two decades of public policy and discourse has focused attention on client demand. In the process it has challenged traditional notions of the professional in a dominant position of power acting on behalf of the client in his/her best interests and providing an expert service for that same client.

Issues and implications

The introduction of a market philosophy into higher education has led to significant changes in the working lives of professionals and these changes in turn raise issues and questions concerning the very nature of professionalism itself. Many of the professional judgements made by academics involve the integration of subject specialist expertise with educational expertise. One of the developments that people feel has diminished their capacity to make autonomous, professional decisions based on this expertise is the introduction of modular, credit-based frameworks. These frameworks are argued to provide students with much greater choice. Trowler (1998) also notes that the credit framework appealed to many academics, who felt challenged by the flexibility it offered and stimulated by the fact that new disciplines could be created, such as audio-visual media studies, which attracted new resources and larger numbers of students. Clearly, where changes of this nature are concerned, there are benefits for both students and staff. However, some academics may feel that they are no longer regarded as disciplinary specialists but rather as Jacks or Jills of all trades. Trowler (1998), in his ethnographic case study of an institution of higher education called NewU, found that many of his interviewees:

> ... felt that they were in danger of becoming mere 'deliverers' of modules, interchangeable teachers perceived as having no special skills or qualities and merely there to satisfy the whims of the student 'market'.

> (Trowler 1998: 133)

Many of the academics Trowler interviewed felt that the emphasis in modular, credit-based frameworks on prescribed learning outcomes led to a diminution of autonomy. The interviewees felt: 'this restricted their teaching and assessment strategies' (Trowler 1998: 128) and contributed to feelings of losing their professional autonomy.

The concept of service is also central to this debate. As Eraut (1994a: 225) notes: 'the service ideal is based on the belief that professional action should be based on the needs on the client'. But this begs the question of who the 'clients' in higher education actually are? Are they the students themselves, their parents, the taxpayer, industry or society as a whole? How able are these parties to identify their needs? And to what extent should any or all of these parties determine the character and outcomes of education? It could be argued that some of these parties delegate their interests to the university, which, in turn, employs lecturers who exercise professional judgement in the service they provide to students. In this interpretation, as Barnett (1997a) argues, professionals have responsibilities and obligations to the wider society, as well as to the individual student–client, as it is this wider society that legitimates the professional to act on its behalf.

Questions like these need to be addressed by the academic community, not least because of the increasingly litigious character of customer–provider relations in the 1990s. The advent of clients who feel increasingly empowered to challenge aspects of all professional work, whether in medicine, law or in education, highlights the need to define who the client or customer in higher education really is and how their interests can be best defined and represented.

Even in considering such brief examples as these, it becomes increasingly apparent that the changing concepts of professionalism require those who teach in and manage universities to re-evaluate professional values and practices and to reconsider how much weight should, or indeed can, be given to the views of the consumers of professional services. As Downie (1990) says, there has always been an element of public representation in education, but in recent years the population as a whole has developed a much greater awareness of individual rights. To reject the views of the consumers of higher education could be seen as paternalistic and, indeed, many in education argue that to do so is unacceptable. Middlehurst and Kennie (1997) and Chadbourne (1992), for example, suggest there is a great need for client-centred professional practice in higher education. But we need to ask to what extent should the views of the consumers of professional services be taken into account by professionals? Whose views count, and in what ways? Downie (1990) argues that consumerism is one form of a general 'rights movement' and, as a consequence: 'the tendency is to require the professionals to supply a service on demand, and according to the perceptions of the consumer rather than to those of the professional' (Downie 1990: 158). In the light of such views, it is the responsibility of those working within higher education to address the implications of the changing balance of power between the client and the professional, and to examine what the new roles and relationships should be.

The introduction of the market philosophy over the past decade also raises crucial issues for teaching staff and for managers. As Barton *et al.* (1994: 532) remind us:

> . . . market forces are alleged to be an efficient means of creating the conditions and relationships necessary for freedom of consumers, for allocating scarce resources, generating diversity and providing the form of flexibility the new order requires.

However, the introduction of market forces and notions of competition into the professions has meant that academic staff in higher education could run the risk of losing professional control over both short- and long-term goals, and policy directions in the definition of their work. Many academic staff now feel that the content of their work is increasingly dictated by the demands of the workplace and industry, and by government, as well as by the demands of the individual student–customer. Several recent studies highlight these concerns. In an Australian investigation of the effects market philosophy has on secondary school teachers, Robertson (1996) found that teachers felt they were no longer expected to work as autonomous intellectuals, but rather as people whose workplace was now the marketplace and whose professional roles as a consequence had changed significantly. Gewirtz (1997) also observes that the culture of the work of teachers is changing significantly. Based on her research evidence, she concludes that teachers are experiencing: 'a loss of autonomy and an accelerated intensification of activity and stress' (Gewirtz 1997: 230).

Downie (1990) argues that the attempt to combine market relationships with professional relationships and to introduce these into education will: 'destroy the independence of the professions; it will lead to a search for commercially-led funding, to cost-cutting and subservience to non-educational values' (Downie 1990: 158). These arguments are powerful but, as Trowler (1998: 142) points out: 'Academics' responses themselves have effects on the direction of change just as much as formal policy does', which is why it is crucial that these issues and their implications are discussed on both a formal and an informal level within the wider academic community.

It is also relevant to recognize the changing nature of the 'student–customers' themselves in higher education today. In the UK, their financial circumstances have changed dramatically since the student grants system was introduced in 1962, entitling all university entrants to mandatory awards for fees and maintenance (even though the latter was subject to parental means-testing). Undergraduate numbers rose steadily between the mid-1960s and the mid-1980s, although the main expansion occurred in the following ten years, when the numbers doubled again to over one and a half million. This second major expansion in student numbers was, however, accompanied by a series of measures, introduced between 1980 and 1992, to reduce public expenditure. These included the freezing of the student maintenance grant in nominal terms, the introduction of a student loans system and the withdrawal of the right of most students to claim housing and unemployment benefit and income support during vacations.

The continued rapid expansion of student numbers in higher education, together with the increasing pressures on scarce public resources throughout the 1990s, culminated in the recommendation made by the Dearing Committee to introduce tuition fees on all full-time, as well as part-time, undergraduate courses (NCIHE 1997). The Labour government converted all maintenance grants into loans as well (Blunkett 1997), thus effectively ending the universal entitlement of students in higher education to State funding. Faced with the increasing cost of participating in higher education, and the subsequent personal sacrifices that need to be made to sustain their studies, it is hardly surprising that many students see themselves as empowered customers operating in a market culture. The increasing acceptance of client rights by the general public, together with the fact that students are provided in higher education with expanding opportunities to exercise their right to choice and take an active role in shaping how, when and where they study, illustrates this empowerment of students (Halsall and Hustler 1996).

The trend towards modularity has added to this notion of student choice, as traditional routes of study have become more flexible and a far greater choice of unit combinations has become increasingly available. This increased flexibility on the part of the higher education has boosted recruitment and led in turn to calls for greater accountability to students as the consumers of higher education provision. As Middlehurst and Kennie (1997) note, one of the principle changes in the operating environments of higher education institutions in the UK during the 1980s and 1990s has been the change from academic autonomy to the accountability to stakeholders. It is, they argue, the notions of quality and accountability dominating professional activity that challenge professional independence, autonomy and discretion.

End word

This chapter has sought to highlight some of the issues that arise from a consideration of professionalism, particularly from the perspective of the academic teaching staff in higher education. It is important that paths are found through the issues raised in this chapter, and their implications, if academic staff are to continue to play a part in defining the structures and practices of higher education. It is also important that those working within, and affected by, the changing contexts of higher education actively debate the cultures within the modern university and where they stand in relation to them. This debate needs to take place in as wide an academic forum as possible, on both formal and informal levels, as we can learn much of relevance to the education of our students for, and in, professional employment by reflecting on our own educational needs as professionals in the light of these changes.

3

University Education for Developing Professional Practice

Tim Katz

Introduction

Implicit in the definition of 'professional' from within diverse domains is an expectation of a number of different attributes and skills. Many of these are manifest in a variety of ways in the different professions but can also be recognized as representing a more generic definition. Although sometimes hidden or disfigured by the weight of the profession's evolutionary development, certain common requirements can be identified in nearly all descriptions of the 'competent professional' at graduate level and beyond.

Breadth versus depth

Rather than considering a large number of professions, or focusing on a single profession, this chapter concentrates on a small group of these professions in an attempt to achieve depth without sacrificing breadth. The three professions – engineering, teaching and nursing – were chosen because:

- they have large memberships and are therefore widely recognized;
- they exhibit a wide variety of practice;
- a lot of information is available about these professions, which have well-defined practices and requirements;
- many universities are stakeholders, providing education and training within the professional institutions' domains and having influence on the setting and maintaining of standards;
- conversely, the explicit requirements of these occupational professions can have a great effect on the higher education institutions – failure to satisfy the professional bodies could lead to financial loss and embarrassment;
- the author has direct experience of two of them, helping to set and maintain standards, and ready access to information and expertise in the third.

Each of the three professional disciplines are considered as specific cases, before common themes are recognized and generic attributes teased out.

Engineering

Chartered Engineer status was the default standard for graduate entry until the latest review of the profession. The Standards and Routes to Registration (SARTOR) three procedures (Engineering Council 1997), reorientated the profession towards an MEng. qualification (four years study) for Chartered status and a BEng. for Incorporated status. These changes broadly follow the Dearing philosophy, but were triggered by:

- the internationalization of standards;
- a perceived dilution of entry mathematics standards;
- a mass higher education system requiring other appropriate exit points;
- doubts about equivalency across the universities;
- the emergence of occupational standards.

The differences between EngTech., IEng. and CEng. are described in terms of knowledge base, job function and responsibility, which are then linked to a developmental ethos through CPD. As membership progresses, the role changes from effective working within well established technologies, through operational development to generating new procedures and processes that advance the engineering profession.

The predominant process within engineering is of serialist analysis and deconstruction, with well constrained parameters that allow conceptual development, hypothesis and synthesis. This is a rugged methodology when applied to scientific and technical problems but means that the default metaphor for the learning process is comfortably taken as the transmission model (see below).

The serialist approach is also evident in the whole formation route: a significant academic input is followed by industrial training, then application to work and, finally, assessment for full membership. It is at this stage that the institution member must prove they can plan their own development and relate this to their working context through CPD.

The CPD aspect has gained in stature to become obligatory (not yet mandatory) with an institutional orientation away from earning points for hours attended, towards ensuring an effective personal CPD plan. Sheila Galloway (1998) discusses this as developing the professional and the institution in a way that is demanding personal awareness and critical self-evaluation.

It is difficult to see how some of the 'delivery' within the academic context is going to support the required cognitive and critical functions only demanded later in engineer's formation. Context is limited to what can be synthesized within the academic course, or commonly restricted to a possibly remote sandwich year in industry between the second and final years. The thin sandwich course is now very rare in the UK but, even there, much of the academic study was content based and not directly relevant to the student's job function.

Teaching

Qualified teacher status (QTS) (TTA 1998a) defines a list of competencies that the candidate has to be able to demonstrate. They are grouped under various professional functions but can be viewed as:

- knowledge and application of the teaching subject content and its structuring for pupils within the framework of educational legislation;
- developing staff and pupils' information technology and other generic skills;
- managing the teaching process;
- interrelating within a professional context;
- being a reflective practitioner.

There is no explicit statement about understanding the learning process or reflecting on the models available but there is a requirement for teachers to evaluate and improve their own teaching. Statements about following the effects of environment, age and other variables on pupil learning allow us to infer a requirement for understanding the process of learning. The critical faculties and learning knowledge are left to be developed by the university course. The QTS requirement ensures that teachers have demonstrated competency, not necessarily expertise, i.e. the approach is focused on 'threshold competence' rather than excellence.

It is when the subject specialist definition is inspected (TTA 1998b) that the operational expertise becomes apparent. The teacher must now take responsibility for the development of the subject within the school, making reference to external good practice and team development. Work with others in their subject domain may also lead to developments within the profession.

Further study leads to the achievement of the defined headteacher's role. Effective professional development of themselves and their staff is explicit within the national standards but contribution to the development of the profession itself is not.

All the above teacher standards are recognized as continuously developing, with a publication of a new set of standards when an appreciable difference has evolved. The mechanism for any changes is facilitated by government and informed by the wider profession, with the contribution of a variety of stakeholders. The character of the development may follow policy leads or research momentum but the direction is not determined by a professional institution.

Nursing

Nursing also has similar requirements of the practitioners that are associated with training. They are defined under the Statutory Instruments (1983), set by act of parliament. Courses must be integrated within practice with a professional preceptor or mentor facilitating the placement. This places their professional education in the context of practice but does not assure that students connect theory and practice. The 'rule' that determines competence outcomes has 13 statements that can be grouped as:

- the social and family implications of illness, disability or child bearing;
- propositional knowledge about healthcare;
- patient needs in illness, learning problems and preparation for death;
- procedures of ethics, law and limitations of the role;
- skills of communication, teamwork, problem-solving and management;
- professional development, using research and reflection on common factors.

Active research is encouraged at this level but the development of the profession itself is left to later stages of registration, or through refereed publication.

Professional issues

In this section issues are highlighted that have a more general relevance to the professions as a whole.

Professional relationships

Professional practice dictates a partnership between the professional and the 'consumer'. The professional needs to move from the position of making decisions in the interests of the clients to working with them and for them. This leads to a change of emphasis towards partnership (Taylor 1997: 5–7) and the ability to operate in an interdependent mode. Towards attaining this end, and due to the rapid changes implicit in society and professional expertise, the professional practitioner must be an independent (or autonomous) learner.

Development of the profession

All three professions considered here have developed along a direction that accepts definitions of competence to determine their behaviour and job roles. Society's shift towards accountability means that they needed to be able to explicitly justify their members' actions in a transparent fashion for protection against litigation. Government pressure has made attainment of these competencies a legal requirement in some cases, with their description decided by advisory bodies within the professional domain. Practitioners and other stakeholders have determined a snapshot definition of the professional activity, which arguably constrains performance to within set boundaries.

Development of the profession, its propositional knowledge base and its competencies is now more likely to come from formal research than through development of personal professional practice: if you are pushing the boundaries in your practice with clients, you are much more exposed and vulnerable in the event of failure or mishap. This makes practitioners more cautious in their approaches, possibly at some cost to innovation and ownership, and raises the importance of a research-based development of the professions.

Practitioners' views, client-based statistics or experimental evidence produce outcomes that inform the development of professional practice. All three professions recognize that the rapid development of knowledge and continual change in our society requires the practitioner to be adaptive. Their definitions of professional behaviour allude to this within their descriptions of the reflective or critical practitioner. CPD and critical thinking are explicit requirements to enable this process. If these components are lacking within practitioners, neither they nor their professions will develop.

Knowledge, skills and professional practice

The relationship between the body of knowledge and professional practice is complex and differs in engineering from the other two professions discussed here (Winter and Maisch 1996: 69–83). All three professions need to ensure the knowledge and understanding (expertise) is implicit and applied effectively. All need immediate responses some times, as well as more measured, delayed responses at other times, to allow time for research and reflection.

Engineers may apply much of their expertise in the latter mode, as the delay between the professional's intentions and their implementation usually allows for much of the underpinning knowledge to be 'off-line'; an engineer can go and check in books and journals or ask others to do so.

Engineering process expertise, however, may well need to be immediate, especially when dealing with operating systems rather than their design or development. This situation is more common in nursing and teaching, where the subjects of their skills are persons (not things) that demand responses that are immediate. Process expertise needs to have its underpinning knowledge and application immediately accessible to the practitioner, so that they may respond effectively when 'on task'.

Making a diagnosis (whether it is a medical problem, a machine fault or a teaching problem) requires the practitioner to demonstrate process expertise. The result of that diagnosis may well entail the practitioner checking stored knowledge. It is important that the expertise is learned in context, so that it may be available immediately.

To develop the professional in terms of their personal knowledge (Eraut 1992), their own experience needs to be incorporated into the learning process. Again context is important to give relevance.

Professional knowledge

Eraut (1992) has proposed that the basis of professional expertise can be categorized as three types of knowledge: propositional, personal and process.

Propositional knowledge is discipline- and specific-practice-based. This has traditionally been the focus for university courses in the professions, where academics accrue an ever-growing knowledge base built on their experiences as practising professionals and researchers. There is a need to recognize knowledge obsolescence within courses, as uncritical acceptance by students will lead to poor choice of relevant knowledge and poor performance as a professional.

Personal (learned, intuitive, impression) knowledge is not as explicit as propositional, needing to be pulled into the professional arena for critical review and dissemination. Process knowledge determines how the professional carries out tasks within their job function to build expertise. It can be divided into: acquiring information, skilled behaviour, deliberative processes (planning, etc.), giving information (communicating) and controlling their own behaviour.

Generic features

The three professions considered here would seem to be typical of most, with few differences in the required attributes of their members or the staging of expected professional maturity. Common features include:

- the understanding and application of an accepted 'body of knowledge', integrating the propositional, personal and the process orientated, to demonstrate professional expertise;
- competence in generic or common skills: communication, teamwork (Brown and Bourne 1996), managing tasks and self;
- reflective practice, using critical thought and informed, ethical judgement to make decisions in a range of contexts;
- responsibility and accountability to others;
- engaging in CPD and lifelong learning to develop the profession and the professional.

From this list it seems that the practitioner needs to be self-aware and self-directed, with personal skills and emotional maturity to take responsible actions with colleagues and clients. They should have the motivation and ability to research and evaluate the outcomes and assimilate them into practice. The universities therefore need to focus considerable attention on these aspects to prepare their students for professional practice.

Learning and programme delivery

To promote effective learning, some understanding of learning processes is needed. Combining learning models and articulated programme aims leads to effective course design and delivery.

Interesting summaries of the development of learning theory, containing many further references, can be found in Brockbank and McGill (1998).

They identify several different dimensions to the learning process that show the area to be complex. Zuber-Skerritt (1992) organizes them as behaviourist (how learning effects action), cognitive (how the mind organizes knowledge internally) and holistic theories (the whole-person perception, construing knowledge) but highlights the differences between pedagogy (child learning) and andragogy (adult learning). Adults are self-directed learners, with a rich experience and personal aims making metacognition, the learners' understanding of their own learning process, much more pertinent.

Learning domains

The three domains of learning identified by Bloom (1956) are the cognitive (knowing), conative (doing) and the affective (feeling). They loosely translate into knowledge, activity in context and emotional development. These three domains can all be developed and should be considered when planning learning.

Many existing paradigms traditionally favour or ignore one or more of these domains, for example, engineering can focus on knowledge and can recognize context and experience but can deny that emotional development is part of its remit. It is tempting to treat the domains independently, with personal tutorials separated from lectures and with laboratory or work experience as a remote activity, or feel the need to compromise. However, these domains are an abstraction from a much more complex and holistic process. Effective learning for the professions must develop all three domains in an integrated context that helps to link them explicitly (Brockbank and McGill 1998).

Learners conceptions of learning

Categorizing peoples' conceptions of learning (Marton *et al.* 1993) has brought out six categories:

1. a quantitative increase in knowledge;
2. memorizing;
3. acquisition of facts, methods, and so on, that can be retained and used when necessary;
4. the abstraction of meaning;
5. an interpretation process aimed at understanding reality; and
6. developing as a person.

There is an implication of increasing depth as the list develops. 1, 2 and 3 are firmly based in the cognitive domain and are easily assessed by recall. The other three categories are more complex and imply an integration of the learning with the world (4 and 5) and personal feelings and behaviour (6). Both the professions and the universities have implicit reference to these later categories within their definitions of autonomy, responsibility, accountability and mission.

Learner positions

The term 'positions' includes preferred orientation, strategies and styles that can be identified within learners. They are not exclusive in their classification: individual learners will have a multiplicity of orientation, style and strategy at their command, to apply as the context and their preferences dictate.

Orientation concerns the intrinsic or extrinsic nature of the learner's approach. Intrinsic orientation will benefit and stimulate the learner directly, while extrinsically orientated learners see the process as a means to an end. For example, vocational training can be seen intrinsically as developing skills for practice, or extrinsically as a qualification. Course designers therefore need to make their provision both relevant (intrinsic) and recognized (extrinsic).

There are two distinct strategies: serial and holistic. With some understanding, self-awareness and maturity, learners could choose a strategy appropriate to context, but may just latch onto one of them for comfort. The holistic approach is inclusive and recognizes complexity (categories 4, 5 and 6), but may over generalize, whilst the serialist decomposes problems into a step-by-step learning process (2, 3 and 4?) yet may miss the point. Providers need to trigger both strategies to reach all their students.

There is acceptance that there are many different preferred learning styles (Honey and Mumford 1992), whether based on activist, reflector, theorist and pragmatist, or other classification. A complex mix of the styles is common; which we use depends on maturity, context or choice. The danger of stereotyping by learning style is now recognized (Brockbank and McGill 1998: 37), but the range of styles needs to be recognized in any learning paradigm: different people learn differently.

Developing learning

The previous section identifies the positions that learners can take without making any judgements about their intrinsic value. Other studies show different developmental paths. The coarsest division identifies surface and deep learning approaches (Marton *et al.* 1984), which delineate between an intention to remember individual bits of knowledge, or look for meaning in context (the message). These can be identified in the six categories of learning described previously. Marton found that a surface approach was ineffective for learning over the long term. Providers can greatly influence the approach taken by the environment, activities and assessment tasks.

The Bateson (1973) model has four stages that are explicitly developmental. They are:

Level 0 – where habitual responses or reflex determine response, so there is no learning;

Level 1 – a constrained context and trial and error strategy for learning facts or skills;

Level 2 – exploring beyond a single context, interpreting and making connections between varied data;

Level 3 – the learner challenges previous perceptions and takes responsibility for their own learning processes.

Other level schema are closely related to the above: Perry (1970) identified that learners progress from dualism (right/wrong view) through multiplicity (recognizing there may not be one correct answer) and relativism (diverse views are accepted) to commitment (position adopted and responsibility taken). Belenky *et al.* (1986) take this forward with a gender dimension that recognizes differences in terms of the affective and the relationships.

Metaphors for learning

The metaphors that are used when describing the process of teaching illuminates the relationships between teacher and learner in our own minds. One of the most common and predominant metaphors is that of transmission, like radio or television. The teacher encodes the knowledge, transmits it via some media, then the student receives and decodes it, storing it for future recall.

This metaphor is extremely attractive, especially for engineers, as it is a serialist, well-defined procedure that mimics signal transmission within the communications domain. As long as lecturers encode and transmit the information accurately, any problems the students might have are purely the fault of their own decoding mechanism: they are 'not up to it'. Also implied is a passive student as receiver of the expertise, which supports a surface approach to learning.

The dialogue metaphor recognizes that learning is a constructive activity, taking place via dialogue and reflection, even when that is internalized. This implies a co-operative environment, with active students engaging with the teachers and each other. Here we have an attractive social construct, with interrelationships, and complexity that needs feedback and dialogue to stimulate reflection. As can be seen from the research into learning reviewed above, this metaphor is far closer to more recent models of the learning process. A holistic orientation and deep learning approach that develops learners to the higher levels and stages is implicit to this metaphor, which informs many of the paradigms discussed in the following section.

Delivery modes

The delivery modes that are either common or relevant to professional education are discussed in terms of their effectiveness in developing the attributes and skills required of professional practitioners.

Didactic approaches with essays and formal examination

The traditional didactic style of education is consistent with the transmission metaphor for learning. Control is with the lecturers, who analyse the propositional knowledge requirements, determine its structure and hierarchy, then deliver it to the students as theoretical abstraction. Case studies, simulation and examples provide context and application of the knowledge base. Critical skills can be assessed within essays and carefully prepared examination questions.

Generic skills are poorly developed, with little relevance to the student experience. Autonomous learners could be interpreted as troublesome, whilst personal and emotional maturity are assumed to develop on their own. Personal tutoring systems try to provide remedial help in response to student difficulties rather than proactively fostering personal development.

Explicit motivators are reinforced by a strict assessment regime, which dominates the student' values, making autonomous learning and personal development difficult objectives to achieve, even if recognized by the staff. Although the delivery of the propositional knowledge is within the control of the course team, the amount that is accessible to graduates beyond graduation is far from clear.

Including some problem-based learning attributes has provided a hybrid problem-orientated style. Realistic case study material and professionally based, real-world problems satisfy some of the contextual requirements. However, the dependent culture from the rest of the course, as well as student and staff expectation, can restrict this potential considerably. A closely supervised dissertation may give integration of propositional knowledge but can still fail to exercise other essential professional requirements: such as planning, critical judgement, self-development, meta-cognition, initiative and autonomy.

Problem-based learning (PBL)

Problem-based Learning was developed at McMasters University medical school in the late 1960s. Dissatisfaction with interns from medical schools at the time led to a reassessment of approaches (Barrows 1996). PBL was designed to integrate the propositional knowledge base within the context of professional practice while the professional processes are developed in a way that enhances autonomous learning and interpersonal skills. It has spread widely as an effective approach in many professional areas (Boud and Felleti 1991).

Gijselaers (1996), gives a concise résumé of the theoretical underpinning and operating principles of PBL. It is grounded in modern cognitive psychology, where learning is seen as constructive, so the teacher's role is to enable and foster that activity. Traditional instruction can be incorporated to help students to become autonomous learners. PBL also recognizes that knowing about knowing (meta-cognition) helps learning, and that social and contextual issues will affect the process.

In operation, PBL problems are encountered before all the relevant knowledge and skills have been acquired (Albanese and Mitchell 1993). Students experience the important professional process of recognizing existing expertise and limitations, then identifying the learning needs and how to satisfy them. After planning their approach, significant time for independent study is given, before reporting back and reflecting on the procedure. Further cycles, with other real-world problems are then initiated.

The tutor's role is to encourage students to participate effectively in their groups, ensure that their analysis is feasible and stimulate the meta-cognition: they must avoid being perceived as the expert. Group work is both an intentional educational and efficiency benefit. Students develop their interpersonal skills and learn to be autonomous within a supportive environment that requires participants to be clear about their preconceived concepts and language, activating existing knowledge.

Enquiry and action learning (EAL) example

This extension to PBL, developed at Bristol University and described by Taylor (1997: 183–4), has a student-centred, problem-based approach, which incorporates an action learning philosophy. It is specifically designed to utilize the diverse personal experiences of its participants and develop learning autonomy within a professional context. The structure of the course is contained within the frameworks of both the university and the professional body.

A number of study units, lasting about two weeks, are built by staff around practice-based problems in consultation with the cohort. Students, in groups of ten, then decide on which part of the problem they need to work for their own learning needs. The study units are designed to satisfy the learning objectives specified by the profession.

Student groups use a classic problem-based learning approach, identifying the knowledge and skills necessary and how they may attain them through suggested activities or their own devices. This is followed up by reflection on the learning, an evaluation of their achievement and planning for the next stage. The study groups are supported by some lectures where appropriate, resources for self-directed learning and block placement in the workplace each year.

The regime encourages autonomy and responsibility for their own learning, putting the propositional knowledge in context through practice-based problems and work experience. Reflective practice, personal development, interpersonal and other generic skills are facilitated within the group study process with critical evaluation exercised in the assessment of objectives.

Action learning

Much CPD in teaching is effectively carried out using an action learning process. It is also used widely in management development, where the learning can be closely allied to the professional activity, providing a work-based model. Action learning regimes are grounded in the reflective, social and holistic nature of learning (McGill and Beaty 1995) and recognize the personal nature of learning within a social context, enabling personal development and reflective practice when successful.

Success relies closely on an explicit process, within small, trusting groups that minimize threat and maximize support. An agreed set of ground rules, developed within the group, helps to impart security where the group members can converse openly and confidentially in order to explore difficulties and promote reflection. Individuals propose and agree their own actions to be carried out before the next session. The group tries to work on developing these future actions and support the learning of each member in turn (McGill and Beaty 1995: 24–39) through application of a set of underpinning values. These are:

- the voluntary nature of set membership;
- an attitude of empowerment to action;
- one learns from experience through reflection;
- the issue owner is the expert on their own issue;
- support via empathetic challenge;
- quality of attention and mutual respect;
- trust and confidentiality to remove threat;
- recognition that development takes time;
- holistic approach embedded in context.

The action learning process maps onto the experiential, cyclic models of learning, whether single-loop (Kolb 1984), which solves a problem, or double-loop (Argyris and Schön 1978), which challenges the model used in the single loop process (see Chapters 6 and 7). In the group (called an action learning set; see Chapter 5), each member is helped to reflect on recent experience, generalize and understand, and develop an appropriate plan of action; the individual carries this out before the next meeting. The group members will help in the realization of these first three stages and occasionally with the paradigm shift implied by breaking out of the box of their own current understanding.

Although originally utilized in work-based development, the strengths of action learning have been realized by course designers who see its application within professional courses (Bourner, Cooper, France 2000). The approach integrates the needs for development of most professions, with all three learning domains exercised holistically. Extended experience of action learning leads to autonomy; enhanced critical, generic and social skills; personal and emotional development; and development of professional skills and of the profession itself.

The use of action learning can be combined with any other delivery mode to form an attractive alternative to the trend towards huge impersonal lectures delivering content within the university sector: knowledge delivery is delegated to learning technology and independent learning resources, whilst action learning integrates the cognitive with the conative and affective (Bourner and Flowers 1998). This is an effective lifelong learning methodology, with an easy transition into its use in CPD.

Work-based learning

Traditionally, in the more vulnerable professions, most of the professional training was carried out in the workplace, after completion of a suitable academic qualification. This is analogous to the craft apprenticeship model, where years of on-the-job experience (often menial to start with) eventually led to a 'master-piece' that allowed transition into certified practice. Nowadays, neither the employer nor the practitioner has the time resource available for a lengthy process in a fast-changing world: it is expected that graduates will be effective from an early stage in their employment.

Eraut *et al.* (1998) use a framework to identify the learning that is indigenous to work. The learning is often a by-product, with opportunities for learning missed in many cases. Although the organizational structure can have an influence, affective parameters were much more important. Learning was rarely planned and arose from challenge posed by the work. The organization and social climate could then either facilitate or inhibit progress. Line managers as staff developers were seldom effective. Universities have responded to this need, innovatively at times, as described below.

Accrediting social services experience and training (ASSET)

Anglia Polytechnic University developed two programmes in the ASSET project (Winter and Maisch 1996); one with the Ford Motor Company and the other with Essex Social Services Department. These are specifically designed for post-qualification higher education, relying heavily on work-based, experiential learning within a well-defined competence-based curriculum. This is of particular interest to universities in that it points towards a future based on partnerships with employers and increased involvement in CPD.

ASSET extends the standards-and-evidence foundation of the National Vocational Qualifications (NVQs) to include the 'lost vocabulary' (Barnett 1994: 99) within higher education. The reflection, judgement, understanding and other 'higher than mere skills' attributes considered missing by Barnett are unified within the competency-based programme (Winter and Maisch 1996: 15) through the module action plan and assessed by a portfolio of evidence. The action plan is developed by the learner and is informed by:

- required workplace competence standards, made from a number of competence elements;
- core assessment criteria that express the holistic requirements of the professional role;
- accredited prior learning;
- support from academic and work-based tutors, trainers and peers.

Here activity is in context, reflectively supported and provides diverse evidence against previously verified criteria and standards. Autonomy is encouraged within a motivational atmosphere of understanding and critical support.

Conclusions

The review of the professional requirements from three disciplines has identified common holistic and affective aspects that have been mostly ignored by universities until recently. The shift from a pedagogical to an andragogical paradigm helps to explain recent developments in higher education for professional practice. All these developments rely on students in a supportive group environment working on real-world, complex problems with reflection and raised meta-cognition. The affective side is now integrated with the cognitive and conative to develop holistic, constructive, critical thinkers with a personal and emotional maturity to continue learning independently in the future. The following case studies show how many of these paradigms appear in practice.

Part 2
Case Studies

4

Partnership in Higher Education

WORKING WITH MULTIPLE PARTNERS IN SOCIAL WORK

Jackie Langley

> To live in a quantum world, to weave here and there with ease and grace, we will need to change what we do. We will need to stop describing tasks and instead facilitate process. We will need to become savvy about how to build relationships, how to nurture growing, evolving things.
> (Wheatley cited in Hanson 1997: 177)

Introduction

This is a case study of partnership in post-qualifying social work education. It considers the reasons for the development of such partnerships, the implications for the role of course leader and the costs and benefits associated with ventures of this kind.

Context

The context of this study is a post-qualifying course for social workers to enable them to become Approved Social Workers (ASW) in accordance with the Mental Health Act 1983. The course also carries a university award of an undergraduate Diploma in Mental Health Studies (60 Level 3 academic credits). It was commissioned by three social services departments, 'won' through a form of competitive tendering against a neighbouring university and is validated by the Central Council for Education and Training in Social Work (CCETSW). It is full-time over one semester and combines university modules with an assessed practice placement. The agreement with commissioning agencies also includes the provision of preparation days for the practice supervisors who supervise students on placement. Overall success on the course depends on reaching a pass level in university assignments coupled with meeting all the practice competences, verified and evaluated by the practice supervisor. The arrangement with the employing agencies is that between them they will provide an annual cohort of between 15 and 20 students and a fee is agreed on a yearly basis. The course attempts to follow what Bines (1992) describes as a 'post-technocratic' model with its emphasis on the acquisition of professional competences, which are developed through practice:

> The practicum is thus the key and integrating element of the course and the professional education tutor and the practice tutor become major educational figures. In addition, course elements outside of the practicum will also primarily focus on issues of professional practice, with cognate disciplines being integrated, contextualized and utilized in the study and development of the competences, settings and problems of professional practice. There is also a greater emphasis on individual student learning and progress and on a partnership of higher education institutions, services and employers.
>
> (Bines 1992: 16)

The first cohort completed the course in June 1998 and all 16 students passed. A *post hoc* survey of students and employing agencies shows that overall the course can be considered a success, with students feeling that it has equipped them for the role of ASW and employers satisfied that this was a cost-effective way of providing this education and training.

Partnership

Partnership has become something of a buzz word in the world of professional education but its actual meaning, usually some kind of collaboration, is often assumed rather than explored. The main 'partners' involved in this enterprise are the employers, the university, a professional body, professional practice (in the guise of placement practice supervisors and practice tutors), mental health service users and the students themselves. This is not a partnership of equals but more a coming together of people working towards a common goal, with all the dilemmas that a diverse group can bring (Moss Kanter 1994). Exploring the reasons for the development of such partnerships in higher education sheds some light on the nature of them and examples from one partnership in action illustrate some of the challenges inherent in them.

Reasons for partnership

Higher education has joined the market economy, and this can be particularly true where professional courses are competing with universities in the vicinity. The National Institute of Adult Continuing Education (NIACE 1993: 8), commenting on their vision of higher education spoke of the change from 'provider to market':

> Where the owners of knowledge (academics, professions and government) once decided what individuals and employers could or should have, institutions now compete increasingly to recruit 'customers' to whom they must respond or die.

Commenting on post-qualifying social work courses, Youll and Walker (1995: 204) say that they are 'strongly shaped by agency demands, which are, in turn, determined by the requirements of legislative and service changes'. It is vital therefore that higher education is responsive to the needs of its 'partner' agencies and is able to provide cost-effective education that meets both employment and academic demands.

There are also sound educational reasons for the development of partnerships in professional education: a growing recognition of the importance of both academic and practice and student and course collaboration.

During the 1980s and 1990s, social work courses have increasingly worked in partnership with practice through agencies who sponsor students and/or who provide practice placements and practice teaching for them. Here the traditional position has been that the university manages the course, which includes managing the professional practice placements. It is essential that the student reaches a pass standard in practice, but somehow this is not equal to academic assessment. Some courses have now developed their partnerships with practice to an extent where responsibility for the course is truly shared between university and practice and where practice teachers or their equivalents are seen as the managers of the practice experience as well as contributors to university learning. This can be seen both in qualifying and post-qualifying social work courses (Harlock and Knott 1998). As an example of this development, CCETSW is increasingly drawing its external assessors from practice as well as from academia.

It has perhaps been the Institutes of Higher Education and the new universities that have embraced this kind of partnership most fully, with its growing emphasis on practice competence and a recognition that there are educational advantages in ensuring that academic study is grounded in the reality of practice rather than just that practice is informed by academic study. The shift is also recognition of the role and expertise of those who teach practice in the field and has been accompanied by a growth in field work education/practice teaching courses.

With the recognition of the importance of student-centred learning and a desire to work in accordance with adult learning principles, the nature of the partnership between students and their course has become recognized as an important ingredient in a successful outcome. Teaching and learning strategies need to be participative, collaborative and based on mutual respect and equality. On social work qualifying courses there is also a new 'value for money' relationship developing between students and the course with the advent of students paying their own fees and, in the case of an increasing number of mature social work students, paying their own way entirely.

Professional validating bodies in social work, nursing and the other healthcare professions are increasingly defining standards for their staff and, to a greater or lesser extent, determining the length, mode of delivery and content of professional courses (Franks 1997). Partnerships with these organizations – CCETSW for social work education – have therefore had to develop. Courses need to demonstrate that requirements have been met, while at the same time seeking to influence the nature of those requirements. For the ASW course, CCETSW prescribes clear competences, which must be met, and minimum timescales in which they can be achieved. The course is part of the CCETSW post-qualifying framework operated through regional consortia. In partnership terms this means that the university also needs to be an active partner in the local post-qualifying consortium.

A new form of partnership

A new form of partnership is beginning to emerge in social work education. This is the growth of partnership with the users of social services. Ideologically this represents a move away from the worker being the expert towards a belief that service users are, in the main, oppressed, disempowered and often socially excluded members of society. They are people who need to be listened to and helped to gain power over their own lives and the resources that traditionally support them but that all too often create dependency. The importance of listening to the experience of mental health service users is highlighted by Miriam Hastings (1996: 43) when she says: 'Approved Social Workers are far more likely to carry out good practice such as this if they have been trained about these issues by the people most concerned and who have direct experience'. Braye and Preston-Shoot (1995: 44) examining partnerships between service users and service providers suggest: 'the apparent consensus about partnership as an uncontroversial "good thing" masks what is in fact a complex and varied aetiology in which several influential factors are combined'. In relation to the new role of service users as partners in professional training, the following questions arise at the simplest level of analysis. Are service users being asked to comment on the course, as written and delivered, and to share their experiences as users with the student group? Or are they being asked to influence and change the nature of the education provided (Crepaz-Keay, Binns and Wilson 1997: 28; Taylor 1997: 179)?

The role of the course leader

What impact do these forms of partnership have on the role of a course leader?

The role of the course leader has been defined as: 'the administrative manager and leader of the course . . . responsible for ensuring and maintaining appropriate academic standards' (General Examination and Assessment Regulations (University of Brighton 1997)). In addition to this role, I would suggest that the more complex the partnership arrangements, the more course leaders need skills in group leadership, negotiation, facilitation, diplomacy and innovation as well as the more usual attributes. They need to be able to see different perspectives and agendas, understand them and respond to them. This requires strategic thinking and action, a 'thick skin', confidence about 'bottom lines', an ability to keep students and the purpose of the course at the centre of their thinking and a willingness to compromise or seek a 'third way'. The task is about developing relationships and maintaining them.

Developing the course

The development team for this course was large and comprised university teaching staff, operational and training staff from the three participating agencies and service user and carer representatives. At the development stage, as course leader, I needed to be aware of what was easily negotiable and what was not. In this case, the number of university, placement and study days had been agreed with the agencies through their acceptance of the university's bid. The competences were not negotiable as they are prescribed by CCETSW. The course would have to operate within the university undergraduate modular framework. Working out what these constraints meant before meeting with a development group helped put boundaries round the planning process and avoid unnecessary discussion. Having said that, if 'partners' to the enterprise bring with them issues that are important for them, they must be given a chance to air them. This is not just about catharsis, it is also an opportunity to see if important points can be catered for differently within the given boundaries.

The training officer from one of the commissioning agencies had previously run the course for that agency at the neighbouring university. She had very mixed feelings about her change in role and the new course coming to this university. The previous course had been longer and, although modular in name, it was not in delivery. Strong concern was expressed about the need for students to have enough input on the law – now seemingly confined to a single module. Although not leaving her entirely satisfied, the group was able to explore ways of trying to ensure that the law was sufficiently dealt with by examining how the practice modules would also address legal issues through consideration of practice. It also considered how another modular assignment and evidence of practice competence would address knowledge, understanding and application of the legislation.

The concept of partnership itself had to be dealt with in the development group. Having already had experience of working with agencies in the development of a qualifying social work course, I thought, perhaps naively, that agency members of the group would want to be involved in writing the documentation about practice and practice placements. However, I was clearly given a message that as the university had been commissioned to run the course it could get on with it! At this stage the 'ownership' of the course rested with the university and if 'working together towards a common goal' was to mean anything there was work to do in bringing the group towards joint 'ownership' of the course. As Moss Kanter (1994: 173) says: ' "Participation" must mean much more than observation and tacit approval of others as they do all the important work'. At the same time as dealing with these agendas, the group included service user and carer representatives for whom this was a new and alien experience. The daunting challenge for me as course leader was to try to ensure that everyone had their chance to contribute and to feel that their contributions were both valid and valued (Moss Kanter 1994).

Over several meetings with everyone gradually getting to know each other and the task to be accomplished, 'ownership' started to develop. As course leader I still felt responsible for everything and accountable to everyone. Out of the agency personnel, key figures emerged who were, or had the time to be, more committed to the process of establishing the course. Perhaps the moment that cemented shared 'ownership' and the common goal was the validation event, where the course team united against some perceived hostile questioning from members of the validation panel.

Partnership in course structures

Although this is a one semester course, it was agreed that the course board should meet twice a year – once during the course and once at the end with an evaluative brief. The board comprises training officers from the three agencies, practice supervisor representatives, mental health service user and carer representatives in addition to the usual university staff. This member-ship helps ensure the continuing involvement and commitment of the part-ners, particularly if they can see that their views make a difference. Recommendations from the course board are then taken forward by the course leader to the management group comprising the senior training personnel from the three commissioning agencies and the head of school at the university. In addition to all the usual academic and university con-siderations, I have to be aware of what the management group may or may not accept and look strategically at the best ways of achieving what is being asked for. On more day-to-day matters I have to gain the agreement of the three training officers.

The course board recommended that the length of the course should be increased – particularly the placement and study days. As course leader I completely agreed with this but needed to think about the position of the representatives of the employing agencies, who have to be concerned with the cost of having their employees away from the agency for longer than originally agreed. A proposal was taken from the course board and, through negotiation, part of the request was met.

Supporting partnership in tutoring

Two tutors who share the teaching on the three practice modules, also acting as personal tutors, come from the commissioning agencies through a financial arrangement with them. The positive side of this partnership is that practice can be taught by up-to-date, experienced and credible practitioners. The downside is that they may not have teaching experience and naturally need a good deal of support in their new role. Neither of the practice tutors from the first year is going to take on the role for a second year. This is for reasons unconnected with their experience with the course, although both felt under great pressure trying to maintain their practitioner role alongside the demands of tutoring. New tutors have to be recruited and supported and therefore there is no consistency in, or development of, the role. Only one agency is wholeheartedly behind this approach and it is difficult, in these circumstances, to feel confident that the practice modules will be developed and delivered as effectively as one would like. The challenge for the course leader is to find the appropriate practice staff through careful negotiation with the commissioning agencies and then to help train and support them in a role far more complex than that of visiting lecturer.

Working with service users

'Feeling our way' the first year, service users contributed to different parts of the curriculum, providing, for example, accounts of living with a mental illness and the experience of being compulsorily admitted to a psychiatric hospital. A significant minority of students thought there was too much service user involvement and asked questions like 'what were they there for?'. Others felt that they shouldn't have to listen to the distressing experiences of service users. This feedback raised all kinds of questions about how students can be moved to a more empowering practice stance – questions being asked nationally as all of us involved in social work education grapple with this new kind of partnership. As course leader, I have been involved in working with one service user representative and one of the training officers in reviewing this aspect of the course. Good practice suggests that, as far as possible, the user perspective should be integrated throughout the course delivery.

For next year, it is hoped that two service users will be present for, and contribute to, half of the course. This will cost money and require support for the service users and tutors involved. As course leader, I am involved in not only negotiating and supporting this kind of development but also in thinking of ways of finding the additional funding for it. It is very gratifying to hear from a service user that they expected 'tokenism' but have felt 'the whole exercise has been one of true partnership'. The extent to which the content of the course will be changed by user involvement is still open to debate and rests not so much with the individual course as with the professional validating body.

The importance of relationships

Although the course leader is principally involved with a particular course, it is vital that they recognize the importance of the relationships being formed. Unsuccessful collaboration may lead to the 'partners' taking their custom elsewhere but effective partnerships can provide the basis for future collaboration. As an example of this, following the successful first cohort of ASW students, two of the employing agencies have now asked the university to develop refresher training for their ASWs.

With the growth in a local student population, students taking qualifying or post-qualifying social work courses are potentially the post-graduate students of the university too. Good relationships also mean that they are likely to want to retain their links with the university by becoming practice teachers/supervisors for future social work students. Although this ongoing alliance has perhaps always been important for course leaders to have in mind, it has a particular significance when working with local professionals engaged in continued professional development.

Practice teachers/supervisors in social work education are always in short supply. They are not financially rewarded for the role and often it is undertaken in addition to, rather than as part of, a full practitioner workload (Franks 1997). Practice supervisors evaluating their experience of the ASW course confirmed that they received little workload relief or support by their employing agencies. Under these circumstances it is vital that the course conveys its valuing of them by involving them, supporting them and generally helping them feel shared 'ownership' of the course. On the ASW course this involves, for example, preparation days, a follow-up half-day at their request and representation on the course board. The hope and intention is that the current practice supervisors will want to take students in the future. If they become managers, a good relationship may mean that they are more likely to agree to student placements and to release their staff to be practice supervisors.

Conclusion

Partnership of the kind described is costly in terms of time and, in terms of student numbers, the benefits may seem small. Care needs to be taken to ensure that, in order to be responsive to our employer partners, the university does not spend time developing expensive provision in which the employer cannot provide continued investment and that is not cost-effective for the university. However, as honest and open relationships develop, it is possible to look at the benefits and costs for all and arrive at considered decisions about what can be done.

What is evident from my experience as course leader in this kind of partnership is that it is difficult and challenging. It requires the development of skills that go beyond those required for leadership of a traditional university course and it poses questions about the definition of course leadership, how staff should be prepared for it and the time needed to carry out the role effectively.

Finally, the venture has been worthwhile and successful. Agencies are seeing the university as a 'safe pair of hands' for this course and for future collaborative developments in this area. The second intake of students has achieved a very high standard and relationships with all the stakeholders are sound.

DEVELOPING A MODEL OF PARTNERSHIP IN PRIMARY ITT

Maggie Carroll and Lorraine Harrison

This case study throws light on those aspects of partnership in ITT that will inform ongoing developments at the university. It emphasizes the need for establishing a well-managed, formal structure within which students are placed to bring together DfEE requirements, those of the university and schools, leading to an informed and refined understanding of the process of ITT.

Background

The development of a model of partnership

In their teacher training courses, students have always engaged in some form of school experience designed to relate the theories of learning and teaching to practice in the classroom. Provision for school-based training (as opposed to just school experience) has evolved significantly during recent years. Models of partnership currently seek to integrate work-based training into the whole student experience whereby the students, over the period of their courses, become ready for work as newly qualified teachers.

Government Circulars, notably Department of Education and Science Circulars 3/84 (DES 1984) and 24/89 (DES 1989), identified partnership to be a mandatory requirement of training (Booth, Furlong and Wilkin 1990). This step strengthened an ongoing professional trend and facilitated the development of a growing, shared philosophy between institutions and schools. The TTA publications, such as *Partnerships for Training Teachers* (Teacher Training Agency 1996), signified the development of a more focused agenda, resulting in the publication of Circular 10/97 (DfEE 1997) and Circular 4/98 (DfEE 1998d). The latter contains details of the standards for the Award of Qualified Teacher Status, ITT curricula for English, mathematics, science and information and communications technology (ICT) and requirements for ITT courses. This publication signifies a policy linking institutional funding and judgements about quality (Blake and Hanley 1998), as evidenced through Ofsted inspections of ITT. Partnership in training must now be embedded in ITT courses.

At the University of Brighton, policies and initiatives within the partnership have been shaped by national developments, university quality assurance mechanisms and School of Education monitoring, evaluation and review. This work provides an overview of the development of partnerships at the university and examines the impact of a case study on the development and refinement of new initiatives. These developments recognize the need to provide high-quality, school-based experiences for students, in order that they are able to become effective teachers capable of providing challenging learning experiences for all pupils.

Partnership arrangements at the university

Partnership arrangements at the university have developed, in part, as a response to government requirements but also as the result of a long association with a large number of schools in the region involved in the process of teacher training.

In 1990, it was agreed that a formal partnership scheme should be developed between the (then) Brighton Polytechnic and primary schools in East and West Sussex. A working party was set up, comprising headteachers, university tutors and appropriate local education authority advisors. The following principles became the basis upon which development evolved. It was agreed that:

- the training, support, supervision and assessment of students would be a shared responsibility between the school and the university;
- the assessment of students would be undertaken jointly by tutors and mentors, the final report being written by the school partner;
- schools would appoint a mentor (or, in the case of larger schools, two mentors) who would undertake an agreed part of the formal supervision of students;
- a training programme for mentors would be set up.

After piloting and evaluation in 1991, the principles of partnership were adopted by all partnership schools. A faculty committee, The Partnership in Education (PiE) (Primary) Committee, comprising nominated headteachers from West and East Sussex and members of staff and students from the university, provided a regular forum for discussion and facilitated the development of new initiatives and policies. For example, Circular 14/93 (DfE 1993) identified a range of competences expected of newly qualified teachers. The PiE committee acknowledged these and created a working party (of headteachers and university tutors) to shape the competence statements into a set of expectations for students on their first school placement. Expectations were then established for the first and interim placements to ensure focus, continuity and progression. The expectations profile allowed mentors and tutors to record the range, quality and evidence of student achievements and encouraged:

- further development of a shared, explicit language between tutor, mentor and student;
- evaluation of student progress across all competence areas;
- identification of those areas where further progress was desirable;
- identification of particular student strengths and areas of expertise.

The shared language and common understanding between mentor and tutor helped students to interpret, reflect and act upon feedback. This led to the introduction of shared observations, where mentor and tutor together observed the same episode of teaching. Agreed oral and written feedback would be given to the student, thus strengthening the model of partnership.

The university also provided a series of partnership training days to disseminate the agreed roles and responsibilities of the partnership, to explore the ways in which school experience could begin to be embedded in ITT and to help ensure comparability of experience for all students. During the first phase of training, mentors focused upon:

- the nature of the partnership;
- the role of the mentor, class teacher and adviser;
- the use of the profile of competences;
- talking to students;
- evaluating students' teaching; and
- report writing.

The benefits of partnership

The formalized partnership became a crucial contributor to the provision of ITT at Brighton. The need for continual development in response to government initiatives was apparent but it was also essential to provide experiences that would be appropriate for the range of contexts in which students undertook school placements within the region.

The recognition of the range of benefits that students bring to schools was a key determinant in the quality of their provision. A case study that would identify those benefits recognized and valued by schools could provide evidence that would inform future developments in the training partnership.

Benefits that students can bring to schools were often reported but had not been explored within the context of partnership provision at the University of Brighton. Reported evidence indicated that student teachers can benefit schools in many ways but most significantly in terms of benefits to teachers, mentors, pupils and the ethos of the whole school.

Class teachers

Research undertaken by Stark (1994) (in which a questionnaire was sent to class teachers, students and tutors during the BEd final school experience), confirmed that the majority of teachers enjoyed working with students, saw it as part of their role as a teacher and recognized the positive impact students had on their professional practice. In some cases, this resulted in further learning on the part of the teacher (Stark 1994). Benefits associated with teachers' further professional development are recognized by Williams (1995) as being of fundamental importance and therefore a significant step in the development of school experience partnerships within the process of ITT.

The presence of a student in the classroom allows a level of flexibility for the teacher that could not otherwise be achieved. The time released (usually dependent on the stage the student has reached) can be used in a variety of ways. For example, the teacher may:

- work with individual and/or small groups of children;
- work alongside colleagues in the classroom;
- develop and review school policies and plans;
- undertake activities to enhance their own professional development (Lock 1995).

Mentors

Benefits can also be extended to mentors who take on a formal role within the partnership arrangements. The skills developed by mentors, often facilitated by training opportunities and recognized through accreditation, are valued and can be of positive benefit within the realms of staff appraisal. They are also of value when supporting newly qualified teachers (Lock, 1995).

Pupils

Students are likely to enhance pupil learning, not least as a result of their enthusiasm for and commitment to their professional role. Lock (1995) recognizes the advantages of increased adult/pupil ratios that can result in greater flexibility of teaching opportunities, especially when individual and small group teaching becomes focused and therefore more purposeful. This situation can often be associated with selected subjects within the curriculum where students and pupils become immersed in a particular field of study, deepening their knowledge and understanding within a specific context. Such initiatives often enable more than one student to work with groups of children, a situation that is recognized by Williams to be particularly advantageous to children (Williams 1995).

Whole school

Involvement with students can be seen to benefit the whole school. For example, their enthusiasm and ability to introduce fresh ideas can have a positive influence beyond the classroom when a student is able to make a contribution to an area of identified strength or subject specialism. The growing expectations from schools that students should become active participants in the school administrative structure emphasizes the importance of two-way learning (Watkins and Walley 1993).

The case study

It became clear that the developing model of partnership at the university, and among providers of ITT generally, resulted in the formalization of arrangements between schools and institutions. At the University of Brighton, four partner schools were selected to take part in the case study. They all had a close relationship with the university in:

• the existence of well established, formalized procedures for supporting students on school experience;
• a willingness to contribute to university initiatives, namely the PiE committee and partnership days.

They also provided a broad, representative range of contexts for school experience placements. Their contributions, therefore, were expected to reaffirm elements of good practice, to be shared among all partnership schools.

Information was gathered using semi-structured interviews, a technique that would encourage sufficient flexibility yet ensure consistency of approach. Interviews were conducted with the headteacher and mentor in each school. Five fundamental aspects of partnership were considered:

1. Management structures – how the management structure is organized to enable the school to provide a framework for the students' training.
2. Responsibility for ITT – the contributions of schools and university and the extent to which joint initiatives can enhance this process.
3. Range of benefits that students bring – with particular reference to class teacher, mentor, pupils and the school as a whole.
4. School initiatives – how students can facilitate the development of school initiatives either directly or indirectly.

5. Partnership initiatives – those initiatives that are of greatest benefit to schools.

Headteachers and mentors were also encouraged to make open comments, relevant to the enhancement of the partnership.

The overall responses indicated that partnership arrangements were effective and considered to be of mutual benefit. The schools and the university were confident that students received well-managed, challenging school experiences that enabled schools to gain a range of benefits. These are presented under the headings used in the interviews.

Management structures

In all four schools, management structures were in place that would meet the needs of students at different phases of their training. Senior management teams allowed for an acceptable number of student placements in conjunction with the school's development plan. Students were placed strategically, facilitating the release of designated staff to work on particular aspects of school policy, through negotiation during the summer term in preparation for the new academic year.

Governors were either informed (three schools) or positively proactive about student placements. In the latter case they made a commitment to the university, viewed students in a positive light and were aware of the school's formal support structures. Information about students was included in the governors' annual report to parents.

All schools provided a range of documentation for students, accessible in school or for personal use. For example, one school provided every student with a pack comprising a prospectus, teaching and learning policy, behaviour policy, health and safety policy and information about planning and assessment.

All schools expected students to operate as a member of staff. Therefore, they were required to:

• plan programmes of work in relation to school policies;
• participate as a member of a planning team;
• assume a professional role and contribute to school life.

These expectations were of fundamental importance to the development of student teachers and raised the status of their professional role, leading to the embedding of professional development within the students' degree courses.

All four schools had well established roles and procedures for mentorship, which were clearly understood and undertaken effectively. The different context of each school gave rise to a range of contrasting, yet effective, mentorship practices. The large primary school, for example, relied heavily on a year-group team to support the student. In contrast, the smaller primary school ensured that the mentor monitored the day-to-day support of the student in collaboration with the class teacher.

Responsibility for ITT

All four schools were clear about their own responsibilities within the partnership and felt that the fundamental roles of the university were:

- to provide opportunities for students to gain sufficient subject knowledge to enable them to teach effectively;
- to elucidate theories of learning and teaching and associated professional issues;
- to develop students' awareness and understanding of current debate in education.

All schools saw their role as enabling students to put their knowledge into practice, allowing them to evaluate, reflect and act upon their strengths and areas for further development. Circular 14/93 (DfE 1993) had encouraged this process to be achieved in a balanced and systematic manner.

The schools also felt that they provided a unique context within the community that made a distinctive contribution to the students' training. Thus, in adapting to and learning from this range of contexts, students can begin to develop a secure, informed philosophy of education, which will shape their readiness for teaching.

Range of benefits that students bring

Students were valued for their enthusiasm, energy, new ideas and sometimes for their expertise. Most importantly, they enabled their school colleagues to reflect on their own practice and develop their confidence in mentoring adults.

All schools were clear about the requirements most appropriate for particular periods of school experience, although a range of opinion was voiced about the nature of benefits gained by partner schools. It was agreed, for example, that students in Year 1 (who work predominantly with small groups), enabled the pupils to benefit from an increased, focused input. Also, class teachers could, through careful planning, benefit from a team-teaching, collaborative approach.

With more experienced students, class teachers enjoyed more flexibility, which resulted in further opportunities for school development. For example, the presence of a Year 3 student allowed time for the mathematics coordinator to refine the school's mathematics policy and work alongside her colleagues throughout the school. (The time gained, however, must be carefully balanced against the university partnership requirement for formal supervision and assessment undertaken by the mentor.)

Class teachers were seen as holding the key to students' development. They offer role models with the experience to facilitate real and effective progress. Although this benefit was recognized by the headteacher and mentor, it was often difficult for class teachers to be fully aware of the positive impact they had achieved.

Student-specific expertise was recognized and developed within the school. For example, a Year 4 student in one school produced a well organized and effective assessment file. She worked with the headteacher to present a selection of assessment strategies during a year-group meeting, which were subsequently disseminated to the remainder of the staff. It was fair to assume that the majority of final year students could make a similar contribution. The presence of students also enabled unusual or difficult situations to be resolved more readily. For example, a difficult child was integrated smoothly into a class with the help of a student, as monitoring and support for this child was facilitated by an additional professional in the classroom. In more general terms, schools noted that behaviour management can become easier when a student is sufficiently experienced.

Partnership in ITT provided opportunities for mentors. All mentors had undertaken the training provided by the university, designed to facilitate professional development and equip them to deal sensitively with students. Mentors had opportunities, throughout the course of their training, to work alongside other tutors and mentors. This was seen to develop skills associated with staff appraisal, talking with parents and governors and managing other staff. Mentors felt valued and were more than willing to share their expertise with students, enhancing the application of key professional skills among teachers. In this case study, all mentors held senior positions, with one headteacher considering the role to be good preparation for promotion as well as an effective means of staff support.

The benefits perceived were most effective when management practices enabled sufficient planning and support structures across the whole school, not just those members of staff directly involved with the student. In general terms, the benefits were considered to outweigh the disadvantages as long as the student support was managed alongside the needs of the school as a whole.

School initiatives

The formalization of partnership arrangements had developed hand-in-hand with the evolution of school initiatives that can support students, such as the expectation that students would attend and contribute to in-service training days. This provided another context where students could increase their knowledge and understanding.

It was often possible for whole school policies to be developed whilst students were placed in schools. The following examples were undertaken as a direct result of student placements:

- One school created a whole-school focus on art, which resulted in linking policy with curriculum planning throughout the school. Staff visited other schools and were able to develop a shared and informed understanding within their own. During this time, all staff (including the student) practised display techniques.

- The mentor in another school raised the whole-school status of English by updating the library, creating a reading and writing workshop for parents, undertaking an audit of reading provision in all classrooms and providing support for writing workshops in selected classrooms. The school intended to continue this work by tracking pupil achievement in English.
- All the non-teaching staff at one school had undertaken courses at the university leading to the award of a Certificate in Applied Professional Studies. Students worked alongside non-teaching colleagues whose expertise and experience were recognized formally.

Partnership initiatives

Schools recognized the contributions that partnership initiatives can make as an effective extension of good classroom practice. It was clear that the university must continue to develop training opportunities and that mentors must be involved, both in planning and delivery. All four schools expressed the need for continued, possibly more flexible, training opportunities.

Conclusions: implications and action

The conclusions drawn from the case study were shared among all partner schools. Their implications, together with the introduction of new government requirements, have influenced the planning and shaped the delivery of subsequent partnership initiatives.

The case study revealed that the requirements of the partnership arrangements had prompted senior management teams to plan time effectively, so that appropriate school developments could occur alongside the support and training of students in the classroom.

The publication of Circular 10/97 (DfEE 1997) prompted the PiE committee to consider the essential experiences necessary for students in relation to the teaching of English and mathematics and in their assessment, recording and reporting. Three working groups were set up to identify minimum requirements for each phase of training. Partnership training days for all mentors facilitated a shared understanding of the requirements and ensured their common interpretation in order to resolve any difficulties. The success of these initiatives depended on efficient management structures within schools and effective support by university staff. More recently, the minimum requirements for the teaching of ICT were launched during a partnership training day, with guidelines to be monitored and evaluated by schools and the university. These initiatives will ensure the provision of comparable subject teaching opportunities for all students, forge closer links between the university experience and school placements and help to raise the capabilities of the students through explicit, highly focused training.

Whilst schools recognized and were sensitive to the range of needs at different phases in students' training, the benefits likely to be brought by individual students and how to develop best practice was less clear. The partnership training days focused on the development and management of structures to facilitate quality learning experiences and the introduction of joint observations to encourage focused, critical feedback. Significantly, the training provision is central to the view of partnerships as potential vehicles for bringing about meaningful change (Erskine-Cullen 1994).

Partnership training has been extended to school subject coordinators in English, mathematics and ICT. The specific expertise offered by the coordinators will be used to develop student effectiveness in the planning, teaching, evaluation and assessment of these subjects. This initiative supports the view that teachers themselves can become effective trainers, provided that they receive appropriate training (Davies and Ferguson 1997).

The recognition of the benefits associated with the role of the mentor has led to the introduction of accreditation as part of the university requirements for mentors. The accreditation contributes to a professional development award and provides evidence of the effectiveness of the mentor, seen to be of fundamental importance as continuing professional development has now become a significant part of the training process.

The small-scale investigation on which this case study is based has been a key activity in determining the development of effective new policies and initiatives. Through this, the university and its partner schools may be confident in enabling students to be ready for work and responsive to change in the ever-demanding context of the primary school.

INTERPROFESSIONAL LEARNING – AN EVALUATION

Graham Stew

Introduction

This is a case study of shared interprofessional learning. It describes the context and the participants' perceptions before going on to explore the lessons learned from this venture involving four health professions.

Before describing this experience of interprofessional education it may be helpful to attempt to define the concept. Not only does 'interprofessional' mean different things to different groups of people but professionals themselves speak different languages that influence both their thinking and sense of identity (Pietroni 1992). In the context of this study the term 'shared learning' is perhaps more appropriate, and has been widely used in the UK. Here, it is applied to pre-registration courses that have a common core programme shared by students of more than one professional discipline.

Barr (1994: 1) suggested the term 'shared learning' can be used to cover all opportunities where two or more professions study together: 'whatever the purpose, form, content or setting'. Several writers have described shared learning initiatives among health and social care professions (Areskog 1995; Carpenter and Hewstone 1996).

It is interesting to examine the claimed purpose of shared learning and some of its implicit agendas. Within higher education, many programmes that share a common core of foundational knowledge have increasingly utilized shared learning for economic reasons. This is part of a trend towards standardization in higher education. Developments such as modularization, credit accumulation and transfer (CATS) and accreditation of prior experiential and learning (APEL) all reflect this growing emphasis on 'operationalism' (Barnett 1994). As a response to the relentless squeeze on funding for higher education during the 1980s and 1990s, it is easy to regard shared learning as yet another symptom of the 'doing more for less' disease (Barr 1994).

Whilst it may be an effective use of resources for universities, shared learning can also be supported for reasons of professional enhancement. That is, the increased mutual understanding between professionals and the dismantling of traditional interdisciplinary barriers should lead to more effective teamwork and improved healthcare. The reality is that everyday practice is influenced by professional boundaries and compounded by issues of power, gender and the rewards associated with each profession (Reeves and Pryce 1998). The shifting boundaries of the professions are influenced by increasing specialization, the changing scope of professional practice and the emergent nature of professional knowledge.

Professional knowledge is not simple or homogeneous; it is dynamic and problematic, and must be considered in the context of its use. Nor are professions static but constantly moving along the continuum of professionalization (Jarvis 1983). Division occurs in professions as knowledge becomes more complex and splits into new subdisciplines, and new occupational groups emerge as specialisms develop. As different segments of a profession appear they seek to demarcate that body of knowledge relevant to their own professional practice, and to educate and train their own practitioners in it (Bucher and Strauss 1961). This 'occupational imperialism' militates against shared learning with other professions, as boundaries of practice and knowledge are constructed. It could be argued that the more mature professions should not be so defensive about their knowledge and skills base and might be more open to sharing with other groups. In practice, however, established power, status and privileges are often jealously guarded by established professions. Interprofessional education promotes the recognition by students, at an early stage in their professional development, of differences in values and attitudes, as well as differences in role, prestige and function (Horder 1991; Hunt 1979).

In an apparent move towards 'interprofessionalism', higher education has responded to changes in wider society by developing faculties and schools of 'health and social care'. Such centres challenge the traditional boundaries of professional practice and disciplinary knowledge and reflect employers' demands that rigid occupational demarcation: 'be deconstructed and recast in new frameworks and forms of knowledge and action' (Bines 1992: 127).

Related to this, support for shared learning may have its roots in the potential to replace health professionals with (less expensive) vocationally trained 'generic' health workers. National vocational qualifications, espousing the 'competence' approach to training, emphasize measurable technical skills rather than critical abilities that are more difficult to assess. Many occupational groups delivering healthcare are facing what could be seen as an aspect of 'de-professionalization' in the pursuit of a more efficient and cost-effective health service. It would seem that the future challenge for professional education in the universities is to provide employers with a competent yet critically aware workforce.

There is little doubt that healthcare in the 1990s does require a multi-professional approach, and the 'social movement' of multi-disciplinarity appears unstoppable. Shared learning is at the forefront of this movement and the assumptions about its advantages need to be evaluated carefully. The Centre for the Advancement of Inter-Professional Education (CAIPE) is among those planning to carry out such an evaluation (CAIPE 1997/8).

Although quite common within post-registration courses, interprofessional education at pre-registration level is still relatively *ad hoc*, under-researched and has not been systematically introduced into mainstream professional education (Weinstein 1994). It might be argued that multi-disciplinary education for qualified professionals is less problematic and is welcomed by the vast majority of students. Here they can bring a variety and wealth of professional experience to bear on educational issues and their different perspectives on common areas of practice are valued.

The context of the study

This study involved four undergraduate courses at the University of Brighton, in physiotherapy, podiatry, nursing and midwifery. First year students undertook three shared modules, in human physiology, professional issues and research. In addition, a number of common modules ran between two courses (for example, social science between physiotherapy and podiatry, and psychology with nursing and midwifery students). As common modules previously had been delivered to more than one course, the main focus of this study is on the shared modules undertaken by all four courses, as this was a major innovation.

The four courses comprised 203 students and key lectures for the shared modules took place over one hour in a large lecture hall, followed by up to ten seminar groups for a further hour in smaller classrooms. The seminar groups were usually multi-disciplinary. Each module team consisted of lecturers from the departments delivering the modules, although the proportion of teaching provided by each department was not always representative of its own student numbers. This was clearly a reflection of the teaching resources available to each of the departments, and is one of the continuing issues.

Methodology

An evaluative study was undertaken at the end of the first year of shared learning, adopting an 'illuminative' methodology (Parlett and Dearden 1981). This approach to educational evaluation tries to describe, interpret and inform rather than to measure and predict. Illuminative evaluation attempts to make a connection between the learning milieu and the intellectual experiences of students. In short, it attempts to portray what an educational experience was like for all the participants, thus providing in-depth information for the purposes of future decision making.

In this type of study the methods of data collection are defined by the problem, not the reverse. Thus, individual and focus group interviews were carried out with student groups, course leaders and module leaders, and written module evaluations were also collected. Most interviews were tape-recorded for later transcription. The resulting data were rich and complex and content analysis produced a number of commonly recurring themes, which are summarized below.

Findings of the study

A summary of the four themes will be provided through a brief introduction supported by excerpts from the interview transcripts.

Organization and preparation

Many lecturers mentioned the formation of teams and the need for proportional representation from participating departments: '. . . we need to have teaching teams that represent the sizes of student groups in our departments . . . the balance of the team was unfair'.

Each team had at least one representative from each of the four courses and met several times to prepare module programmes and content. Each team needed to agree on the learning needs of student group, both in relation to the subject matter (for example, human physiology) and also the academic level (CATS level 1 represents first year undergraduate study): '. . . there was little common understanding of what is meant by level 1, and we had to hammer out what we understood by shared learning and what we expected from students'.

Module teams had to produce module handbooks and plan lecture and seminar formats. Room bookings were arranged through course leaders, a modularity coordinator and representatives of the estates department. One course leader said: '. . . it felt like we had to do everything ourselves; shared learning is certainly not an easy option . . . the organization needs to recognize this'.

The experience of shared learning

The environment of the lecture hall and seating arrangements were the subject of much comment from students. One typical comment was: '. . . it was not that comfortable . . . how do you expect anyone to concentrate in a noisy, crowded lecture hall?'

One lecturer stated: '. . . it was fascinating to note how the students sat together in their own groups; there seemed to be little interaction between the courses'.

Seminar groups were usually multi-disciplinary and they attempted to take the concepts from the key lectures and apply them to their own spheres of practice. One student mentioned that: '. . . it was interesting to meet other students, but in our seminar group it would have been better to have only our course in order to apply the material from the lecture to our own discipline'.

Comments regarding the differing styles of lecturing came from both staff and students and the organization and explanation of module assignments were also noted: '. . . in group presentations for assessment, it's important to have everyone pulling their weight, otherwise a few do all the work . . . the meetings in our own time just didn't work'.

The module assignments have all been subsequently evaluated and the teams have made improvements where necessary. Nevertheless, the pressure of modular programmes was a topic that arose frequently: '. . . we all became obsessed with the next module assignment to be completed . . . it's like a conveyor belt . . . we're being processed, not educated'.

Professional identity

The need for a sense of identity and belonging to a discipline was evident among many students and, similarly, lecturers talked of the importance of 'professional socialization' early in the courses: 'I wanted to identify with my chosen profession early on, and resented the pressure to mix with other courses in my first semester'.

The timing of the shared sessions attracted such comments as: 'I think we ought to develop a sense of what our role is before we can appreciate other health professionals' roles'.

Lecturers differed in their responses to this issue but several felt that the first year of their courses was too early for students to appreciate other professional roles. Perhaps there is a need to develop a sense of one's professional role first, before appreciating where others 'fit in'? One lecturer considered that a sense of professional identity was already formed: '. . . perhaps they want to be socialized into their own profession before they share modules, but then the role boundaries are fixed? . . . somehow, I think their professional identities are already there before they start their courses!'

Another felt that in the multi-disciplinary seminar groups for the research module: '. . . students needed to learn their own professional language, another language for research methods, and work with the professional languages of others in the group, as well as sorting out the group dynamics . . . it was all too much for them!'

Practical application

The need for the taught material to show relevance and application to practice was widely expressed: 'We do need to see the point of what's being offered in these sessions . . . if I can't see its relevance to my practice I'll just switch off!'

Not all comments were negative. There were accounts of good teaching and enjoyable learning, particularly in the common modules shared between two courses: '. . . where the module team obviously got their act together the sessions were great . . . generally well prepared, with good support from the handbook'.

Where factual material was taught, and some students had entered the courses with A level qualifications in the subject (for example, physiology), there were perceived difficulties. One lecturer said: '. . . much of this material they knew already . . . there's a problem with mixed ability and hitting the right level for the majority'.

Following key lectures, some students received tutorial support in the specialist application of material to their field. Teaching staff also perceived the need to cater for multi-disciplinary needs within their key lectures: '. . . there's a need to prepare with some practical examples from their areas of professional practice . . . talking about one's own field all the time is THE way to lose them'.

Discussion of findings

This evaluation has clearly shown that simply putting 200 students from different courses together for an hour in a lecture hall does not produce interprofessional learning; what is needed are clear educational objectives and a rationale for such innovation. There are specific lessons that can be drawn from this study and these concern the organization, planning and delivery of shared learning.

Small module teaching teams appear to have an easier task in planning and delivering the module, and those modules taken by only two professional groups seem to be more successful. There are issues concerning the disproportionate representation by lecturers of the professions participating in the module and the resource questions surrounding this. The view that delivering multi-professional education in any way requires less effort and resourcing was quickly dispelled; in fact it represents a considerable undertaking by all concerned.

Time spent in agreeing the content and level of the module would seem to be very beneficial. Where uncertainty arose, as in one module, the students were quick to spot discrepancies and were rightly critical. Assumptions were made about 'core' content for each of the four courses but the application of this common material to specific disciplines (as in physiology) requires careful preparation. Unless the application of theoretical concepts to specific areas of practice is emphasized, the transferral of knowledge can be inhibited (Bradshaw 1992; Bridges 1993). The question of whether the smaller seminar groups should be uni- or multi-disciplinary continues to generate debate and should be carefully evaluated in future. One valued feature often mentioned was the continuity of lecturers in facilitating seminar groups.

Despite these initial difficulties, a considerable amount of learning seems to have taken place, and not just among the students. Lecturers have discovered unforeseen benefits in collaborating with other disciplines. Individuals with specialized knowledge and skills have been identified to other departments, communication has been opened up and stereotyped images have been challenged and dismantled. In many ways the whole experience has been a 'celebration of differences'; whether it will have any effect on students' developing practice remains to be seen. It is the impact of these initiatives on the quality of healthcare that is in urgent need of further research.

Perhaps in their final year students will realize the importance and relevance of interprofessional education. Despite the initial problems identified in the evaluation, it has been decided to continue with the shared modules for a further year and to review progress again, weighing up the resourcing and logistical demands against the perceived educational advantages.

Conclusions

This small study has highlighted some general features of shared learning that need further development and evaluation if these initiatives are to be successful; these are summarized below.

The motives for shared learning need to be clarified to identify the stakeholders. Two questions should be addressed: (i) in whose interests is shared learning? and (ii) are these initiatives being driven by ideological pressures? Ostensibly it is the students' educational needs that are paramount but one should always bear in mind the economic pressures (in terms of more effective use of resources) that promote shared learning.

Who has a vision of shared learning in the health professions as the way forward? If it is the course and module leaders only, then an uphill struggle seems inevitable. It is vital that within both higher education and the leadership of the professions at interprofessional level is committed to the development of shared learning. Collaboration across departments, schools and faculties can break down many of the practical and bureaucratic difficulties that exist. Professional statutory bodies, with varying registration, funding and practice requirements, sometimes present constraints that need imaginative and tactful negotiation. Government policy for future healthcare will promote further integration of community, hospital and social services, and interprofessional education would appear to be a logical way forward into the twenty-first century (Taylor 1997).

If course leaders and module teams can share a clear vision of the purpose and processes of interprofessional learning, can enjoy equal status and, when necessary, have the confidence to explore differing and conflicting views, the chances of successful cooperation are increased. Collaboration should also be regarded as shared ownership, with each participating group 'signing up' to the venture as an aspect of their formal educational policy. This will involve commitment and support for any extra resources required and the development of a truly multi-disciplinary culture within the organization.

Investment in shared learning involves focusing upon the processes of key lectures, followed by smaller multi-professional group work, conducted by confident, experienced teachers. Practical considerations such as the geographical location of lecture hall and seminar rooms, and the local support of learning resources and catering facilities are all ingredients of successful shared learning. It may also include use of distance learning materials, the world wide web and creative timetabling. Adequate preparation of both staff and students necessitates effective channels of communication, as well as time available for planning meetings and evaluation studies.

The traditional divisions between the health professions have had a negative effect on teamwork, with stereotypical attitudes reinforcing rigid role boundaries, with a resulting impact upon patient and client care (Larson 1995; Leiba 1993). There is evidence that interprofessional education can increase mutual understanding and respect within teams and can enable the breaking down of 'myths, misunderstandings and inappropriate expectation between professions' (Barr and Waterton 1996: 7). However, research into its effects on standards of healthcare is much needed. The Council of Deans and Heads (1998) has asserted that it will support the development of interprofessional education if research shows that it enhances teamwork and patient care. It is incumbent upon the NHS and the universities to establish this connection and then to support this model of education with more than policy statements. Without this central commitment it would seem that shared learning between health professionals will remain little more than a good idea. A quiet revolution is occurring in the division of labour amongst health professionals; the challenge for professional education is to respond to these changes to produce skilled and adaptable practitioners for tomorrow's health service.

5

Independent Learning and Reflective Practice

PRACTICE FOR LIFELONG LEARNING THROUGH INDEPENDENT LEARNING

Jenny Smith

Introduction

> It is not usually difficult to persuade lecturers that some forms of change in courses are desirable. It is much harder to persuade them that it is possible.
>
> (Gibbs 1992: 170)

This case study provides a practical example of how the university can develop the capacity of professional practitioners to engage in lifelong learning and continuing professional development as autonomous learners.

In response to local clinicians who wished to study occupational therapy at Masters level, the University of Brighton developed an MSc in occupational therapy. This incorporated innovative and well-founded theories of teaching and learning, which promoted deep as opposed to surface learning and lifelong learning skills (Boud 1993; Boud *et al.* 1993; Tait and Knight 1996). During 1996–7, whilst this course was being developed, a change in patterns of recruitment within Masters programmes in the school began to be noticed.

Previously, clinicians had been interested in enrolling on professionally oriented courses, for example, MSc in occupational therapy, whereas now they appeared to be more interested in programmes of study related to clinical specialisms, for example, hand therapy, child and adolescent psychiatry and developmental paediatrics.

Until the late 1980s, such courses of study for occupational therapists had been validated and accredited by the College of Occupational Therapists (COT). When this service ceased it was anticipated by COT that special interest groups within the profession would develop courses in partnership with higher education institutions. A hiatus occurred because special interest groups were insecure in this role and it was difficult for a relatively small profession within health and social care to identify sufficient numbers of personnel, interested in a particular area of study within a geographical area, to make it viable for higher education establishments to develop courses.

Changes to the systems of delivery of health and social care in the early 1990s also led to a change in management structures, with the emphasis being based on consumerism and leading on, in more recent years, to the development of evidence-based practice and clinical governance (Department of Health and Social Security [DHSS] 1989a, b; Department of Health [DoH] 1997). Therapy interventions were now being evaluated for their effectiveness and outcome measures became a very important tool. On the horizon, too, was the high probability that future legislative changes affecting the licensing for practice of occupational therapists (and other professions allied to medicine) by the Council for Professions Supplementary to Medicine (CPSM) would build in the requirement for clinicians to engage in CPD.

Taking into account all these factors it seemed sensible to build into the emerging MSc in occupational therapy a means of enabling clinicians to develop their clinical practice. It also seemed logical to enable clinicians to undertake this means of study as a 'stand alone' module in a form that could count as CPD.

Discussions with other course leaders within the Graduate Programme in Health and Social Sciences indicated that other professions, notably nursing and physiotherapy, were experiencing similar difficulties in meeting the needs of clinicians wishing to improve their clinical practice. It was decided to develop a module with a multi-disciplinary approach, to enable a variety of clinicians to enhance their clinical practice by using independent learning strategies. The emphasis would not be the content but the process: the content of the individual's curriculum would be modified by their student needs (Reeve 1993).

The overall aim would be to produce a skilled clinician who could contribute to a lifelong learning culture within organizations, who could manage his/her own learning whilst facilitating the learning of others (Eraut *et al.* 1998). He or she would, at the same time, have the confidence to disseminate the new learning by well honed oral presentation skills or by publishing work.

For clinicians who wished to move their practice forward in a given specialism, independent experiential learning was combined with work-based learning (Henry 1993; Marsick 1990). Staff, peer and self-assessment methods were all used in the design of this single or double module of study. The planning phase of the module was very exciting and it was interesting and reassuring to note that, when researching later, the procedure for instituting change outlined by Gibbs (1992) had been applied.

The module was validated in April 1996 as part of the MSc in occupational therapy but is offered to any student within the Graduate Programme in Health and Social Sciences. It is used as a double module (carrying 20 Masters level crediting points – 20m) or single module (carrying 10 Masters level credit points – 10m) of study and has been adopted as core for some Masters programmes, for example the MSc in occupational therapy and MSc in clinical studies. Other students have elected to study the module as an option.

Process

Students select an area of study, write a learning contract, seek a mentor and then embark on a voyage of discovery where they explore their chosen topic area in depth. The module is designed to improve patient care through the enhanced knowledge of the clinician and to develop in the student the skills and attitudes of the lifelong learner. Learning in the individual student is supported by a personal tutor, a mentor, membership of an action learning set and the university's library and information technology resources.

Area of study

Prior to commencing the module the student has usually broadly identified her/his area of study but this usually requires some refinement to prevent it becoming too large to be addressed within the timescale of the module (one semester [10m level credits] or two semesters [20m level credits]).

Learning contract

Anderson *et al.* (1996) describe the practical applications of learning contracts. In this form of study the learning contract is the key element against which the student's progress and success is assessed. Students must define their existing knowledge, skills and experience, which can be employed as a resource. They must then go on to define deficits in their knowledge, skills and experience. Learning objectives must next be set out which are both attainable and measurable, but also valid and relevant for the area of study.

The student then needs to identify learning resources and strategies that will enable him/her to work towards these objectives. It is very important to set out a schedule for task completion at this stage so that students can be realistic in the size of the commitment.

Students then need to show what they will produce as evidence of their learning by defining the final product they will produce for assessment. They also need to set out the assessment criteria, that is, how they will know that they have been successful.

Learning support

Action learning set

Action learning is a well established form of experiential learning that empowers the students to manage their own learning. The process has been defined by many but notably Revans (1982), Bourner (1989) and McGill *et al.* (1989) but common features involve individual students working on a project or task using the group as a means of guidance and support (see Chapter 3).

Students are allocated to action learning sets of approximately eight students according to the geographical area where they are based. The method of allocation ensures that the sets are multi-disciplinary as far as possible and that the students allocated to each set come from a broad range of work settings. During set meetings each student is allocated a period of 'airtime' when he/she can reflect on progress towards goals, identify barriers to learning or progress and use the rest of the set members as a resource.

Set members are expected to contribute to the support of other set members by open questioning to enable them to move forward and help them to acknowledge progress. The sets are facilitated by university tutors who have been trained in this form of facilitation skill by the International Foundation for Action Learning (IFAL). The role of the set facilitator is not to act as a subject expert or to dominate proceedings but to disseminate information regarding the module process, to act as a resource for learning, to question carefully and to ensure that the students are using the process of the sets correctly and are moving forwards towards their goals.

The action learning set meets three times per semester. The early set meetings tend to be preoccupied by the students narrowing down their areas of study and developing their learning contracts. Subsequent sets are used by the individual students to develop their ideas or recognize their progress and personal growth.

Mentor

It should be emphasized at this point that this form of study acknowledges that the university tutor is not the 'subject expert'. The students may well already be experts in their own field, choosing to use this form of study to move their practice even further forward. The university tutor can therefore monitor and guide the learning process but is unlikely to be able to comment or advise on the content of the student's individual curriculum.

Prior to embarking on this method of study the student is advised to seek the support of a mentor. Students are advised that this should be a well known national or international figure who has published extensively within the chosen area of study. The role of the mentor is to be used as a learning resource or 'expert' in a consultancy role. They can act as a guide for the student to avoid repeating work already undertaken by others or becoming entrenched. The student is required to present the mentor's curriculum vitae for approval at the same time as the learning contract. The student is allotted five hours of mentor time in total, which is funded out of the course fees by the university. It was considered important to give each student a 'budget' of mentor time in order to encourage them to prepare for mentoring sessions, manage the mentor as a resource and use the time effectively.

Personal tutor

Each student is allocated five hours of personal tutor time. The personal tutor for the purposes of this module is the facilitator of the action learning set to which the student is allocated. The personal tutor's role is to act as a resource for the student, facilitating and enabling her/him to move forward through the module's process. Again, it was considered to be important to restrict this time to encourage the student to manage their personal tutor as a resource and use the time effectively.

Other learning resources

Students have access to the university libraries but may also choose to spend time studying in other more specialized libraries. The university libraries allocate each student a number of interlibrary loans and will be supportive in seeking out texts and journal articles to support the student's learning. The students are also inducted into the rich delights of the Internet (if they are not already regular users of this source) and they are given access to the Internet via the university's computer pools.

Assessment

Assessment was designed to meet the learning outcomes of the module and is embedded within the process of the module. The assessments vary depending on whether the student is undertaking the single module (10m) over one semester or the double module (20m) over two semesters.

Portfolio of evidence

The portfolio is tutor-assessed and will be worth 50 per cent (10m) or 33 per cent (20m) of the final mark. It will include the following:

• A copy of the individual learning contract – although previously agreed with the personal tutor and the action learning set early in the process of the module, this may have needed adjustment during the course of study, after negotiation. This will be linked to a plan of how learning will take place.

- Reflective reports – these could be on critical incidents, meetings or conferences attended in conjunction with the module.
- Précis and evaluation of journal articles – these might identify articles or other publications that have influenced the individual student's thinking and direction.
- Statements of relevance – these will reflect on the proceedings of the action learning set meetings and will cover the contributions that the individual student has made to the sets and the effect this has had on others, as well as what the individual student has derived from the set meetings in the way of support and guidance.
- Evidence of achievement of learning outcomes – this will be a summary of the student's progress and, although they may not have achieved implementation of service changes, the student may have reached a point where an action plan, fully supported by research-based practice evidence, could be provided for the employing organization.
- References – a wide range of references, including Internet web sites, is required as well as a list of searched databases.

Ten-minute seminar presentation

This is peer assessed and will be worth 50 per cent (10m) or 33 per cent (20m). This is a presentation of the student's work and will be followed by 15 minutes of the individual student facilitating discussion. The assessment is based on both the content and presentation skills.

An article or poster for publication

The article (which is required only for 20m) will be approximately 3000 words and will follow the publishing guidelines of the journal selected by the student for publication. A poster presentation will follow university guidelines for publication.

Evaluation

The first cohort completed the module very successfully in the summer of 1998 and the second group are well advanced in the exploration of their topics. A longitudinal research project is being undertaken by the author into the motivation of individual students to undertake this form of study and into its effects on their skills in managing their own learning and facilitating that of others within the workplace. The first evaluation of data was undertaken in the summer of 1997. The aim of this study was to evaluate why the first cohort of students wished to undertake this module of study and what they were hoping to attain (Smith 1997).

Fourteen students from a range of health and social care roles and settings were surveyed by a brief semi-structured questionnaire as they embarked on the module. They were asked about their professional backgrounds, clinical specialisms, reasons for selecting this mode of study and their hopes for what this module would equip or enable them to do in the future. The results of this questionnaire were analysed using a qualitative, thematic coding analysis. A brief summary of the findings of the study were that the students wanted to undertake this form of study because it directly and specifically related to their area of professional/clinical work. Some students undertook the module because it was prescribed by the Masters qualification, whilst others felt it was the only module of study available within the graduate programme that related to their work setting in this way. They all wished to advance their clinical practice and valued the opportunity that this module would offer in providing protected time, space and the resources to attain their objectives.

Lessons and recommendations

In opening up this new and exciting form of study within the Graduate Programme in Health and Social Sciences, some valuable lessons have been learned:

- Time – the students often take more time than is anticipated to finalize their learning contracts and identify and recruit a mentor. It was anticipated that they should be able to do this by the end of the first month of study. This is essential in order to complete their project within the one (10m) or two (20m) seminars of the module. It is felt that students possibly need more guidance to begin this process before they embark on the module.
- Assessment – peer assessment was used to assess a 10-minute seminar element. This was found to have inflated the mark of some students, notably the weaker ones. The module team are currently deciding with the external examiner the best way of dealing with this difficulty but are currently leaning towards using peer assessment formatively in the form of comments and advice from fellow students but counting the tutor mark as the summative assessment.
- Success – the module was evaluated by students, tutors, mentors and other course leaders alike as having been a huge success. It has been largely used as part of a named route towards a Masters level qualification but it has great potential to be offered as CPD module, which need not be restricted to health and social care professionals. To this end, a shift in focus of marketing is required. Work is currently being undertaken to offer this module along with others to students via the Internet.

Conclusion

In conclusion it seems appropriate to quote a reflection from one of the first students to study this module:

For a learner who has come from a background of teacher controlled education, where the goals are set by the institution and students receive rather than explore, it was a marked change in the process of learning. Initially I thought it was easy, as no-one would control my pace of education. But when I started on the planning of it I realized the great responsibility that had come on me. I realized that I was answerable to myself for whatever I did to achieve the goal of learning. It was very difficult to plan for my own education, to work out objectives and to write evidence to prove that learning had taken place. Once the objectives, the goals and the plans were established, it gave me satisfaction of being a part of the project. I felt ownership of the project.

I can see the benefits of independent learning. Whatever is learnt can be implemented in clinical practice. It motivates the learner to achieve goals because of ownership of the project. The other learners and facilitators become a resource for learning. It is an interesting and challenging way of learning. It can be a way to promote lifelong learning.

A MASTERS DEGREE BY LEARNING OBJECTIVES

Patrick Palmer

Introduction

The MSc by Learning Objectives is normally completed part-time as a work-based learning programme but is flexible enough to be adapted to a variety of situations.

It begins with the development of a learning contract based on a number of negotiated goals. The final goal is the presentation of a dissertation, which has to include a reflective quality. This can be onerous unless the contract has been conceived and implemented with reflective practice in mind throughout.

This case study provides a report of the philosophy and practice of the MSc by Learning Objectives offered by the University of Brighton since 1996. Responses to frequently asked questions are used to provide an account of this Masters degree.

Questions

How would you briefly describe a Masters degree by learning objectives?
A self-managed period of postgraduate level learning, driven by a learning contract determined at the start and concluding with a relatively short dissertation.

To what areas of study can it be applied?
It was initially developed for work-based learning in an engineering context but it is equally applicable to any area of study and can include the interests of unemployed or retired people.

Is it a taught degree or a research degree?
It tries to gain benefit from both these traditional routes. Like the taught degree, there is a programme of study determined in advance and there may or may not be taught elements to it; and like the research degree, it is self-determined and may involve some research. The point about the taught part and the research part is that if they are appropriate to the aim of the student, and agreed by the parties to the contract, then they are included.

Can you give some examples?
Three examples from the recent past have been:

1. A small manufacturing company making electric motors wanted to develop a new motor for use in electric wheelchairs. Although this had been done before, advances in technology needed to be brought together to incorporate improvements in performance and cost-cutting to make the product competitive. The learning contract was focused on this problem and had a research and development orientation.
2. An architectural firm used an MSc student to develop a computer database that would incorporate their growing expertise in office design, thus enabling them to advise clients quickly on the optimum design for particular sites. Initially, the student, who had studied architecture, knew nothing about computer databases but she learned about the various types, set up a database and developed a training scheme for the staff of the firm.
3. A student was employed by a very large organization as an electrical engineer but, because of a physical disability, he had a need and wish to reorientate his career in a management direction. With the agreement of his employer, a learning contract was developed that broadened his engineering knowledge to include building engineering, so that he could better manage multi-disciplinary construction contracts. He also trained in a variety of computer-oriented skills so that he could lead and implement a raft of changes concerning the use of computers in the company.

What is the purpose of the learning contract?
The learning contract is a written agreement between the student and the university. An employer may also be a party to the contract. At the beginning of the process, the purpose of the learning contract is to concentrate the minds of those involved (particularly that of the student) on the aim of the contract and how it can be practically implemented. A well-written contract generates the circumstances in which higher level learning is most likely to occur. During the period of study, when the other elements of a student's

Figure 5.1 Hierarchical structure of learning contract

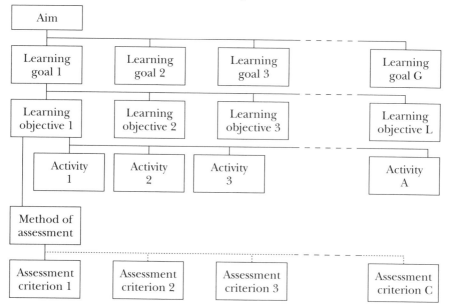

The learning contract also identifies the assessors and any special resources needed to achieve each learning goal.

life often provide obstacles to progress, the learning contract acts as a rudder, reminding the parties of the essential aim and the means of getting there. At the end of the programme, the learning contract both serves as a measure of what has been achieved and provides the framework for assessment.

What are the characteristics of the learning contract?
As can be seen in Figure 5.1, to achieve an aim, a number of learning goals are identified, usually in the range six to twelve. Each learning goal is broken down into a number of learning objectives (typically three or four in number), the successful completion of which result in that goal being achieved and assessed. A learning objective can be thought of as the smallest assessable piece of learning. As each activity contributes to a learning objective; the method of assessment and the criteria for assessment can be defined in advance.

An example of an aim, from the learning contract of a student employed in a manufacturing company, is: 'to establish principles and criteria for the successful design of generic products in a mechatronics context'.

An example of a learning goal is (one of eight for the aim given above): 'to establish a design methodology for the generic product range'.

The learning objectives associated with this learning goal included background reading and facilitating brainstorming sessions. The activities divided the tasks into even smaller units. One of the assessment criteria was to obtain company agreement to a clear definition of the term 'generic product'.

How is the need for additional study at undergraduate level accommodated and accredited at Masters level?

This question is best answered with an example. Joan Smith's MSc (not her real name) was in the area of management by continuous improvement. Some of the learning objectives required her to use statistics packages on the computer but she had never studied statistics beyond General Certificate in Secondary Education (GCSE) level. In this case, it was appropriate for Joan to attend a short, taught undergraduate course in statistics and its application using a standard computer package. The attendance at this short course was one of the activities for the first learning objective that required the use of statistics. The important point is that the Masters level of the goal was expressed as the application of this learning to the situation she had at work. The goal would have been unacceptable as a goal set at Masters level, had not the learning objectives included the application of the statistics in the workplace. The assessment criteria also expressed Masters-level work by requiring the application to be successful in demonstrably saving money as part of the continuous improvement.

How difficult is it to develop a learning contract?

Learning contracts are covered widely in Anderson *et al.* (1996) but, in our experience, the contract drafting team experience difficulty in one or more of the following areas:

- finding an aim that will endure;
- building in some flexibility;
- writing assessment criteria that are at MSc level.

Whereas some students find relatively little difficulty in defining their aim in generic terms that will never waiver, others prefer to begin by visualizing the activities, the learning objectives and goals that such activities imply, and finally develop the wording for the aim, which was known all the way along but which was so difficult to articulate! It usually takes a period of around two months to develop a learning contract but the effort is worthwhile if its endurance is to be a measure of its strength.

The need for flexibility arises for such reasons as illness, redundancy or even a radical change in the ownership and aims of an employer. It is possible to build in a procedure for renegotiating learning contracts. Our experience is that about half the contracts are renegotiated in some respects. Generally, it is rare for the aim to change but changes to individual goals or learning objectives are fairly commonplace.

Defining the criteria for assessment at MSc level has proved to be one of the most difficult areas of implementation of this degree and remains a developmental aim of the university. The easiest starting point is to refer to the standards commonly adopted on traditional Masters courses and to undergraduate and doctoral programmes. Many supervisors and learning contract drafters nevertheless find it difficult to put into words the criteria for Masters level standards. What is available to date is a set of 'indicative criteria' to include ideas such as insight and independence. A demonstrable recognition and use of previous knowledge should be evident. If it is insisted that reflective thinking be part of the assessment regime it would have to be acknowledged that some very able people show a limited capacity; they feel uncomfortable when forced to do so, unless they can be prompted with questions such as 'what, with hindsight, would you have done more/less of?' None the less, good reflective writing characterizes the best dissertations. However, the course seeks to develop the capacity of students to learn from reflection on professional experience in order to achieve continuous professional improvement. Here, the generic criteria developed by South East England Consortium (SEEC) can give appropriate cues to the contract designers (SEEC 1997).

Who decides what is in it?
A team involving the student, the academic supervisor and the workplace supervisor (if any) composes the best learning contracts. But someone has to start the process; it is usual for the student to table the first draft.

Why is there only one aim?
To have a single aim, well expressed, avoids the doubt implied by having more than one aim. Where multiple aims are being considered we have found that it is better to think of them as learning goals and to then find a single aim that embraces all these goals. The benefits of doing this arise in the many cases where unforeseen circumstances cause changes in direction of the learning contract. If the aim has been well composed at the start it will have lasting value for the duration of the contract. One of the many characteristics of postgraduate study is the self-doubt that afflicts many students, especially when they are working alone. In this situation, a strongly written aim acts as a beacon in the darkness to which renewed efforts at achievement can be directed.

How long does it take?
Although a notional time of 1200 hours spread over two years is expected, many students vary this quite substantially. It is possible for retired or unemployed people to study full-time and complete the work within one year. For those who are working, and relating their MSc to their work, a flexibility commensurate with the demands of business life is needed for successful completion.

How do you do it?
The process is essentially as follows:

- The first goal is to negotiate a learning contract (about two months). Each contract has an aim and a number of learning goals that point towards that aim.
- Complete each learning goal in turn (between one and three months per goal); any changes to the contract that become necessary are negotiated

and agreed as you go. Goals are assessed as they are completed. Goals can overlap in time, if necessary.
- The last goal is to write the short dissertation (about one month, say).
- Examination by viva and dissertation of about 4000 words.

Why is the dissertation so short?
The dissertation will typically be about 15 pages long (about 4000 words) but the evidence for all the learning is not so short and may also be presented at the viva that concludes the MSc. A short dissertation forces the student to summarize the content and the relevance of each learning goal, as it relates to the single aim. It also concentrates the minds of the examining team at the viva.

Where would the work be undertaken?
Anywhere relevant to the pursuit of the aim. If a taught course is required, then the place of that taught course is where that part of the work is undertaken. One answer to this question is 'the brain of the student', an excellent example of a portable place, fully equipped with ideas processor, to do the work.

Why would anyone do it?
Our students' motivations are diverse but have included: professional self-development, contributing to the attainment of a firm's mission, MSc, satisfaction, insight, possible promotion or a new job.

How will it enhance the student's professional development?
The pursuit of this Masters degree contributes to the attainment of a firm's mission, gains an MSc or MA for the student and may lead to promotion or a new job. The degree comprises directed learning in which the student, university (and, possibly, the employer) have a partnership expressed in the learning contract. The student is then well placed to improve knowledge, apply that knowledge and gain an understanding of how the work relates to what the rest of the world is doing in that field and closely related fields.

What sort of help can other people offer the student?
Any resourceful student is likely to draw on other people for help in assembling data, interpreting it and formulating a new direction to follow. Some students need help with developing their communication skills. The climate of learning is greatly assisted by the support given by family and friends. The ethical question is, then, who should be awarded the degree? Has the student acknowledged the assistance given by others and is it clear which parts of the work are his or her own? This is a particular issue if the student wants to study remotely, in another country, say.

The dissertation is one important location for the accreditation of reflective learning. Reflective activity leads to ownership and this can be tested rigorously at the viva.

Can it be extended to a PhD or other level of qualification?
The model of the learning contract could be applicable to some, if not all, of a doctorate programme. It is particularly appropriate as a platform for the newly emerging professional doctorates. Some learning contracts for the MSc by Learning Objectives have proceeded as smoothly as foreseen at the time of drawing up the learning contract. But many do not, and require the contract to be amended 'on the hoof'. This is a likely outcome in a research orientated study programme if it is to include any creative element that may cause the programme to change its expected route. The learning contract is suitable for shifting sands as well as for firm ground.

How is it known whether the learning is at Masters level?
This is one of the most difficult areas to define in the learning contract. Referring again to Figure 5.1, the criteria for assessing any part of the work would ideally be clearly at Masters level. One criterion is the demonstration of new insights; yet such a criterion may well be argued for levels of education other than Masters level. Brockbank and McGill (1998) have promoted the idea that the assessment of reflective learning needs to consider both the outcome and the process. The viva has an important role to play in assessing both and can refer to the SEEC criteria for confirmation (SEEC 1997).

Can non-graduates be successful on this programme?
Most undergraduate degrees prepare for Masters level study by having at least one major dissertation to complete in the final year of the degree programme. This formative experience of research and presentation of a major study is an important prerequisite for success at Masters level. If an applicant has no such experience on a degree course they may well be able to offer equivalent experience in their place of work. In the absence of this, it is possible in some cases for the early goals in a learning contract to concentrate on developing the skills that will be need for the successful completion of the dissertation.

How does this development fit into the past, present and future of professional development?
The current form of this MSc was based on a model articulated by the Teaching Company Centre Directorate (TCC 1996).

In one sense, this is just a modern form of what must have been going on for centuries; that is, think about what you want to learn, write it down and then go and learn it. Then prove you have learned it, through an academic procedure, which will then accredit you with that learning. Its 1990s expression is found in the MSc in the learning objectives described and in closely related educational frameworks.

What does the future hold?
At the time of writing (1999) the future seems to be very much more electronic. Communication between people around world is so much easier

and the sharing of ideas so much richer than hitherto. In all this it is as well to remember that a Masters degree is only an indicator of accomplishments, not the accomplishment itself. The future of professional life is set to be as interdisciplinary as ever it was. It could well be argued that all Masters programmes start as interdisciplinary and then become a discipline as they age.

Conclusion

Since implementing this degree, some 30 or more students have graduated with their MSc obtained in this way. Additionally, the thinking described in this chapter has entered other parts of the higher education curriculum.

Some of the lessons learned at this early stage are related to *any* innovation, for example, leadership is needed to help novice supervisors in the preparation of suitable contracts. The lessons learned for the course, once the novelty has passed by, are that the quality of external examining can have a profound effect on the standards achieved; and, in developing reflective writing, many students need guidance and encouragement on a continuing basis. Hence, the quality of supervision also impacts on the outcome of the programmes. The most successful programmes have engaged employers as willing and active participants, to their own benefit, as well as that of the students.

The learning contract model provides a strong framework whose motivating attributes and adaptability are well suited to focused professional development. It is possible to recognize work as being at Masters level and to write into contracts the criteria for that recognition. Although the assessment is a difficult issue, it is secondary to the very real achievements that have been made by the many students who have been successful.

INDEPENDENT REFLECTION IN TEACHER EDUCATION

Angela Pickering

Introduction

In this case study I report a personal 'journey', which began when a number of problems were identified in relation to the reflective practice component of a teacher education course for which I was responsible. The account traces the process by which I was led to consider two issues: the role of reflective practice in teacher education, particularly for teachers with limited experience, and the means by which reflective processes and reflective outcomes might be facilitated.

I begin by recounting my own teacher education context and the problems it has highlighted. I go on to present a conceptual framework that has helped me to revise my approach to reflective practice. I conclude with a summary of the curriculum changes I have made in the light of my analysis and a consideration of the extent to which my conclusions are transferable to other professional contexts.

'The more I teach the better I will become'

Looking back over the last two years, it has been interesting, hard work, the blood, sweat and even a few tears . . . I realize I still have quite a lot to learn yet . . . It is coming slowly and obviously the more I teach the better I will become.
                    (Student teacher, Diploma in Teaching English to
                              Speakers of Other Languages (Dip. TESOL),
                                              University of Brighton)

What constitutes a teacher's craft knowledge, and the process by which it is acquired, are subjects on which most teachers have an informal theory. The role of teaching experience in the development of effective teaching ends to occupy an important place in such theories. However, the process by which experience leads (or does not lead) to effective teaching, is far from clear. And yet beliefs about such a process are central not only to most teachers' informal theories about teaching but also to the design and delivery of teacher education programmes. Such programmes need to have a guiding approach towards two key areas: what a teacher needs to know and the process by which this knowledge is acquired. They also need to address the tension between learning about teaching from training programmes and the learning that takes place as a result of practice (Van Manen 1995: 37). This tension is particularly strong in the world of teaching English to speakers of other languages (TESOL), where a very high premium is placed on learning from experience. Customer attitudes to TESOL qualifications are defined by the weighting their assessment procedures give to practical teaching.

A teacher education context

Background: reflective practice as a syllabus imperative

As Course Leader for the Diploma in TESOL (Dip. TESOL) at the University of Brighton, I am responsible for the design of a teacher education programme that serves English as a Foreign Language (EFL) teachers who come both from the local community and from overseas. The Diploma is not an initial teaching qualification and students who enrol on it will normally have had some recent teaching experience.

In 1994, while redesigning the existing Dip. TESOL programme, a decision was taken to build a reflective teaching diary into the curriculum. This had been prompted by an informal survey of influential training models, such as the RSA/UCLES DELTA (Royal Society of Arts and The University of Cambridge Diploma in English Language Teaching to Adults) syllabus, which had focused attention on reflective practice in TESOL training.

In the revised syllabus, Dip. TESOL student teachers were required to approach experience systematically and to draw upon a variety of knowledge sources in order to reflect on teaching. Reflection was oriented to the past and future and aimed to enable the student teacher to gain context-related insights by means of clearly defined cognitive processes, such as thinking, introspecting, looking back and evaluating. Reflection on practice was seen as an important context for learning from practice, in which 'knowing about' and 'knowing how' were united. Practice consisted of EFL lessons taught by the student teachers themselves (which might have been videoed, observed by peers, observed by tutors or unobserved) and peer-teaching activities.

The problems

Over the years following the implementation of the revised Diploma syllabus, a number of concerns were voiced by tutors and student teachers. Between 1994 and 1997 an informal analysis of reflection outcomes and processes, which was based mainly on teaching diaries and tutor evaluation of teaching diaries, raised a series of concerns that were related to: what it is that teachers need to know (and therefore reflect on); how it is that teachers learn and develop (the process and outcome of reflection); and the extent to which reflection on practice can help student teachers develop their teaching skills.

For example, student teachers were often required to focus on their own strengths and weaknesses. In doing so they tended to adopt a shopping list approach to teaching skills and the checklists produced were often either context-bound and not used to generalize from or so decontextualized as to be difficult to relate back to practice. Many also found it difficult to move beyond 'the problem' or 'success' they had identified.

Reflective narrative could be defensive in tone. Justifications for action tended to rehearse arguments from methodology or second language acquisition theories but did not relate these to specific teaching problems. An important paradox was identified in connection with this. In spite of the frequent reference to espoused theories, students (and particularly those with limited experience), tended to see most of their problems in terms of an impoverished knowledge-base of skills and techniques, which could most effectively be improved by experience or exposure to best practice.

The process of written reflection was seen by a number of student teachers as a time-wasting academic exercise, which did not capture the reality of decision-making within a lesson itself. Descriptive accounts were the norm and analysis tended towards superficiality. Student teachers often felt that they were saying what they thought their audience wished to hear, quoting aspects of academic theory, for example, of which they suspected their tutors would approve. Student teachers who had difficulty with the diary-writing process were mostly unable to make experiences 'their own'. They also felt uneasy about the isolated introspective process of diary-writing, which seemed very different in character from the informal discussions with colleagues in which a student teacher might normally engage.

Such *ad hoc* findings were found to resonate with research findings. A tendency to display survival orientation, instrumental motivation, an unwillingness to consider the wider context, a difficulty in being self-critical in threatening situations, a lack of a language of reflection and a lack of a skills repertoire were all problems that had previously been identified (Borko *et al.* 1988; Calderhead 1987; Hatton and Smith 1995). The reflective product had turned out to be influenced by a large number of variables, such as the student's own learning orientation, which influenced the need for self-discovery (Korthagen 1988), the degree of previous experience (Calderhead 1988; Copeland 1981; Russell 1988), the degree of subject and case knowledge (Shulman 1986), role perception (Hatton and Smith 1995; Valli 1992), and the barriers of the student's own beliefs (Russell 1988; Zeichner, Tabachnik and Densmore 1987). Teachers within a predominantly oral culture experienced difficulty in addressing the task of written reflection (Eraut 1994b; Hatton and Smith 1995).

A trigger for the analysis

In the process of implementing the Diploma programme it had become clear that reflection is neither an automatic nor an easy process and that, although it is possible to define reflective outcomes, it is less easy to describe the reflective process. Reflective practice, although it is becoming a teacher education orthodoxy (the various approaches to which are summarized in Hatton and Smith 1995), was felt to be a slippery concept that held a lot of potential for confusion.

The trigger for my analysis had been the mismatch between the perceived needs of the Diploma student teachers and the extent to which the Diploma programme was providing for these needs. The analysis that follows was guided by the (often emotional) responses of the student teachers themselves, such as the following comment:

> . . . I wasted a lot of time going over what went wrong in my lessons and it made me lose a bit of confidence for a while. I don't need to write things down to know what went wrong . . . I hate the feedback after the lesson is finished. What I need is help and suggestions while I am teaching . . . I also feel that more experience will help build my confidence . . . and I need more ideas.

Reflecting on reflection

A flirtation with Schön

In the process of revisiting reflection it was essential to engage with that most influential of theorists – Schön. Schön's epistemology (Schön 1983, 1987) is a philosophy of practice that is very attractive to teachers. His central concept of 'reflection-in-action', described as 'a reflective conversation with the materials of a situation' (Schön 1987: 31), is particularly attractive because of its rejection of the rationalist, didactic theory into practice approach in favour of a non-logical and intuitive approach to professional development. For example, it helps to explain the process of 'thinking on your feet' and other intangible skills. His description of the competent professional as someone who operates in a constant experiential mode, in which 'practice is a kind of research' and 'knowing and doing are inseparable' (Schön 1987: 165), is seen by many to represent a truth about professional practice.

When the Dip. TESOL student quoted earlier noted the need for help and ideas, it might be useful to consider which processes and which knowledge bases she was hoping to access. Was she, for example, attempting to implement reflection-in-action? In considering this issue I found it useful to consider whether it was feasible to describe what is actually occurring within the 'hot' atmosphere of the classroom as reflection. It has been argued that, if too closely bound up with action, cognitive processes may not serve the function of enlightenment, particularly where the individual's knowledge base or manipulation of that knowledge is limited (Bengtsson 1995). Diploma student teachers had found that survival, enjoyment, desperation and other emotional responses were often uppermost in their minds in the classroom context, and so reflection on problems was difficult and crisis management was the order of the day.

All teachers know that the average 'classroom' situation is an environment in which time and timing are crucial factors. The 'engaged intimacy' (Van Manen 1995: 35) with which the teacher must behave is characterized in the experienced teacher by an ability to extemporize, to cope with 'front stage' action (Goffman 1959). But it is precisely in this context that deliberative action is difficult. Decision-making in the 'classroom' often occurs within a rapid time frame.

Now I return to the issue of the knowledge base of my student teachers and the extent to which an impoverished knowledge base might act as a block both to reflection while teaching and to retrospective reflection. While retrospective reflection may be more deliberative and less emotional, a reflective outcome, qualitatively different from the rapid decision making that occurs within the teaching situation, is not easy to achieve. The reason for this difficulty might lie in the circularity of a reflective process that relies heavily on the quality of the individual's perception of the situation on which he or she is reflecting and the access that individual has to alternative perceptions. In short, although reflection on practice is considered to be an important source of knowledge about teaching, gaining access to that knowledge through reflection is difficult.

The Diploma programme had enshrined the importance of learning from practice through reflection but the retrospective reflection with which students were involved had failed to result, for a significant number of students, in enlightenment or self-discovery, and had actually resulted in loss of confidence and disillusionment in many.

A framework for the facilitation of reflective outcomes

In the process of re-examining the problems highlighted by the student teachers and tutors on the Dip. TESOL course it seemed that a significant number of the issues raised could be reframed in terms of three concepts; the notion of perspective, the ownership of knowledge and the creation of relevance.

The importance of perspective

Von Wright (1992) has identified the concept of distance as being crucial to the achievement of qualitatively superior reflective outcomes. In retrospective reflection, distance is both temporal and spatial. However, it may be more useful to consider the process of distancing as a multi-dimensional concept, in which distance is a 'way of seeing', or 'perspective'. Student teachers, particularly those with less experience, had felt that they needed to improve their craft knowledge but they had found it difficult to 'look habitually for the learning' (Jamieson 1994: 40) in their experience. It was helpful to consider how professional education programmes such as the Dip. TESOL might facilitate the acquisition of 'perspective'. The key to this process seemed to lie in the way in which knowledge was defined. My conclusions were informed by insights gained from the literature on professional development and are centred on an eclectic description of knowledge.

The ownership of knowledge

Ronald Barnett has argued that the professional practitioner should be able to operate within a critical framework and that the ability to operate critically depends to a large extent on an individual practitioner's access to a wide variety of knowledge. He argues that the professional context should not be seen as the boundary of either what a professional needs to know or the process by which he or she develops (Barnett 1997b). Knowledge, in this sense, can be both public and private in character. Michael Eraut (1994b: 74) has highlighted a 'practical paradox' in relation to public knowledge (or theory), which is very relevant to the teacher educator:

> If public theory is taught but does not get used, it gets consigned to some remote attic of the mind, from where it is unlikely to be retrieved, as it has already been labelled irrelevant. But, if public theory is not taught, teacher's ability to theorise is handicapped by their limited repertoire of available concepts, ideas and principles.

There have been various attempts to define the way in which private knowledge and personal theories are created but the most convincing attempts are those that take into account the filtering function of personal perceptions. Knowledge has been described by Calderhead, for example, as something that interacts with the 'belief systems, implicit theories, schema (and) images . . .' (Calderhead 1989: 47) of an individual teacher.

If knowledge is therefore both a public and private entity, if it is filtered through a complex web of beliefs, attitudes, emotions and conceptual frameworks and is, in turn, bounded by what an individual 'knows', then it is useful to consider how a teacher education context might facilitate the acquisition of the kind of knowledge that an effective practitioner needs. It might be helpful, for example, to assume that knowledge, ideas and beliefs can interact with other knowledge ideas and beliefs as fruitfully as they can interact with practice. The value of knowledge would then be a factor not of its source but of its perceived relevancy, and it would be by the perception of relevancy that knowledge would become accessible, insights would be reframed in practical terms and knowledge would be owned.

The creation of relevance

Theorizing has been described as a process by which relevance can be created (Eraut 1994b). Theorizing involves making knowledge one's own through its interaction, not only with one's self and one's experience but also through its interaction with other theories and, one could add, with other practitioners' theories. In my own context I have interpreted theorizing as being an intellectual process that involves critical faculties and which may use a variety of knowledges (both experiential and non-experiential). This is an attractive concept because it addresses the notion of the different developmental needs of the professional practitioner and widens the context in which learning about teaching might take place. In many reflective practice models, reflection tends to be interpreted as an individual introspective activity that is isolated and isolating. An advantage of theorizing is the extent to which it has the potential to reinforce the notion of a community of professional practitioners, as theorizing and the creation of relevance can actually be facilitated by interaction with others. In this context it is interesting to observe the growing significance attached to 'dialogue' in reflective learning (Brockbank and McGill 1998).

Conclusions

I have described a journey that was prompted by the recognition of a practical problem. The journey has involved me in retrospective reflection on my own practice. I needed to distance myself from my problem, to engage with a variety of knowledge sources, which were filtered through my own personal beliefs and theories, and to perceive the relevance of my analysis to my own context. I have concluded that, in relation to my own teacher education context, there is no easy solution to the facilitation of reflective outcomes. I believe, however, that it is important for teacher educators to acknowledge the need to move away from the straightjacket of the individual classroom event and to embrace experiential learning (Kolb 1984) in its widest sense, in which experiences are not only directly related to the individual teaching event but also include opportunities to theorize, to create relevance and to own knowledge.

Changes and modifications

The Dip. TESOL curriculum has always undergone fine-tuning and has changed gradually over time. Reflections on reflective practice have led to a number of modifications in my own practice:

- Opportunities are given to students to theorize on the process of learning as well as teaching. Components are delivered in ways that mirror the EFL methods that student teachers themselves will use with their students. Experience as learners then provides a valuable context for filtering knowledge about learning through the individual's own personal beliefs about teaching.
- Future needs are predicted through problem-based learning tasks and the devising of action plans, which offsets the deadening effect of retrospective reflection. This process has been termed prospecting.
- A mentor system has been set up, in which a relationship with an EFL class can be developed without the pressure to 'perform', and can therefore become the basis for developing the skill of 'looking for learning'.
- Students are still required to keep a reflective diary. In order to help them to achieve greater insight, diary-writing is supplemented by opportunities to theorize with peers. This helps individuals to assess the relevance of knowledge to personal developmental needs. Interaction with interested others allows students to filter public theories and other students' personal theories through their own personal beliefs and attitudes. This is a process that is useful at any developmental stage. Talking with peers also helps in the development of a professional voice and mirrors the oral culture of teaching.

A wider context

I began by noting the intangibility of the process by which a teacher develops craft knowledge. The importance of the facilitation of reflective outcomes is, however, relevant to a wider professional audience. Currently, with increased awareness of the importance of lifelong learning, there is a greater need for professionals to embrace change and innovation and to learn and develop independently. In any professional context, therefore, if reflective outcomes are desirable, professional educators need to consider how practitioners might be enabled to reflect. It is important for professional educators not to neglect facilitative processes and to acknowledge that, where individual practitioners do not find it easy to achieve reflective outcomes, bridges can be provided. I have found it useful to recognize the need to nurture perspective, to offer opportunities for practitioners to recognize the relevance of a variety of knowledge sources and to help them to own this knowledge by systematically reframing it in terms of their own changing beliefs.

6

Using the New Learning Technologies

INTEGRATING LEARNING TECHNOLOGIES INTO PROFESSIONAL DEVELOPMENT PROGRAMMES

Katie Herson, Michael H. Sosabowski and Andrew W. Lloyd

Introduction

Continuous professional development (CPD) is becoming increasingly important in the medical field as changes in technology occur ever more rapidly. Effective medical provision relies on primary healthcare professionals having up-to-date knowledge and experience. However, financial constraints within these services often limit the available resources for professional development and there is an increasing need for more effective means of delivery. The integration of learning technologies into professional development courses could offer remote access to learning support material and a means of facilitating active learning. Although the use of learning technologies has been shown to be particularly beneficial for distance learning courses (Kaplan *et al.* 1996) this approach is limited by the need for access to the necessary computing equipment and the provision of basic training. Consequently, there is a growing need for training in the use of learning technologies for future professionals, early in their careers. This case study describes the approaches taken by the School of Pharmacy and Biomolecular Sciences at the University of Brighton to utilize learning technologies in undergraduate and postgraduate courses and provide requisite training for future professional pharmacists.

Within the School of Pharmacy and Biomolecular Sciences at the University of Brighton we have developed various distance learning courses for CPD including the Postgraduate Diploma/MSc in Industrial Pharmaceutical Sciences and, more recently, a Postgraduate Diploma/MSc in Community

Pharmaceutical Healthcare. Both courses involve the completion of distance learning training modules and the attendance of triennial residential training sessions. These courses attract pharmaceutical scientists and healthcare professionals from across the UK and, in some cases, Europe. Although the students have the opportunity to meet and interact as part the residential training sessions, they suffer to some extent from the inability to communicate effectively with each other and benefit from group learning. In addition, the modules are paper based, which limits the ability to readily update the material in order to provide an insight into the latest development within the healthcare fields. In an attempt to overcome these problems the course development team for the Postgraduate Diploma/MSc in Community Pharmaceutical Healthcare decided to try to use learning technologies, based on the current work with undergraduate courses.

Current undergraduate learning technologies

The School of Pharmacy and Biomolecular Sciences has developed and implemented a range of learning technologies as part of the learning and teaching programmes on undergraduate courses over recent years. This work focuses on three of these, namely:

- computer-assisted learning (CAL) packages;
- school intranet;
- newsgroups.

In addition to the direct learning benefit on specific courses and/or modules, the students' utilization of these technologies at an undergraduate level will prepare them for more effective use of the technologies as part of postgraduate professional development programmes. The benefits of using such technology-based learning support materials is perhaps more important outside the university, where access to other learning support is more restricted.

The following sections briefly describe these learning technologies:

Computer-assisted learning packages

These were developed as part of the HEFCE Teaching and Learning Technology programmes in the fields of pharmacy, pharmacology and chemistry and have been subsequently integrated into course curricula to provide both direct and additional learning support material on undergraduate courses. The packages are designed to be interactive and under complete student control. This allows the student to work at his or her own pace and to revisit parts of the package as often as necessary.

An extensive evaluation of both the perceived learning benefit and actual learning benefit has been undertaken by our group in conjunction with others and shown that direct integration of the CAL material into the course curriculum (Timmis *et al.* 1998) is best. This involves providing both timetabled slots for usage and technical and academic support. Weaker students, who perhaps lack some background information, also benefited from studying the packages as part of their independent study.

School intranet

We have defined our intranet as 'a private Internet operating on an internal network enabling the exchange of information through a centralized structure'. Intranets originated from within industry (Morrell 1997) and are fairly new to higher and further education (Blackmore 1997). An intranet makes use of the availability of inexpensive or free commercial web-browser and web-server software to allow access to information resources from any type of workstation. Intranets also allow a simple, uniform hypertext interface to many kinds of information and application programs. Within this school we have introduced the concept of an educational intranet that provides a focused learning framework to integrate administrative documentation and learning support material (Sosabowski *et al.* 1998a).

Figures 6.1 and 6.2 show introductory screens for the school intranet. The school intranet is structured around degree courses and individual modules within those courses.

Typically, module pages include: course information, past exam papers, links to relevant sites, worksheets, tutor contact details, syllabi, timetables, lecturers' notes/handouts/overhead projections (OHPs).

The lecturers' material is provided to allow students to download and study material prior to the lecture. This facility also benefits students who

Figure 6.1   The Pharmacy Intranet

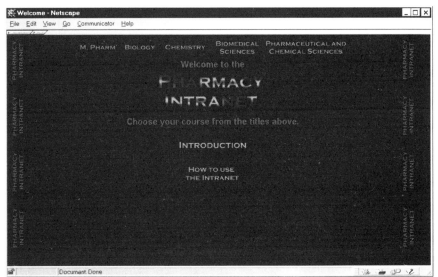

Figure 6.2   Accessing module pages on the Pharmacy Intranet

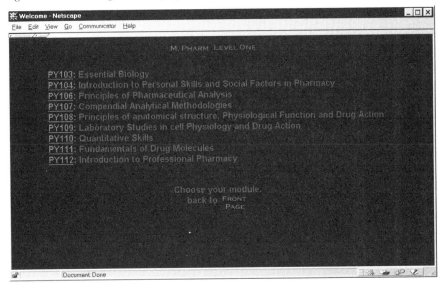

are unable to attend specific components of the course for whatever reason. A potential criticism of this approach has been that it may encourage students to download the material rather than attend the course lectures. A recent analysis of this provision for a first-year pharmacy cohort found this not to be the case; the students were in fact found to value these lecture notes more than lecture handouts (Sosabowski *et al.* 1998a,b). In having to locate and download the lecture notes the students felt that they had a greater ownership of this learning support material.

Newsgroups

Newsgroups are an extension of electronic mail whereby individuals are able to post information to a single newsgroup, where the information can be read and responded to by all individuals within the group. This means that students are able to exchange ideas, questions and comments with all members of the learning group and the tutor. Students on a particular course or module communicate electronically with all other students on that course/module, as well as with all the lecturing staff. Students or staff initiate 'threads' by posting an appropriate question or comment to the group under an appropriate header. Other members of the study group reply with possible answers, allowing the thread to develop. The academic tutor is able to monitor the answers being submitted and, if the thread is moving too far away from the 'right' topic, can 're-tune' the thread. The perceived benefit of this type of approach is the absence of an immediate

Figure 6.3 Newsgroup viewed using the Pine interface

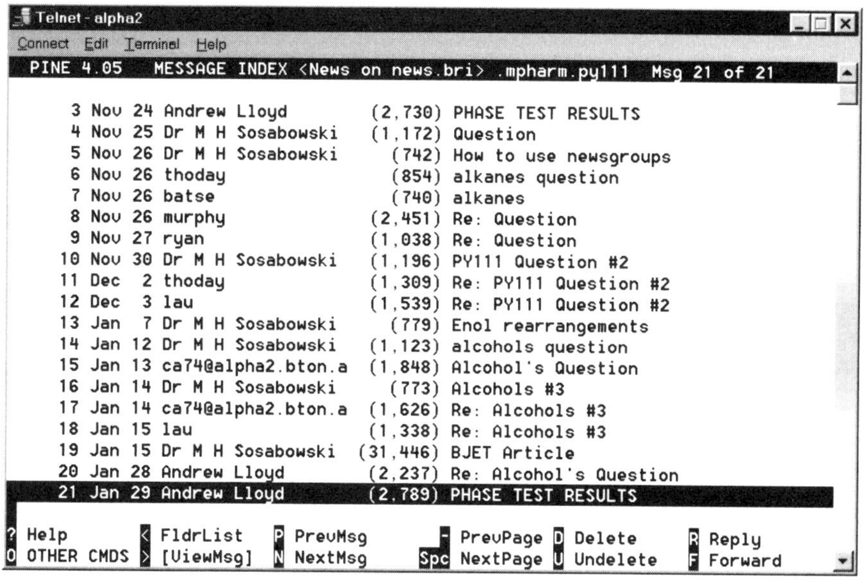

```
Telnet - alpha2                                                          _ □ ×
Connect  Edit  Terminal  Help
 PINE 4.05    MESSAGE INDEX <News on news.bri> .mpharm.py111  Msg 21 of 21    ▲

      3 Nov 24 Andrew Lloyd      (2,730) PHASE TEST RESULTS
      4 Nov 25 Dr M H Sosabowski (1,172) Question
      5 Nov 26 Dr M H Sosabowski  (742) How to use newsgroups
      6 Nov 26 thoday             (854) alkanes question
      7 Nov 26 batse              (740) alkanes
      8 Nov 26 murphy            (2,451) Re: Question
      9 Nov 27 ryan              (1,038) Re: Question
     10 Nov 30 Dr M H Sosabowski (1,196) PY111 Question #2
     11 Dec  2 thoday            (1,309) Re: PY111 Question #2
     12 Dec  3 lau               (1,539) Re: PY111 Question #2
     13 Jan  7 Dr M H Sosabowski  (779) Enol rearrangements
     14 Jan 12 Dr M H Sosabowski (1,123) alcohols question
     15 Jan 13 ca74@alpha2.bton.a (1,848) Alcohol's Question
     16 Jan 14 Dr M H Sosabowski  (773) Alcohols #3
     17 Jan 14 ca74@alpha2.bton.a (1,626) Re: Alcohols #3
     18 Jan 15 lau               (1,338) Re: Alcohols #3
     19 Jan 15 Dr M H Sosabowski (31,446) BJET Article
     20 Jan 28 Andrew Lloyd      (2,237) Re: Alcohol's Question
     21 Jan 29 Andrew Lloyd      (2,789) PHASE TEST RESULTS

? Help       < FldrList   P PrevMsg    ▬ PrevPage D Delete    R Reply
O OTHER CMDS > [ViewMsg]  N NextMsg    Spc NextPage U Undelete F Forward   ▼
```

audience providing a route for constructive discussion for all students, not just the confident ones. The underlying theory therefore is to present a non-threatening, peer-based learning environment from which all members of the group should benefit through participation.

Despite the attraction of this approach to facilitated learning, several papers have recently highlighted various problems encountered in the use of such technology for undergraduate learning (Brailsford and Davies 1997). We recently investigated the implementation of newsgroups into a second year Biomedical Sciences undergraduate module 'Chemistry for the Life Sciences', which ran in Semester 2 1997–8 (January–June 1998), and is taken mainly by BSc. Biomedical Science (BMS) students (Sosabowski *et al.* 1999). Our study showed that university-based students are reluctant to utilize this method of learning. Furthermore, those that did use the newsgroups tended to treat the interaction formally; laboriously researching, checking and rechecking their contributions as if they were items of assessed coursework.

The failure of the newsgroup approach may reflect the ability of the students to communicate with their peer group on a day-to-day basis obviating the need to utilize the electronic platform. Such technology may therefore be more appropriately suited for use in a distance learning course where students often work in isolation with minimal communication with their peer group and tutors.

A second issue arose from the interface used by the students to access newsgroups. Students accessed the newsgroup using Pine on a Unix system (Figure 6.3), instead of a Graphical User Interface (GUI). The students accessed the computers as a 'guest' and their individual setting could not be saved. Most critical commands in Pine (for example, send and cancel) involve Ctrl-key combinations, which are inconvenient and unintuitive. A GUI interface is much more user friendly (it is the interface of choice for accessing newsgroups) and is provided as a standard component of web browsers. This will allow distance learning students to use a single, standard package to access intranet-based learning resources, newsgroups and wider Internet-based resources.

Training

As these network resources have become a more integrated component of teaching and learning within courses there has been an increased need to provide effective technical training for undergraduates. This training is regarded as important for both encouraging the students to utilize these resources as undergraduates and also as training for their future use as healthcare professionals.

Although many undergraduates are reasonably computer literate, with some computer experience of word processing, data analysis and graphical representation, and many have access to the Internet and world wide web, we have found that, in order for them to gain the maximum benefit from these learning resources, they need direct training in:

• the effective use of the intranet;
• the use of electronic mail and newsgroups; and
• accessing CAL packages.

This was achieved through a 90 minute, hands-on induction programme during the first week of term. In order to encourage the use of the resources, students were actively encouraged to use specific CAL packages, newsgroups and the school intranet during the first semester of Year 1. The school intranet and newsgroups were also used to post relevant course notices such as phase test results. As a consequence, the undergraduate students now recognize these resources as an integral component of the learning and teaching support material and actively encourage staff to provide information via these platforms.

In contrast, postgraduate students on professional development courses in this school were given a brief 30 minute overview of: (i) connecting to the university computer networks; (ii) using a web browser to access both the Internet and the school intranet; and (iii) accessing and utilizing newsgroups. They were provided with access to the University of Brighton computer network and a newsgroup was specifically established to support the course and the students. As the course was part of the initial induction weekend, held at a hotel outside the university, it was only possible to give very limited hands-on training in the use of the technology.

During the first year, minimal use was made of the newsgroup by any of the students on the CPD course, despite their desire to be able to communicate regularly with other course members and the course tutors. This was attributed to a number of factors:

- Insufficient hands-on training in accessing and utilizing the technology. These professionals had very limited experience of the use of computer technology, except perhaps for word processing. Unlike the undergraduate students this group is, to some extent, less familiar with the technology and has limited experience of the Internet and other forms of electronic communication. An extended hands-on training session would therefore have the advantage that each member of the group could 'play' with the computers.
- Lack of resources. Although all the course attendees were professional community pharmacists working within the community, who routinely use computer-based systems for stock control, patient records and labelling, few actually had access to the Internet. Many therefore required more specific training on how to set up a personal computer through an Internet provider. Although limited guidance could be provided during the induction, there is a clear need for a simple means of providing Internet access for these users. Furthermore, the maximum benefit from such a resource will probably only be gained by each user having home-based access to the Internet. This is an aspect that will undoubtedly be addressed over the next few years, as the computer increasingly becomes another standard household appliance.
- Staff-based issues. We found that teaching staff were initially reluctant to 'buy in' to the intranet concept, unless they could see a 'payoff'. Moreover, the posting of material that would otherwise be non-public-domain caused some anxiety. Two parallel approaches went some way towards addressing these issues: (i) initial strategic supply of material to key module pages created student-led demand for further material; and (ii) a policy of 'leading by example' by key personnel. Staff training further eased the implementation process, culminating in a rolling programme of training workshops in web design that resulted in staff being able to update their own pages.

Conclusions

Educational establishments need to develop a culture of providing training in the use of learning technologies for future professionals, both at undergraduate and postgraduate level.

The resources available through a web interface provide an open-access platform that can provide integrated systems to support professional development courses. The development of communication technologies through the use of web-based newsgroups means it is also possible to facilitate group learning and more effective tutor–student interactions. The benefits of these resources will only be realized when professionals have the appropriate training and access to maximize the utilization of the technology.

Despite the availability of the technology to support these developments, effective utilization is limited by the lack of specific training for students embarking on distance learning courses. The development of a learning technology induction course that provides students with the necessary guidance on: (i) the establishment of network communications at home; and (ii) the utilization of these technologies is therefore necessary for the present generation of medical professionals. However, with the integration of learning technologies into undergraduate courses, future professionals will be better qualified to use this technology as part of their continuous professional development.

THE USE OF VIDEOCONFERENCING TO SUPPORT MENTORSHIP

Duncan Cullimore and Avril Loveless

Introduction

The context of this case study is a teacher-training 'partnership' with approximately 200 secondary schools, mainly located in South East England, but actually covering all areas of the UK. These schools take trainee teachers for placements that normally last for three months and, for most of this time, the trainees do not come back to the university but are trained and assessed by mentors in the schools. The mentors are teachers who have been identified by their managers as being good role models and as having appropriate mentoring skills.

It is the responsibility of the School of Education at the University of Brighton to ensure that all of the trainees receive a high quality experience and a system is in place to support and monitor partner institutions. Evidence from university evaluation reports suggests that, whilst many students receive a good quality training, there is a need to work more closely with partner institutions in order to integrate the university and school-based parts of the course. There are also other issues raised in the current system.

Students, teachers and tutors need to be aware of, and explicit about, the ways in which the different elements of the course support and supplement each other. During their school experience, for example, students are required to work on a series of learning packages – tasks and assignments that focus on a range of areas of general professional practice, from classroom organization to the use of ICT in teaching. The purpose of these packages is to enable the students to draw upon, make explicit and reflect upon their practical classroom experience in the light of the broader professional requirements. Although developed by small groups of teachers and tutors in the partnership model, the rationale of these learning packages needs to be discussed by teachers, tutors and students in order to support their purpose and avoid their being viewed as 'bolt-on extras' to practical school experience.

There is, therefore, as in any partnership arrangements, the need for a continued discussion, debate and shared awareness of purpose and sense of direction – particularly in a fast moving and frequently changing field such as teacher education in the UK. The current model attempts to keep all partners informed and involved through a combination of detailed documentation, visits to schools by tutors and occasional one-day conferences for mentors. Partners outside of the local area frequently find it difficult to attend the conferences organized for their benefit. The travelling time involved can make such activities unattractive to all but the most enthusiastic. Another possible difficulty arises with tutor visits, which can be time-consuming and expensive, a visit to a school in Essex, for example, may cost the university several hundred pounds in tutor time and travelling expenses. Time and distance are important factors in the value and success of these strategies for mentors and tutors.

There are clearly alternative ways of working more closely with distant schools, such as through local support groups, locally organized conferences and newsletters. These ideas are being used but another avenue in which we have been interested is that of videoconferencing. Videoconferencing has the potential for training and liaison over a distance without the costs associated with travelling time. It has the advantage over a telephone of enabling users to observe body language, share software with documentation on it and actually observe teaching performance. Our initial thinking was that videoconferencing technology would be effective when solving a real and shared problem of communication that required visual immediacy, both to establish contact and maintain a sense of communication and community (Wright and Cordeaux 1996, cited in Dillon 1998; Nummi *et al.* 1998). There was, however, a concern that it would not be able to replace the quality of face-to-face contact in certain situations but play a role in the preparation for such meetings (Myhman and Eriksson 1997).

The TTA supported initiatives to develop partnerships between training providers and schools in order to promote the quality and consistency of the mentoring and assessment of trainee teachers. Having identified the constraints and difficulties of time and distance that the University of Brighton partnership faced, the School of Education set up a project to investigate the potential of multi-point videoconferencing to strengthen links with mentors and enhance the quality of training they provide. The project was undertaken between the university and the mentors of four partner schools to videoconference on five occasions for 45 minutes on each occasion (Homer 1998). This case study describes the strategy used in the investigation and analyses the outcomes.

The strategy

Participating partners

The stakeholders in the partnership include teacher trainees, university tutors and mentors in schools. It was decided on this occasion to focus on the communication between mentors in schools and tutors in the university. Enquiries of other projects in five other UK universities established that this was the only project that focused particularly on the link between mentors and tutors, rather than tutors and trainees. In order to promote the strengths of group discussion and interaction, whilst overcoming difficulties of time and distance, the project was set up as a multi-point videoconference between the mentors of four partner secondary schools and tutors in the university. A multi-point videoconference enables a number of groups to participate at the same time. There are different types of display available for multi-point conferencing, including a 'celebrity squares' version where all participants appear on the screen, and ones where just the speaker appears. The version used in this project was one where each group could see a small image of themselves on the screen as well as a larger image of the person speaking at the time.

Apart from using the videoconferences for conversation it was also hoped to use filesharing facilities, which would enable discussions concerning stored information about, for instance, student lesson plans/evaluations. As well as this, it was intended to investigate the 'whiteboarding' facility, which would enable data to be manipulated on screen.

Three to six mentors in each school were therefore involved in a videoconference on five occasions for 45 minutes on each occasion. The coordinator of the project and university tutors also participated in the videoconferences and the university provided specific technical support in the schools to prepare for and support them.

Supporting the schools

There are clearly greater benefits in real life from using videoconferencing technology with distant schools rather than those in close proximity but, in terms of the practicalities of providing the technical assistance for a pilot project, it was thought sensible to use schools close to the university. Four schools were therefore selected that were within a 20-mile radius.

There were technical as well as training issues involved in the strategy. The schools involved had the necessary specification of computer with access to Integrated Services Digital Network (ISDN) lines as well as the technical expertise available to support the conferencing process. The university funded a loan of the videoconferencing equipment and provided technical advice to the schools. Visits were made by a university technician to ensure that all parties understood how to work the equipment. The University Computer Centre provided considerable advice on the activity and booked the multi-point conference channels through United Kingdom Education and Research Networking Association (UKERNA).

The planning process was time consuming and involved the evaluation of videoconferencing equipment as well as its purchase. This evaluation was undertaken with the assistance of the University Computer Services, as well as tutors in the School of Education. Schools were approached to discuss the requirement and implications of participation and there were some who, although enthusiastic, did not have the necessary technologies.

Setting the agenda

The nature of the discussions in the videoconferences were clearly important in so far as they had to add value to the work of mentoring. However, it was also important to respect the needs of mentors in setting the agenda and although the discussions were led by a university tutor there was flexibility in the programme design. The professional centre coordinator and a university tutor, who was an experienced mentor seconded to the School of Education, highlighted key areas of concern and designed the initial programme. The final conference programme covered the following topics:

- pilot – a discussion of school-based professional studies assignments;
- school placement files;
- mentors' recording procedures;
- moderation of teaching standards; and
- revisiting moderation and project conclusions.

Each session was supported by a sheet that clearly identified the aim of the session and key questions to be discussed.

The outcomes

The project was recognized as a preliminary investigation, focusing on the experiences of the mentors and tutors in order to inform discussion of ways forward in developing the quality of moderation and assessment of trainees.

Technical issues

Five conferences were planned involving multi-point conferencing with four schools and the university. On three occasions the technology worked for all institutions from the beginning of the conference and there was effective communication between them. On the other occasions there were different degrees of disruption, varying from a colleague dialling the wrong number but eventually making contact to no multi-point contact being available on one occasion. The cause of the last problem was never identified.

During the successful conferences mentors and tutors were able to converse effectively and the quality of sound and vision was satisfactory. However, the volume was erratic at one school, which had chosen to use its own equipment. No other electronic features could be used during the multi-point conferencing, however. For instance, we were not able to use the 'whiteboard' facility or exchange software because of the technical specifications of the equipment used.

Colleagues quickly adapted to using the videoconferencing equipment although seating arrangements were frequently cramped and feedback suggested that a 'celebrity squares' multiview facility in which all groups can be seen at once would be better than the single view of the speaker. Technical assistance also proved vital to the whole operation.

Training issues

Considerable planning went into the design of the agenda for the conference. Information was sent out to prepare for the experience of the videoconference and issues such as seating arrangements, dress and protocol in gaining attention within the conference were raised. The teachers said that they were comfortable with the medium, after an initial period of self-consciousness and some amusement. The issues of time and availability for a videoconference meeting were still difficult in a busy teaching schedule and needed careful coordination.

There were differences of opinion between the groups of mentors as to whether the videoconferencing supported the development of moderation and assessment of trainees. Some felt that the detailed documentation already provided by the university was supporting consistency whilst others felt that the nature of the discussions on the videoconference helped them to develop a broader view of their own practice.

Four uses of the videoconference were widely supported:

1. To link mentors in schools with subject tutors in the university to develop subject-based discussions of standards and expectations. This would also afford the opportunity for subject mentors to discuss general developments in the area with the subject tutor as a form of professional development. This direct subject link could not be provided on such a scale by face-to-face visits.
2. To support the university link tutor's communication with a group of mentors in school. The videoconference would play a role in preparing key issues to be addressed in the face-to-face visit, dealing with administrative matters or questions beforehand, leaving time to make the personal visit more focused and effective within the school.
3. To promote direct collaboration between schools as they delivered the professional studies programme.
4. To develop links between secondary and feeder primary schools for trainees on Key Stage 2 and Key Stage 3 courses.

Mentors in one school, however, not only expressed their interest in working with an unfamiliar medium but also their doubts as to the contribution of videoconferencing techniques to their own support and development. It was felt that the personal and professional links between the schools and the university were already good and that videoconferencing did not add anything to the partnership relationship that had been built up. The headteacher noted that the face-to-face meetings served purposes beyond that of initial information sharing and discussion.

The distinctiveness of this project lay in its focus on videoconferencing as the support for mentors, rather than trainees. Much was learned about the procedures and technical support required to set up videoconferencing links and the possibilities and constraints of multi-point communications and file sharing. The project also provided the opportunity for mentors to identify a wider range of groups that they felt would help them to develop their role but that were not included in the current support programme. It was clear that the tutor–mentor link was already being addressed by other means but that videoconferencing provided possibilities of links with groups for whom the time, distance and cost of meeting face-to-face were problematic. Issues of moderation and consistency in the mentorship relationship are complex and need to be supported by a range of interactions and discussions.

Conclusion

It was felt that the videoconference itself could be a medium for raising awareness and promoting discussion between mentors and tutors, but that it should augment, rather than replace, face-to-face meetings. The distinctive characteristics of the medium that enabled immediate visual communication and file sharing could be developed in appropriate contexts. Its use should also be developed within the context of a range of media for communication using ICT, from e-mail to audioconferencing. To this end the project team is now investigating the use of a range of electronic media to support communication in the partnership.

ASSESSING LEARNING IN ITT ON A BUSINESS INFORMATION TECHNOLOGY MODULE

Duncan Cullimore

Introduction

This case study focuses on the assessment of learning in a second level undergraduate ITT module entitled 'IT in Business Education'. The module aims to prepare students to use information technology in the teaching of business studies and economics.

The module is being constantly updated to take account of new information technology and its impact on teaching and learning in business education. The challenge is to ensure that assessment continues to be valid and continues to promote learning.

Validity is always challenging but it is particularly so in this module because it relies on a vision of what ought to be happening in the classroom rather than what is actually happening (reality). Validity is dependent, to a certain extent, on the accuracy of the vision. Only if the potential uses of the new technology have been correctly interpreted by the assessor may the assessment be valid.

The issue of collaboration is important because it is a powerful tool for learning about the uses of information technology. Recent developments in the use of the intranet have enabled collaboration over distance as well as in the classroom. The intranet also enables new monitoring opportunities for both the teacher and peers.

This case study particularly considers the two separate issues of ensuring 'reality' and collaborative learning in the context of an assessment strategy. It evaluates the extent to which the 'reality' issue and 'collaboration' are currently managed in this one module and suggests how improvements might be made.

Throughout this case study the term information technology (IT) is used rather than the more recently adopted information communications technology (ICT) (or CIT). This is because the title of the module is still 'IT in business education' and schools are still using this term. In order to provide some contextual background, the case study starts with a brief description of the resources used, the learning outcomes and the teaching approaches in the module and then evaluates the two main issues regarding assessment.

Resources

The module is taught in 13, two-hour sessions. Students work in a room of networked personal computers (PCs), which are all linked to the Internet and which also have most of the software required for the module. The room is not ideal in so far as it is small and most computers do not have a printer attached, but it does offer the basis for familiarization with the software. The only major resource not available in the room is that of CD-ROMs, but this is available elsewhere and students are given access when it is required.

Most students have a good level of general IT awareness and have a working knowledge of generic software packages. Most have PCs at home and most are regular Internet users at the university. A few have an Internet link at home.

Learning outcomes

The module has to address two major issues in so far as students need to be taught a curriculum content for schools as well as how to teach that curriculum. The proposed learning outcomes of the module are as follows:

- confidence and competence in using the range of hardware and software for teaching economics and business education;
- appreciation of the potential and limitations of using IT as an aid to learning business and economic concepts and skills;
- understanding of IT in the National Curriculum and the role of the IT coordinator;
- competence in planning and presenting lessons where IT and/or business skills could be developed.

Evidence from assignments, external examiner comments and end of semester evaluations suggests that most students achieve these outcomes and find the module useful in their teaching placements. Two students last year produced learning materials that were promoted by the Economics and Business Education Association as exemplar material for school teachers on its web site.

Teaching approach

The intended learning outcomes described above are not equally represented in terms of teaching time. There is an initial focus on the curriculum requirements for IT, as well as theory relating to learning and teaching, including the potential and limitations of its use. However, the emphasis in taught sessions is on students investigating software and considering its use in learning about business. Considerable time is therefore spent familiarizing students with specific software such as simulations, business databases, the world wide web and CD-ROMs. The issue of planning and preparing lessons and reflecting on the application of software is addressed largely through individual and group work, which takes place out of classroom time.

The assessment strategy

The assessment at the end of the module comprises the development of a disc-based activity with supporting paper-based materials designed to enable pupils within the 14–16 age range to develop their IT skills and to learn business skills/concepts. The full assignment is identified in Appendix 1 at the end of this case study but a brief description is given in the paragraph below.

Students have to utilize a range of tools including the Internet, spreadsheets, databases and desktop publishing. They have to identify which skills their pupils will develop and how they will find the evidence for their development. They also have to identify how the materials will be used for teaching and learning and how they will be evaluated. The assignment is presented to the group at the end of the semester. This presentation is not assessed but is undertaken mainly to share their work with their peers. It is also useful to give the assessor more information about the material they have produced.

Students are given the assignment at the beginning of the module and they have the opportunity to develop their ideas as the sessions progress. This strategy is aimed at enabling reflection and discussion on the part of students.

Assessment issues

An evaluation of the assessment process needs to involve a consideration of the assessment objectives and the validity of the assessment strategy used is valid. The assessment objectives for the assignment are identified below:

- The electronic and paper-based materials are of a quality that could be used in the classroom.
- The materials are stimulating, matched to pupil needs and could enable learning.
- Students demonstrate an understanding of what the materials contribute to National Curriculum IT and National Council for Vocational Qualifications (NCVQ) key skills.
- Students demonstrate an understanding of the issues related to teaching with the materials and assessing pupil learning.
- Students demonstrate an understanding of how the material would be evaluated.

Issue 1: the assessment objectives and the reality of classroom life

The assessment objectives are designed to define outcomes that are measurable and that should integrate the learning of software with the pedagogic issues associated with teaching it. At a superficial level, the assessment objectives would appear to be in line with the learning objectives and might therefore be assumed to be acceptable. However, there is a major issue over the interpretation of the words 'which could be used in the classroom'. This is explicitly stated in the first statements but actually runs through all of them to some degree. The difficulty is that such an assessment is based on theory rather than practice or experience because of the current use of IT in the classroom.

Hurd (1995: 3) found in his survey of the use of IT in the teaching of business and economics that: 'a high proportion of computer time is used to enhance the presentation of coursework'.

Davies (1996) suggests that teachers are tending to waste time with IT in business and economics by focusing on what the technology can do rather than thinking about how children can learn more effectively about the subject. He too notes that pupils tend to use computers to improve the presentation of work rather than to learn anything about the subject (or IT). This view is supported by Cullimore *et al.* (1996) and, to a certain extent, by the Ofsted review of Inspection Findings (1995), which noted that in general (not specifically in business and economics) some computer applications require: 'only modest levels of IT capability'. However, the same report notes that: 'some fine teaching . . . on such topics as survey construction, privacy and the security of computer-based data' (Ofsted, 1995: 11–12).

Whilst Ofsted has clearly identified these general issues there is evidence of low expectations on its part. In a piece of small-scale research focusing on seven Ofsted reports of good schools, which included a report of IT in business and economics, Cullimore (1996) found that very little credit was given in reports for anything other than the use of IT for presentational work. There were actually many omissions in the reports. There was no reference to the use of anything other than generic software, no mention of simulations or database interrogation, no mention of the use of the Internet. The ratio of computers to children was given in only one report and there was no information about software used by different departments or the average use of IT by pupils in lessons or at home. The implication of these findings is that Ofsted does not look for anything else. It could be said that inspectors cannot report everything but, generally speaking, the inspections are systematic and the indicators used reflect priorities as well as standards.

It seems that the expectations both of teachers and of the quality assurance inspectors regarding the use of IT has been quite limited and certainly below the potential use. This may have been because of past disappointments. Hurd (1995) noted a marked shift away from using computer games and simulations reflecting their limited availability and doubts on the part of teachers concerning their cost effectiveness. Another reason for the underuse of IT in schools may have been because of a narrow, 'skill-based' interpretation of its potential.

Davies (1996) argues that the National Curriculum descriptors of IT capability are very useful in the context of business and economics and are better than the foci of IT in General National Vocational Qualification (GNVQ) and GCSE Business Studies, which are skill-based (that is, related to techniques/routines). He suggests that business and economics teachers have tended to use these latter foci rather than those of the National Curriculum and he recommends that they should pay closer attention to the concept of IT capability:

> In contrast to some other descriptions of IT capability, the National Curriculum emphasizes the skills of processing data in the light of what the data mean . . . Economics and business are rich in contexts which provide suitable data for the development of these skills. In addition, pupil skills of data processing can be harnessed to help them recognize patterns, to challenge their preconceptions, and to build models of relationships in economics and business.
>
> (Davies 1996: 174)

An important and constant component of the teacher training curriculum is the experience that students have in schools. This may be from their own experience as pupils or from placements from university. Oliver (1994: 141) notes that: 'new teachers are very much inclined to teach in the way that they were taught and to model their practices on those that they judged to be effective from personal experience'.

It is clear from the above discussion that role models of the sort that we need for teaching IT are unlikely to be found in schools. It is therefore imperative that the teaching and learning styles used in the university cur- riculum should provide a role model for students:

> If we truly want student teachers to adopt and integrate new techno- logies into their teaching, they need to be taught in a fashion that models this and in a fashion that will cause the students to ascribe value to the use of computer technologies as instructional tools.
> (Oliver 1994: 141)

ITT students will typically not teach with IT unless they have experience of being taught 'effectively' with it. Furthermore, the possibility of having been taught with it as a pupil or seeing someone else teaching 'effectively' with it on a teaching placement is unlikely, unless the teachers concerned were at the forefront of developments. We therefore have to construct the teaching, learning and assessment programmes in a way that will model what we think should be happening in schools.

The content of the module is based on existing materials and practice and it draws on accepted evidence of what represents good practice, as discussed above. However, when we are considering the assessment of stu- dents work at the university there has to be a certain act of faith that student learning packages 'could' be taught in the classroom by the stu- dents concerned. It is unlikely that something similar is being taught in many classrooms as the ideas have not yet permeated that far.

In order to be truly valid, however, the assessment system needs to be revised and would benefit from implementation and assessment by more than one person. It would be worth investigating whether the material could be trialled with some pupils. An evaluation could then be undertaken with the assistance of a classroom mentor and improvements recommended. This might be possible at the end of the semester in which the module is taught. If not, students could have an initial assessment, then take their package into a school and test it whilst on teaching placement in the following semester. They could then redesign and improve it in a subsequent related module.

Issue 2: collaborative learning and an intranet

Collaboration has long been recognized as an important strategy for learn- ing to use information technology: 'The research of Johnson and Johnson (1986) and others suggests that pupils are likely to learn more from their IT work if they are encouraged to work together' (Davies 1996: 188).

Collaborative learning strategies have frequently been used in the 'IT in Business Education' module to work on understanding the implications of a piece of software for classroom use. However, the assessment has always been of an individual's own piece of work and there has not been much emphasis on people working together to develop it further.

The major recent innovation has been the use of an intranet to facilitate collaborative learning. In the 'IT in Business Education' module students have been split into groups of about three people. Davies (1996) notes that Johnson *et al.* 1986 suggest that this represents the optimum size of group working on screen-based activity.

Students are taught in one session how to write simple Hypertext Mark-up Language (HTML) screens and to transfer material from the web onto their intranet sites. The function of the small groups is designated principally as providing support for the writing of the assessed assignment. The assignments will still be marked as individual attempts but the idea is that students will bounce ideas off their group members and therefore provide mutual peer support. All students have access to view the web sites of their classmates but only those in the specific intranet group can edit the screens of their peers under agreed rules.

There are two issues for the writer here. The first is to identify how closely the groups should be directed. There is considerable disagreement about how much freedom students should be allowed to work with software. A summary might be that too much freedom and they become involved in irrelevancies but too little and they may become bored. Davies (1996) notes that DiSessa (1986) argues for 'pupil freedom' as an essential ingredient in pupil use of software. The students in question, however, need to use the intranet facility in their own time on a basis that is similar to distance learning, and, to this extent, they may need tighter controls. Chang and Chen (1997: 3) have focused on the use of collaborative learning for distance CAL systems and they argue that:

> If generic network tools are to be used for learning, the teacher should participate in the discussion and assign roles, notify students, enforce schedules, guide students to what he/she should do, and accumulate information to understand the performance of students.

The writer has therefore tried to be fairly prescriptive about how groups use their intranet site. They have a clear goal in terms of the end product and they are working mainly in discrete friendship groups. The tasks are also clear in so far as they are collecting relevant material from the web and designing their own learning package. Many are working effectively on the project out of lecture hours at a distance from each other although they spend 10–20 minutes of lecture time each week discussing issues and progress.

Issue 3: objectives and the SEEC criteria

The assessment objectives noted at the beginning of this section are designed to describe measurable outcomes for the module but they also have to meet the requirements of the university undergraduate modular scheme, which offers modules at three levels. One method of identifying relevant descriptors of the desirable outcomes for these levels is to use the 'generic level descriptors' identified by SEEC (the South East England Consortium). The 'IT in Business Education' module is accredited at Level 2 in the modular scheme and the relevant level descriptor is shown in Appendix 2 (page 104).

It is suggested that the headings (1) 'Operational Contexts' and (2) 'Cognitive Descriptors' can be recognized within the module descriptor and the assignment. It is more difficult, however, to recognize all or even many of the descriptors in (3) 'Other Transferable Skills Descriptors'.

Issues such as 'self-appraisal', 'planning and managing learning' and 'interactive and group skills' did not occur naturally in the assessed assignment even though they (hopefully) appeared in the teaching and learning programme. However, this year the programme has been modified to enable some formative assessment through the peer group activity on the intranet described above. The use of this vehicle and the process are in line with the objective of the module in so far as they promote the effective use of IT in teaching and learning. They should be extended next year to enable the peer group assessment to be used in the final module assessment.

Conclusions

This case study has addressed issues related to the teaching and assessment of the module 'IT in Business Education'. It is taught to a group of IT literate students, who have access to quite good learning materials, and yet there are still considerable challenges to the successful assessment of the module.

The context of a rapidly changing technology environment is a major issue and means that the curriculum content represents the future rather than the present. The conclusion relating to a consideration of this issue is that the assessment strategy needs to take account of the many unknown issues and to actually test the materials in the field before they are assumed to be effective.

The other issue is the development of teaching and assessment strategies to cope effectively with peer group learning and assessment with an intranet-based learning system. It has not been feasible to undertake a formal evaluation but the intranet clearly offers considerable potential at this stage. It is clear that the desired outcome of peer group support in out-of-class hours is happening, with most students very enthusiastic about the technology. They are tending to use their sites to build links with other web sites, rather than to generate a lot of original material, but this can be relevant in terms of producing a teaching package. It is also easier to build links than to generate original material and to this extent it is to be hoped that students will progress to generating new material in time. Anecdotal evidence suggests that they are finding 'browsing' their peers' web sites useful and it is certainly helpful for the lecturer to be able to monitor what they are doing by browsing. The intranet offers a powerful vehicle to support collaborative learning but much needs to be learnt about its impact on pedagogy.

Appendix 1: Assignment brief

IT in business education – assignment

You are to develop a disc-based activity with supporting paper-based materials to enable pupils within the 14–16 age range to develop their IT skills and to learn business skills/concepts.

Your project should utilize a range of tools including the Internet, spreadsheets, databases and desktop publishing. Pupils should be expected to demonstrate a broad range of National Curriculum skills (that is, some of – analysis, presentation, modelling, measuring and controlling). You must identify which skills are being developed and at which level you are identifying them. You should also identify which NCVQ key skills should be developed and where the evidence might be found.

You must clearly identify in your paper-based materials:

• the learning objectives for both business and IT;
• how the learning package will be used by the teacher and pupil;
• what the timescale for use is;
• what the resource implications are;
• how the learning will be assessed and recorded for business and for IT;
• how you would expect to evaluate it.

The project will be submitted on Thursday 4th June and students will be asked to demonstrate their software to the class on that day although the presentation will not be assessed.

Assessment objectives

1. The electronic and paper-based materials are of a quality that could be used in the classroom.
2. The materials are stimulating, matched to pupil needs and could enable learning.
3. Students demonstrate an understanding of what the materials contribute to National Curriculum IT and NCVQ key skills.
4. Students demonstrate an understanding of the issues related to teaching with the materials and assessing pupil learning.
5. Students demonstrate an understanding of how the material would be evaluated.

Appendix 2: SEEC generic level descriptors for Level 2

Details are shown in Figure 6.4 (page 104).

Figure 6.4 SEEC generic level descriptors for Level 2

	Characteristics of context	Responsibility	Ethical understanding
	Characteristics of context are:	Requirements of responsibility are:	Requirements of ethical understanding are:
1. Operational contexts	Simple but unpredictable *or* complex but predictable contexts demanding application of wide range of techniques.	Management of processes within broad guidelines for defined activities.	Awareness of the wider social and environmental implications of areas(s) of study. Ability to debate issues in relation to more general ethical perspectives.

	Knowledge and understanding	Analysis	Synthesis/creativity	Evaluation
2. Cognitive descriptors	The learner: Has a detailed knowledge of (a) major discipline(s) and an awareness of a variety of ideas/contexts/frameworks that may be applied to this.	Can analyse a range of information within minimum guidance, can apply major theories of discipline and can compare alternative methods/techniques for obtaining data.	Can reformat a range of ideas/information towards a given purpose.	Can select appropriate techniques of evaluation and can evaluate the relevance and significance of data collected.

	Psychomotor	Self-appraisal reflection on practice	Planning and management of learning	Problem solving	Communication and presentation	Interactive and group skills
3. Other transferable skills descriptors	The learner: When given a complex task, can choose and perform an appropriate set of actions in sequence to complete it adequately. Can evaluate own performance.	Is able to evaluate own strengths and weaknesses; can challenge received opinion and begins to develop own criteria and judgement.	Adopts a broad-ranging and flexible approach to study; identifies strengths of learning needs and follows activities to improve performance; is autonomous in straightforward study tasks.	Can identify key elements of problems and choose appropriate methods for their resolution in a considered manner.	Can communicate effectively in a format appropriate to the discipline and report practical procedures in a clear and concise manner with all relevant information in a variety of formats.	Can interact effectively within a learning group, giving and receiving information and ideas and modifying response where appropriate. Is ready to develop professional working relationships within discipline.

Source: SEEC, 1997.

7

Using the Internet and the World Wide Web

DESIGNING MULTILINGUAL, MULTI-DISCIPLINARY DISTANCE EDUCATION

Tony Hartley, Thierry Nodenot, Lyn Pemberton and Raf Salkie

Introduction

When speakers of English use computer software, they expect it to communicate in English. For instance, when they start their computer they expect to see words like *Start, File* and *Help* on the screen. If instead the words *Commencer, Fichier* and *Aide* appeared they might start to worry, and if the computer offered a choice between *Uusi, Avaa* and *Sulje* (Finnish for *New, Open* and *Close*) they would probably get hopelessly lost. They also assume that the manual for the software will be written in English, and the same goes for any on-line help or dialogue boxes on the screen.

If your working language is French or Spanish you will not want your computer to use English. Increasingly, even users of less widespread languages expect standard wordprocessing and drawing packages to be available in Latvian, Basque, Xhosa or whatever, and the software companies (still predominantly English-speaking) are responding to this demand. Not surprisingly, the young generation are the driving force: a few Japanese or Venezuelan teenagers might be willing to play Mortal Kombat or Carmageddon in English but the majority want it in their own language. Language is a barrier to globalization, and a multiple one at that, with some companies marketing their products in 22 languages.

A simple translation task, you might think: pay people to translate the English words into each language and the problem is taken care of. In reality things are not so straightforward. To take a simple example: the *Find* command can be translated into French so that the word *Chercher* appears on the screen. Suppose instead that you want to use the keyboard: an

English user types *CTRL+F* (*Apple+F* on a Macintosh), where the *F* conveniently stands for *Find*. For a French speaker that is not at all convenient: it would be more helpful to use a letter that appears in *Chercher*. This means that the software has to be reprogrammed for French users. Think of all the keyboard shortcuts that have to be modified in this way, add on the redesigning of menus because the German expression for *More* happens to contain 16 characters (*Weitere Optionen*) and will not fit in the available space, and the need for bigger buttons because the Polish equivalent of *Exit* is more than three times longer (*Koniec pomocy*). Consider languages in which the writing runs from right to left, or cultures where the egg-timer that appears on the screen while the computer is busy means nothing to anyone.

Beneath the surface, the program itself must handle different sorting orders for different languages (Swedish *ä* sorts after *z* and *å*) and respect varying conventions for the format of dates, times, numbers and currencies. In the documentation, national sensibilities too must be respected: for example, a flight simulator game that credited the Wright brothers with the first powered flight could offend customers in Norway and Brazil, who hold different opinions.

In the software industry, the features of the user's environment that are dependent on language, region and cultural convention are collectively known as the *locale*. Translating and customizing a software product so that it feels natural in a specific market is known as localization.

Software firms aiming a new product at the global market will first develop a generic program core whose design makes no assumptions based on a single locale and whose documentation is similarly neutral. This process, termed internationalization, is intended to avoid the delays and expense of re-engineering the product and rewriting the documentation.

The demand for people who are skilled at localizing software has increased enormously in recent years. Ireland produces over 40 per cent of all software and 60 per cent of business applications sold in Europe and takes localization very seriously. The Localization Resources Centre, based at University College, Dublin, acts as a research and support centre and is leading a major training initiative – the Certified Localization Professional – with software companies and training providers, including ourselves. The University of Limerick was the first in the world to offer a postgraduate degree in localization. But to our knowledge, no training whatsoever in software localization was available in the UK until we started the OLE project.

The motivation for OLE (on-line localization in Europe)

Producing software for more than one locale requires expertise in two areas: software engineering and translation. Good practice sees localization not as the last link in the chain of production but as one that loops back into design. It is the job of the localization manager to set up processes that ensure that design, programming, writing and translating mesh smoothly. In large organizations, these processes may shield engineers and linguists from the others' particular concerns: the thinking that goes into the framework pre-empts problems. But where the localization effort is distributed among smaller firms, probably specializing in software engineering and translation respectively, it may be that nobody has the necessary 'super-awareness' of the complexities of the enterprise.

The key training task, then, is to foster such awareness. The approach we took was to devise productive ways for these two groups of professionals to work and talk together.

The catalyst for experimenting with these ideas was the annual call from the European Commission for funding under the Socrates scheme to develop new course modules in partnership with other European educational institutions. One of us already had strong links with the Institut Universitaire de Technologie (IUT) in Bayonne and the University of the Basque Country in San Sebastián, thanks to several rounds of joint intensive courses in computing. It seemed natural to extend this collaboration into languages and linguistics by proposing a course in localization that teamed students of software engineering and human–computer interaction (HCI) in France and Spain with linguists in England, collaborating via the Internet.

We started from the premise that after graduation 'their' computer scientists were likely to become involved in developing global software and 'our' linguists in translating software. We wanted to give the members of each group the benefit of seeing the bigger picture and, through that experience, the potential to act as a localization manager.

The logic of the project was convincing to us. Moreover, it was consonant with our philosophy of language learning in that it promised our students a real purpose and a content of substance for their collaboration and for the end product. However, the motivation wasn't exclusively altruistic. We welcomed a chance to experiment with novel teaching and learning methods that used the Internet, to get a grip on new developments in our own fields and to learn from the experience of neighbours whose patch had not previously bordered on our own. It was also a way of refreshing existing links – between the three of us and with European colleagues – by setting our sights on different targets. The prospect of working in three languages and the social contact were further incentives.

The proposal for funding was written by the University of Brighton as the deadline loomed and, while a late draft was seen and approved by the head of international relations in Bayonne, our partners effectively signed a blank cheque in putting their names to the project plan. OLE (On-line Localization Europe) proved persuasive in Brussels and all that remained was to translate the words into deeds.

Cycle 1 of OLE

The Socrates funding covered travel and subsistence costs only, for one meeting at each site, to set up the localization projects for groups of students, carry out an interim review and then reflect on the whole process. From the outset, we envisaged two cycles of the development process: the first would be necessarily experimental, allowing the staff team to climb a fairly steep learning curve and to get to know one another better; the second would benefit from the lessons learned.

Rather than building a software application from scratch, we decided to work on an existing application. Bayonne located some French shareware that met our selection criteria in that the interface and information screens contained a lot of text and the text itself was very much anchored in the French locale. It was an educational ecology game designed to teach users about the national and regional parks of France. Bayonne obtained the author's permission to use the source code and text – rules of the game, information on the parks, test questions and answers. The texts were in fact embedded in the program code, which meant that internationalization couldn't proceed without extensive re-engineering. The texts were all translated in Brighton by students working in pairs. In effect they overtyped the French versions and the translations were delivered in their original format both to the software engineers and to the author of the software. The translators were also given an HCI seminar and workshop on the principles and practice of interface evaluation, based on Draper and Oatley (1991) and produced, as part of their assessed work, reports on the suitability of the software for adaptation to an English locale. These too were sent to the author.

The student experience

In both disciplines the students learned at first hand just how deep a problem localization can be, particularly when the original design doesn't take into account the possibility of localization into other languages.

The translators were pleased with an experience that looked good on their CVs. However, the software engineers were demotivated because the scale of the task – familiarization with the field, deconstruction of the software, reconstruction – exceeded the time available in the curriculum. So although they progressed towards the ultimate goal of having an educational game that worked for both French and English players, they were disappointed that there was no end product. Indeed, the HCI analysis revealed that the adaptation of the game for English users would require an investment that could never be recouped commercially. More worrying in the eyes of the tutors was the lack of e-mail communication between linguists and computer scientists in the transnational teams that had been set up. This was because the two aspects of the task had been effectively uncoupled by circumstances and so the students had no pressing reason to confer. Moreover, the project web site was too sparsely furnished with materials on software engineering, HCI, translation and localization to provide a shared reference point.

The lessons we drew from this first round were numerous: students needed to be set smaller, well-defined intermediate tasks with inputs from both disciplines; the localization project had to be realistic; it had to be capable of completion within the time available; communication via a bulletin board, which is more public and more dynamic, was likely to work better than e-mails within teams in providing a common focus.

The staff experience

Despite the hint of disappointment, everyone remained keen to renew the experience and was pleased when the funding was continued. We had been rewarded by some excellent student projects in both areas and by a realistic grasp on the pitfalls of localization. The source of any difficulties was neither the multi-disciplinarity of the project nor its multilinguality; at meetings everyone could speak and be understood in their own language. Rather, it was the lack of familiarity with institutional variables, such as the patterns and timing of teaching and assessment. OLE was having to find its niche in three very different academic settings.

Cycle 2 of OLE

Our critical task was to create a scenario that would present our students with a localization project that was both motivating and feasible within the constraints of the curriculum at all three universities. We turned again to the Internet. Only 20 per cent of the Global 500 (the world's biggest companies) have web sites solely in English; growth rates for Internet usage in Latin America, Asia and Europe are such that organizations will ignore multilingual markets at their peril. Increasingly, web sites serve not only to publicize but also to conduct e-commerce. The interest for translators in localizing the content of a corporate web site has been evident for some time and now the challenge of designing interactive, transactional sites presents an equal interest to software engineers.

Bayonne agreed to identify local small and medium-sized enterprises (SMEs) willing to participate in a scheme that would deliver them a proto-type multilingual web site. In return for a small investment in providing data and feedback, they would have a working mock-up as a basis for further development.

This direction offers many advantages over the scenario of the first cycle. The students start from scratch, unconstrained by existing program code and having control over the design of the software and its content. More original, the task is more motivating while remaining realistic, in so far as its scope can readily be tailored to the resources available. HTML is transparent to linguists, who are able to engage in text design as well as translation; it also enables work to be easily shared, irrespective of the particular computer that students happen to be using.

The project partners have embarked on this second cycle with introductory seminars that include a number of common references on localization in general (Esselink 1998; Glossasoft Consortium 1994; Kano 1995) and multilingual web sites in particular (Bishop 1998). A project management web site on the lines described by Siegel (1997) will act as a repository for work in progress, for ancillary materials and as a central focus for communication. The involvement of 'client' SMEs brings into the ring additional participants who have to be consulted on both linguistic and programming concerns, which requires the 'service providers' for their part to ensure that their efforts are concerted. In other words, the students face a real need to interact across disciplines and across languages via design documents, interim reports, draft translations and so on, all of which constitute manageable subtasks. The prospects of delivering a working prototype to the company are both real and motivating.

On the staff side, the links with the local, and not so local, community contribute to the universities' mission to enter into partnerships beyond the campus. OLE's innovative approach has attracted support from companies like Corel and Lernout & Hauspie, who have provided software designed specifically to aid the localization process. It has also brought some recognition of its architects in both professional and academic circles.

General lessons for designers of multinational, multi-disciplinary courses

Although the second cycle of OLE has yet to run its full course, we are already in a position to summarize a number of conclusions of general interest.

Students need genuine reasons to communicate at frequent intervals. This is best sustained by a motivating, long-term goal that the students feel confident they can achieve. Having an external 'client' is one good way of putting both needs and motivation in place. Communication will fail if no one group has a good working knowledge of the others' languages but effective communication can be negotiated even with imperfect linguistic competence. A greater obstacle to communication is a lack of respect for the contribution of the other project partners, due either to an underestimation of the technicalities or to simple stereotyping. This could be a danger between translators who have an arts background, study a second language and linguistics, have only a basic knowledge of computing and are predominantly female, and software engineers who have a science background, know little about translation and linguistics, study computer science and are mainly male.

Familiarization with the new disciplines can be achieved through traditional class teaching and also by setting up a project web site as a locus for common references and intermediate versions of the 'product' being jointly developed. Videoconferencing is a good means of putting faces to e-mail names and creating some rapport.

What is true for students is equally true for staff. As early as possible, colleagues are advised to exchange seminars on their respective fields, knowing that even within the same discipline the perspective might vary from one country to another. Arguably, it is even more important that everyone understands their partners' institutional constraints so that ambitions are both compatible and realistic. Finally, a face-to-face session, where everyone states openly their personal agenda in being involved, lays a sound foundation for building a project where everyone can find the rewards they seek.

AN INTRANET FOR THE BUSINESS SCHOOL: DEVELOPING A MODEL OF TECHNOLOGY - ENHANCED HIGHER EDUCATION

Steve Flowers, Becci Newton and Cameron Paine

Introduction

This case study examines the development of an innovative model of technology enhanced higher education: specifically the creation of an intranet within a business school. It focuses on the system's development, implementation and operation and does not include any detailed discussion of the technologies employed within the project. The key issues of the management of the innovation are discussed and the case concludes with an indication of the main management challenges in moving to a technology-enhanced model of higher education.

Background to the intranet project

The intranet at Brighton Business School was developed against the background of an intense debate within the academic and business literature of the potential and opportunities offered by the adoption of web-based technologies within organizations. Whilst much of the early literature in this area tended to be speculative and presented without any consideration of the real-world challenges that would be faced in attempting to adopt such technologies (Leggat 1993; Searl 1993), other literature made clear the potential pay-off for business education in making such a move (Alavi, Wheeler and Valacich 1995; Ives and Jarvenpaa 1996). It was clear from the start of the project that there was speculation but little firm evidence or documented experience of the creation of such a system within a business school. It was also likely that much of the literature promoting organizational intranet use was flowing from intranet 'early-adopters', a group who, in embracing a new technology, often seek to make dramatic improvements to existing processes by applying novel ideas to core activities, in some cases simply to see if it can be done (Rogers 1995). Given this position prior to the start of the project, there was a clear understanding that the creation of a Business School intranet would involve significant challenges, some of which could not be predicted.

It was within this context and with a clear understanding of the risks of working at the leading edge of technological change (Flowers 1996) that the development of the Business School intranet was initiated.

Technology enhanced education: the business school intranet

The initial concept of the intranet was the combination of a range of existing course-related material (for example, teaching schemes, lecture notes) with a series of links generic business web sites, more specialist subject-specific web sites and a series of forums for course and subject-related discussions. The list of resources is outlined below:

- Course-specific resources:
  - on-line course notice boards;
  - links to generic business-related web sites;
  - student handbooks, university regulations, and so on;
  - method of assessment;
  - course and examination timetables.
- Module-specific resources:
  - module schedules;
  - module materials, including lecture slides, reading lists, links to other web sites;
  - past examination papers.
- Generic resources:
  - Internet research tips for assessment, and so on;
  - links to one or more library catalogues;
  - e-mail links to the course administrator.

The original intention in developing this system, in true 'early adopter' fashion, was to build the foundations for the creation of a new model of technology-enhanced educational infrastructure for learning and teaching. It would enable greater flexibility in provision for both staff and students and provide a wide range of new educational opportunities. However, the limitations of this approach were identified at an early stage and the very real risk that colleagues working in the mainstream with more traditional learning and teaching approaches might decline to be involved was recognized.

In order for the project to be successful it was very important to sensitively manage the introduction of the system so that the core aim of maximizing involvement could be met. The ways in which this was achieved and the fall-back positions that were established if this involvement was not forthcoming are examined below.

Positioning the intranet project

The intranet development was positioned as a small-scale pilot project that would be made available to a single cohort during a single academic year (1997–8). After consultation with course managers it was decided that the Business School intranet (BSI) project would focus on the modules contained within the second year of the BA in Business Studies degree, involving some ten modules divided over two semesters, with the potential involvement of over 20 academics and more than 200 students. Whilst this appears to be a large group of staff and students to manage for a pilot study, the importance of effecting a cultural change and encouraging a debate on the role of technology in learning and teaching was one of the primary aims of the project. Given the importance attached to achieving this aim, the prospect of confining such an initiative to a single module was not considered by the project team to be a worthwhile option.

The positioning of the intranet development team as an experimental pilot that would evolve over time was intended to have the effect of lowering both expectations of what would be delivered and the fears over the impact that such a system might have on the working lives of academic staff. This was viewed as an important issue since much of the rhetoric surrounding the use of IT within higher education was, until relatively recently, based in the automation paradigm in which technology could be used to substitute for much of the work traditionally undertaken by academics.

During the initial stages of the project, the development team worked as a closed group as the prototype went through a series of iterations towards the first release version. During this period there was little attempt to actively involve other academic staff, other than to discuss, in outline terms, the broad goals of the project and to emphasize the importance of their involvement when the system went live. At the same time, influential colleagues and other important stakeholders within the Business School were identified and a series of approaches implemented that were intended to nurture their support for the project.

A major part of this process was a series of formal and *ad hoc* discussions with key influencers and stakeholders to create a shared conceptual framework and develop, as far as was possible, a shared understanding of the purposes and goals of the intranet project with those outside the development team. During this time, and since, the technologies underpinning the intranet played very little part in discussions with colleagues with, in accordance with experience elsewhere (Norris and Dolence 1996), the major focus being placed on the 'learning vision' and the benefits available to both staff and students.

The most contentious issue within the development was the proposal to collect all lecture/seminar materials used within a module and make them available over the intranet. When this possibility was discussed the immediate reaction of both staff and students was: 'Why would students go to lectures?'. This was the key issue for most, if not all, academics despite the fact that, for some time, most academics within the Business School have provided a hard copy of their lecture slides to students at the time of the lecture.

In attempting to understand the source of this resistance further discussions revealed that, for academics, there were two main issues of concern. Firstly, the control over student access to the materials and the implications, in terms of the role of the academic in the lecture/seminar module delivery format, of a move to a situation in which students could access all lecture/seminar materials from the outset of a course. Secondly, the move to a more transparent working environment in which colleagues (and managers) could have access to a lecturer's materials was a significant shift in working environment and viewed as a threat by many.

In contrast the students with whom this issue was discussed initially viewed the provision of lecture materials on the intranet as a diminution of the role of academics as providers of information and saw potential opportunities for the avoidance of attendance at lectures.

In order to engage in a meaningful discussion with academics and students about this issue it was important to widen the focus to examine the role of lectures and the lecturer within the learning and teaching of a discipline and, in turn, the part the printed content (in this context the lecture slides) plays in that process. During extensive and repeated discussions with academics and students the realization emerged that the content or lecture slides would usually play an important but relatively minor to very minor role in a lecture. Far more important was the role of the academic in interpreting, synthesizing and mapping out the topology of a discipline, as well as introducing students to the specialized language of a discipline area.

Reactions and usage of the intranet

The discussion of the reactions of the academics and students involved in the Intranet project will be divided between the views expressed prior to implementation and those expressed once the system had gone live. The views were collected during informal and semi-formal discussions with all academics and a significant number of students.

Prior to implementation

During the initial stages of the development, whilst the system proposal was being completed and the conceptual design was being finalized, the views of students and academics were almost diametrically opposed. The students, represented by a small project group who, through a series of meetings had significant influence over the conceptual design of the system, were strongly or very strongly in favour of the system being developed and could see very large advantages to students from the facilities being proposed. In contrast, many (non-IT) academics with whom the system was initially discussed were either negative or apathetic towards the creation of such a system. As the development progressed, however, this attitude was to change as a greater understanding of the purpose and potential of the system was developed.

Post-implementation

The reaction of both students and academics to the intranet was overwhelmingly positive, with the change in attitudes amongst staff being most marked. An important example of this change in attitude was the strong support for the project being voiced by individuals who were not directly involved in the project at all. This is not to say that support was unreserved – far from it. The very powerful visual design of the first release, intentionally so in order to make a strong impression on the undergraduate users, was not approved of by many academics. An unfortunate side-effect of this design, rectified in the second release, was to make the system rather slow to load, and this too was criticized. A further criticism was the occasional delays, due to the heavy workload of a key member of the intranet project, in mounting the content provided by academics. Despite these criticisms academics were, in general, supportive of the system.

From a content point of view, the success of the intranet largely depended upon the academics involved making their course and assessment outlines and lecture notes available to the project team, who would then place them on the system. Of the ten modules involved in the pilot study only one failed to provide any material at all, with the rest providing, at a minimum, course and assessment outlines, and eight providing either some or all of the lecture/seminar materials used.

The students involved in the pilot study were not the same as those who had been involved in its design who, due to the timing of the project, had by this time moved on to the next year of their course. The students who were to use the systems had thus had no input into the overall system design. One result of this was that the facilities to obtain on-line feedback from students, the module discussion areas and social 'chat' areas (put in at the behest of the student project group from the previous cohort), were largely ignored by the students who were ultimately to use the system. Despite this, students were generally positive towards the system in concept, although they were critical of its slow speed and patchy content provision. The most heavily used module-related areas on the intranet related to lecture slides, past exam papers and module-specific web sites. The most heavily used non-module feature was a horoscope facility!

Key issues in moving to the intranet model

During the period of the Business School intranet pilot project a large number of valuable issues were identified, allowing those involved in the system's development and operation to appreciate some of the implications of its large-scale adoption. The following is a reflective commentary on some of the most important lessons from the project.

Organizational and professional culture

The biggest and most important single issue identified during the intranet development was that of attempting to manage the myriad factors that arise relating to cultural change. One agenda of the intranet project was the creation of an environment in which the long-established culture of learning and teaching based on the lecture/seminar model could begin to be challenged and alternative models of educational provision developed. In this the project was successful. However, within a collegiate culture, in which academics have a high degree of autonomy, it is important that the system should be able to demonstrate obvious and early payoffs to those who are to be involved.

At an early stage of the project it is important to celebrate rather than condemn academics' individualistic working practices and recognize that they may have very different priorities, both between themselves and to those who must manage the intranet as a stable and ordered system. The chances of success are thus considerably greater if the development team understand the culture of the academic and student group into which the intranet is to be implemented and are thus able to reflect that culture in system design and management. An example of this may be found in the lack of use of discussion groups within the system.

Within the group of academics and students involved, the use of discussion groups was, at that time, a largely alien concept and no effort was made by the project team to introduce either group to their use. For students it should be recognized that they are more highly motivated towards activities that are assessed, with optional (albeit worthwhile) activities more likely to be neglected. The importance of assessment in determining student behaviour, as noted elsewhere (Maki and Maki 1997), should not be ignored in any attempt to introduce discussion groups.

Managing personal and professional change

The most important change management lesson is the need to spend a great deal of time with academics in order to develop a shared concept of the purpose and goals of a system such as an intranet. It is important to engage at the level of learning and teaching and focus on the immediate benefits rather than discuss the technology and stray into discussion of the longer-term, and thus far more speculative, implications. A key insight gained within this process was the fact that many academics are likely to be far more at home discussing developments within their discipline than they are engaging in debate over the purposes and goals of higher education or the relative merits of didactic and facilitative approaches within programmes of study. In this situation the importance of the gradual education of staff is paramount, in order that a base level understanding is achieved and a meaningful discussion of the role and potential of a system, such as an intranet, in learning and teaching may take place. It is also important to recognize that it is likely that staff will be at different places on the learning curve in this area and that some may (or may not) welcome assistance in developing their understanding of the issues.

The potential insecurity of academics in what may be a far more transparent manner of working should not be underestimated and it may be likely that academics will feel exposed by placing their lecture slides on an intranet such that they are open to inspection by colleagues and others within the university. This insecurity is likely to be exacerbated if staff are accustomed to working alone.

Finally, it is important to recognize that as the use of IT to automate work is still widespread in all sectors of industry and commerce, it is likely that academics may fear that, by participating with intranet developments, they could be working themselves out of a job. This perception is likely to play a factor in the willingness of academics to participate in projects of this kind.

The design and development of the intranet

It is vital that any intranet system is able to accept materials in a wide range of formats as, in the final analysis, the content is largely dependent upon academics providing material by consent rather than by direction. With this factor in mind, it should be clearly understood within the development team that to enforce a standard format for many course documents would be likely to alienate the very individuals upon whom the system is dependent. This issue of recognizing and respecting others' ways of working also applies to the intranet development team itself, as the range of skills required to manage its design and implementation is such that it is important that time is spent to develop a clear understanding within the team of the differing roles.

Lastly, it should be understood that there is a great deal of work being carried out on the area of on-line courses and web-based learning support environments in many parts of higher education and it is thus vital to develop a knowledge of best practice in the area. This is important for all members of a development team as the frontiers of knowledge and understanding are expanding rapidly.

Achievements and challenges

The Business School intranet project was an experiment that fulfilled its promise, albeit in slightly different ways to those anticipated by its designers. A major achievement of the project was its role in moving the learning and teaching culture within the Business School to the point that an informed debate on the role of technology in learning and teaching within higher education could begin to take place. The challenge for managers and academic leaders within higher education is to move this debate forward in such a way that maximizes the involvement of academics, course managers and the technical support personnel, creating a new model of organizational structure capable of supporting the emerging models of technology-enhanced higher education.

The learning from this project indicates that it is very likely that, at least within business schools, the role of academics will move away from simply information-giving towards more facilitative approaches that perhaps more actively manage student learning. Any move towards the intermediated world of technology-enhanced higher education may also require a new definition of the roles and responsibilities of the multi-skilled teams that will design, deliver and manage courses. The challenge for academics, administrators and technicians alike is to work together to effectively facilitate the significant personal, organizational and pedagogic re-evaluation and change that will result from engaging with new models of technology-enhanced higher education.

Technical note

The Business School intranet was a bespoke system using standard HTML combined with Javascript and Perl and was designed around NetScape Enterprise Server software v3.5.1 running on a Pentium Pro NT4 server. The system used Lasso to integrate existing FileMaker Pro databases and had a custom-designed user interface that was created using Adobe Photoshop, Freehand and Extreme 3D. The system was designed to be usable by Netscape Navigator versions 2 and above. The next generation of Business School intranet is to be based on Lotus Domino.

An earlier version of this paper was presented at the Computers in Teaching Initiative – Accounting, Finance and Management (CTI-AFM) Conference, Old Ship Hotel, Brighton in April 1999.

A WEB-BASED, STUDENT-DRIVEN MODULE

Gordon Bull and Mike Smith

Introduction

The Faculty of Information Technology at the University of Brighton structures its undergraduate courses within a modular programme. While many of the modules are compulsory, students are also able to elect to study certain modules including those outside of this main field of study. One such modules is entitled 'On-line Information Networks'.

This module had been delivered using a traditional lecture-based course backed up with supervised practicals and tutorials. In 1997 the decision was taken to run the module in a different way. This decision was based on student feedback and an analysis of the benefits that students were getting from the lectures. Teaching notes had been created that supported the lectures and it was noted that much of the material in these notes had been produced from information obtained from the world wide web. It was concluded that the value being added by giving lectures did not warrant their delivery. It was also concluded that the students would benefit from seeking, evaluating, assimilating and presenting the information which the authors had found on the web. This decision led to the redesign of the module delivery while keeping the aims and objective much the same as before.

The original version of the module

The aims of the module are to explore ways of:

• exploiting technology to search effectively for information;
• presenting information for others using a range of media.

At successful completion of the module students will be able to:

• understand and use a range of tools available for locating and retrieving on-line information effectively;
• evaluate approaches to finding the information required;
• design appropriate systems that deliver information via the networks; and
• appreciate current issues of concern in the use of information networks.

The lectures were used to introduce such things as network fundamentals, search engines and search strategies, web technology, commercial use of the Internet and the web, underlying standards and issues relating to such topics as security, copyright, pornography and censorship.

The module was assessed using two items of coursework. In the first the students were required to write an article, of the form found in personal computer magazines, comparing and rating search engines. This was designed to ensure that students understood the different kind of search engines available and to get them to explore their strengths and weaknesses as well as to decide on the criteria they would use to assess the engines. The second was for each student to create a web site displaying information on a topic of their choice. This involved them in designing the structure of the information, the navigation aids to help users find their way round the site and the appropriate format for the presentation of the information. They had also to produce a workbook describing technologies and tools explored or used, the legal and technical limitations encountered, a critique of their own web pages, reference to other appropriate material and a full list of the sources of information used.

The students found it difficult to present a magazine-style article and, although there was evidence of learning taking place, the overall quality was not as good as expected. The second piece (the created web site) engaged the students (primarily because they were engaged with the subject matter of their web site) and led to some excellent work.

Developing the module

The first version of the module

Given it had been concluded that the lecture course added little value, a radical rethink was undertaken as to how the original aims and objectives of the module could be achieved in a different way.

Work started by considering how to best assess the module. As the creation of web pages had been successful and highly motivating it was decided that this should be retained to assess that students could design appropriate systems that deliver information via the networks. As a number of the students had noted in their workbooks that issues had arisen over copyright of material, this coursework also gives them an opportunity to appreciate current issues of concern in the use of information networks.

It was decided to replace the first piece of coursework with an exercise which both substituted for the lecture course, by getting the students to create some of the material that would have been covered in the lectures, and assessed their ability to understand and use a range of tools available for locating and retrieving on-line information effectively and to evaluate approaches to finding the information required, by using the tools and evaluating the material found in a critical way. This piece of coursework involved selecting two topics each from two different lists (one based on the technology and the other on non-technological issues) and finding information on the Internet to support the writing of an essay of 1000 words on each of the chosen topics.

A final piece of coursework involved students participating in a bulletin board discussion group chosen from a list. At the beginning of the module, students were required to mail an ordered set of choices to the module leader to indicate in which discussion groups they wished to take part. Based on this an attempt was made to give each student their top choice whilst balancing the number of students in each group. This led to some not getting their first choice and not all topics running. The feedback received was that this method gave most people what they wanted and created groups of sufficient size to ensure that the discussion was maintained.

Each student was required to write a 1500 word report on their participation in the discussion group. This included a description of how the group worked, their individual contribution to the success of the group (by including in the report examples of their contributions) and a critique of bulletin boards as a medium for conducting discussions. The assignment assessed both approaches to finding the information required and the appreciation of current issues of concern in the use of information networks as, in order to sustain the discussion, students needed to obtain information from the Internet (and other places if required) and to participate in debates about a current issue. The bulletin boards were 'seeded' with web site addresses where relevant information could be found, as well as a couple of provocative statements to get the discussion going.

The second version of the module

Having run the new version of the module twice, the outcomes were reviewed and ways sought to improve the assessment.

The feedback received from the students was that the discussion groups were working well but that the report required was not serving its purpose. Moreover, this assessment overlapped with the essays in that both assessments were testing similar learning outcomes. On the basis of this it was decided to combine the two pieces of work.

Seven bulletin boards were established (see below). The purpose of the bulletin boards was two-fold: (i) to provide a communication medium with which students needed to become familiar in order to meet the course objectives; and (ii) to support the students' research into the topics about which they were to write their reports. Students could participate in as many of the bulletin boards as they wished but had to participate and contribute to the ongoing discussion in at least two of them as the two reports would be based on the topics of two of these newsgroups and because they would be assessed on the contribution they made to the discussions of these groups.

The topics of the reports were drawn from the following list:

- censorship on the net;
- the information 'haves' and 'have-nots' and the social problems this can cause;
- Microsoft's domination of the net;
- electronic commerce (e-commerce);
- distance learning using the net;
- electronic libraries; and
- security.

The students were told that the majority of the information on which the reports were based should be obtained from the world wide web/Internet and from the discussion that took place on the newsgroup relating to this topic.

Students were also asked to write a 1500 word report on their participation in the discussion groups. This was to include a description of how the groups worked, their individual contribution to the success of the groups (by including in the report examples of their contributions as before) and a critique of bulletin boards as a medium for conducting discussions.

The outcome of this change was an improved set of essays/reports and a clearer understanding of how bulletin boards could be used to support discussion and information gathering.

The third version of the module

All the students taking the module had been from the Faculty of Information Technology. These ranged across a wide variety of courses – computing and information systems, computer studies, computer science, software engineering, information and library studies and information media studies. An approach had been made from the School of the Environment to make the module available to students of geography and environmental studies but none had taken up the offer. At a later date an approach was made by the Institute of Nursing and Midwifery (INAM) to offer the course to their students.

Discussions with the course leader from INAM led to minor changes in the course delivery. The main change was to offer different discussion group topics, namely:

• censorship on the net;
• the information 'haves' and 'have-nots' and the social problems this can cause;
• public access to healthcare information;
• health information strategy;
• confidentiality of health records;
• year 2000 compliance and healthcare.

Nurses and midwives at the University of Brighton are taught across three counties, centred both in hospitals and on campus in the university. This development was the first time the module genuinely had students at a distance and distributed across a wide geographic area. This made the use of newsgroups more realistic.

This revised version showed that the basic structure of the module and its assessments were sound. The new topics were agreed in less than an hour and the details, web sites and issues were created in another hour, e-mailed round for comment and agreed.

Learning support

The main support given to students on this module was a web site that set out the details of the module and what the students had to do, together with full details of the coursework requirements that included such things as hand-in dates and the assessment criteria. A copy of the current web site is given in Appendix 1 at the end of this case study.

Because many of the students on the module were, by and large, unused to participating in on-line discussion groups and might find the technology a barrier, a help newsgroup was created to which students could turn to get advice and support from their fellows, outside the main discussions. To encourage others to support those who needed help a bonus of 10 per cent was offered to any students who could show that they had helped their fellows to overcome problems. So far no-one has qualified for the bonus.

It was made clear that throughout the module students could e-mail the authors to ask questions or to gain support: none of them have.

Lessons learnt

The work handed in by the students indicated that a great deal of learning had taken place. Although the quality of the essays varied, as one might expect across a group of students, the best showed a level of understanding of the topic, skill in finding the relevant information and the ability to select quality information that demonstrated they had met the objectives of the course. The report on the discussion group work again led to a range of grades but also identified that reporting on such an activity was new to this group of students and they struggled to find the right way of presenting the information. Nevertheless, the groups worked well, showed clear signs of a good debate taking place with people changing their positions in response to other peoples' arguments. Most felt that the medium was appropriate and many comments were positive on the ability to deal with the group comments at times to suit the individual rather than during a fixed seminar slot.

One student gave some truly excellent feedback on the use of newsgroups. Drawing on both his own experience and published material on success factors for groupware, he identified areas where improvements could be made, including ensuring that the group sizes were large enough to generate sufficient activity (under the new arrangements there was no attempt to balance the number participating in each discussion), making explicit the benefits for contributing to the discussion and providing training in what, for many, is a new technology. All these issues are now under active consideration.

Through the various versions of this module, it has been hard to get students to make proper reference to the source of their material. Having identified this problem with certain groups of students (and not with others, such as those on the BA Information and Library Studies), discussion with the course teams has taken place to find ways of introducing students to both the importance of, and methods for, citing references.

Students reported that they soon adapted to a module with no face-to-face contact and used e-mail to keep in contact with each other and resolve problems (which may explain why the *Help* bulletin board was not used). The feedback received was that they at first found it difficult to allocate time to the tasks and found themselves taking part in the bulletin board discussions towards the end of the time allocated (that is, close to the hand-in date for that assignment), a common feature of students faced with coursework throughout higher education!

The clear message from our students was that they can be independent and succeed.

Records were kept of the time taken both on the original lecture-based version and on the new version. Although the objective was not one of efficiency, it was found that there was an efficiency gain.

The original lecture-based approach for *n* students on the module took the following time:

2 hours per week of face-to-face contact for
13 weeks 26×60 minutes

2 assignments, taking on average 15 minutes
each to mark $2 \times n \times 15$ minutes

The two later versions took the following time:

3 assignments, taking on average 15 minutes
each to mark $3 \times n \times 15$ minutes

The break point comes when marking the extra piece of coursework is more costly than delivering the lecture course; that is when $n \times 15$ exceeded 26×60 or when *n* is greater than 104. Similar sums can be done on longer or shorter times for marking. Neither of the above set of figures includes preparation time for the lecture course nor the time to devise the new version of the course and create the web site to support it. In this context, however, it is interesting to note that it took much less time to design the version for the students in nursing and midwifery.

Lessons for others

As the experience with INAM shows, the approach taken in the design and delivery of this module is applicable in other areas. Providing the students are confident in using the web before they start, all of the elements of the assessments are subject independent and could be adapted for another subject area, that is, the information searching exercise is subject independent, the discussion groups are subject independent, whilst the contents of the web page could be made to reflect the subject area.

The following example shows how the assignment to create the web pages could be adapted. It is taken from another module run by one of the authors, the assignment is to create a web-based information resource:

It is useful to have a reference source that grows with you. The objective of this coursework is for you to build an information resource of key concepts and topics as they relate to this module.

As you will know, the information on the web is not all good quality or reliable. Your task is to choose twelve of the entries below and, for each, find a range of high quality pages that give relevant information on the selected topic. You may choose other topics relating to this module if you wish. Where there is a wealth of information available you may care to create lower-level directories to assist in navigating around the information. Each page included should have a brief synopsis so that the user can decide if the page pointed to would be relevant or likely to contain the information required. This commentary might also include comments on the quality, trustworthiness and correctness of the referred information.

You are to hand in a set of files, which are readable by Netscape Navigator, that contain the pages you have created. You are also to hand in a 1000 word report on the process you used to find the pages and the way you created the directory pages.

Many students attend in part-time mode. Such students find great pressures on their time and often find that pressures of work and family make attendance on a regular basis difficult. A course structured in this way enables such students to undertake their study in patterns and at times to suit them, rather than at pre-scheduled times in the day or the week. Many part-time students travel long distances to attend classes. Modules delivered in this way can reduce the demands for travel.

Conclusions

There is strong evidence that high quality learning has taken place on this module since it has been changed. The students have indicated that they enjoy the approach, now feel more confident in using the Internet and have acquired many skills, over and above those in the aims of the course.

The approach taken has been shown to be adaptable to other subject areas and as such offers a model for others to experiment with.

Students have reported that although they initially find the management of their time a challenge, they enjoy the flexibility this approach offers them.

The approach taken in this module has led to learner independence whilst at the same time creating an interdependence that encourages team work.

Although not one of the reasons for making the change, the method of delivery turns out to be efficient in the use of staff time.

Students can take this module in their placement year to redeem failure in a module taken during their second year. Otherwise there may be a need for attendance at the university, which may be difficult if the placement is not in Brighton.

Overall, an approach such as this can enrich the learning experience of students. The authors would not advocate widespread use of this approach for students who normally attend a university or other educational establishment but it has its place in encouraging and enabling different approaches to learning and teaching.

Appendix 1: IS207 information networks academic year 1999–2000

This course is assessed by two separate pieces of coursework, which are described below, together with a test at the end of the course. In order to pass the module you must pass each of the three assignments separately.
The aims of the coursework are as follows:

1. To ensure that you understand some of the important topics associated with information networks.
2. To ensure that you are able to present information in a format appropriate for the audience you are addressing.
3. To introduce you to a form of communication that supports group working.
4. To ensure you are able to contribute to an electronic discussion forum.
5. To ensure that you are able to critically evaluate a communication medium.
6. To ensure that you are able to design and construct web pages.
7. To ensure that you are able to evaluate web pages created by others and yourself.

The work may completed on any suitable machine. For example, a machine running the Unix operating system, Windows 3.1/95 or the Apple Mac O/S.

Mode of operation

This course is a self-study course using electronic communications for support if and when required. This means that, other than an introductory presentation in week 1, there will be no formal lectures or tutorials. In particular, this means that you can complete the course at your own pace on days of your own choosing. However, during the course there are several milestones that have to be met. These milestones are the delivery of three completed course work units. The coursework units are in essence the driving force of the course.
You should devote about six hours a week to the course. However, as you can study the course at your own speed you may choose to study less some weeks and more others. Remember, you must make sure that you allocate yourself enough time for the course during the semester. In particular, it will not be possible to pass the course by trying to complete all the work in the last week of the semester

Allocating your time

This is perhaps the most difficult of all decisions that you will have to make during the time that you study this course. It is important to allocate time for the following core activities:

• searching for information
• reading and assimilating the material found

- preparing material for the coursework
- completing the coursework.

The course has a notional requirement of 80 hours of your time during the semester. The mark allocation suggests that you should spend about:

- 40 hours in total preparing for and completing assignment 1.
- 40 hours for assignment 2.

We urge you to schedule a fixed time each week to work on this course otherwise there is a danger you will get behind as other courses and activities take priority. The exact time spent on each activity is of course your decision, however spending too much time on any one activity will probably result in a poor mark or failure in the course.

Support

Support is available electronically by e-mailing your problem to either of the following people:

Gordon.Bull@brighton.ac.uk

M.A.Smith@brighton.ac.uk

Remember to include your name and the course you are on in your e-mail message. Although not instant, we hope to be able to provide a solution or path of study to help you with your problem. However, this should not be used for requesting information that could otherwise be found by searching information sources either on- or off-line. There is a also a general news group help for requesting help or seeking information about a particular aspect of the course. This newsgroup also allows you to share knowledge or solutions to problems with other members of the course. In providing a solution for others you will also help you in clarifying an area of knowledge and as the basis for material for the coursework. See the bonus section.

Resources available

The BURKS CD (a double CD) produced by John English is a complete local web site of useful information for computing students. The double CD uses Netscape 3 (PC edition) to browse material on the CD. The CD can be obtained from the computer shop for only £5. Alternatively you can browse the contents on-line on `http://burks.bton.ac.uk/`. In particular the section: `http://burks.bton.ac.uk/burks/internet` has various articles taken from the web about the components and technologies used in and by the Internet. This is a useful starter for your exploration and investigation of the Internet.

Accessing the WWW

When using and accessing the Internet, of which the world wide web is part, it is important to remember:

- Access is world wide. Network traffic from North America increases considerably after midday.
- The material on the web is held in many different countries and generated by many millions of people whose laws/cultures/values may not be the same as yours.
- Many people in the university will also be using the Internet, of which the web is a part.
- The university rules for use of computer equipment and resources.
- The laws of the UK.

Assignments

This course is assessed entirely by coursework consisting of three separate pieces of coursework, which are described below. The aims of the courseware are as follows:

1. To introduce you to a form of communication which supports group working.
2. To ensure that you understand some of the important topics associated with information networks.
3. To ensure that you are able to present information in a format appropriate for the audience you are addressing.
4. To ensure you are able to contribute to an electronic discussion forum.
5. To ensure that you are able to critically evaluate a communication medium.
6. To ensure that you are able to construct web pages.
7. To ensure that you are able to evaluate web pages created by others and yourself.

The work may be completed on any suitable machine. For example, a machine running the Unix operating system, Windows 3.1/95 or the Apple Mac O/S.

Assignment 1

The assignment, which consists of two reports and a critique, must be handed in by 12 noon on the Friday of the eighth week of the semester.

Seven newsgroups/bulletin boards have been established (see below), which are accessible using the newsgroup reader within Netscape Navigator (version 3 or higher on either Windows-based or Macintosh platforms). The broad topics of these discussion group are listed below.

The purpose of the newsgroups is two-fold. Firstly, to provide a communication medium with which you need to become familiar in order to meet coursework aims 3, 4 and 5. Secondly, to support your research into the topics about which you must write reports. You may participate in as many of the newsgroups as you wish but you must participate and contribute to the on-going discussion in at least two of them as your two reports will be based on the topics of two of the newsgroups and because you will be assessed on the contribution you make to the discussions of these group.

Before entering into the selected discussion group be sure to read the notes that form part of the course web page under the heading ethical, legal and copyright issues.

You are to write reports on two topics from the following list:

- censorship on the net
- the information haves and have-nots and the social problems this can cause
- Microsoft's domination of the net
- electronic commerce
- distance learning using the net
- electronic libraries
- security.

Each report is to be about, but no longer than, 2000 words. In addition there may be no more than two diagrams if required. You must include aword count at the end of each report. You must identify clearly the target audience you are preparing the notes for and this should be stated at the beginning of the report. The reports are to be in the form of factual information such as one might produce to hand out in support of a lecture on a topic.

The majority of the information on which the reports are based should be obtained from the world wide web/Internet and from the discussion that took place on the newsgroup relating to this topic. You must give references to the sites (and any other sources) on which the information is based as well as acknowledging any contribution from your fellow students via the newsgroup.

You are also to write a 1500 word report on the your participation in the discussion groups, which includes a description of how the groups worked,

List of discussion groups	Discusses
`help`	General help and useful information.
`censorship`	Censorship on the net – should there be any, can it be applied, should access be controlled to 'undesirable' material?
`distance-learning`	Distance learning using the net – they way of the future?
`electronic-libraries`	Electronic libraries – does the future lay this way?
`electronic-commerce`	Electronic commerce – will it take off and what is required to make it happen?
`security`	Security – is the release of encryption algorithms a threat to national security?
`social`	The information haves and have-nots and the social problems this can cause.
`news:brighton.test`	Use this group to try out news.

your individual contribution to the success of the groups (by including in the report examples of your contributions) and a critique of bulletin boards as a medium for conducting discussions.

This assignment is worth 50% of the marks for this module.

Make sure of the following   That each report is no more than 2000 words, has a word count and has no more than two diagrams. There is an absence of typographical and spelling errors and the English is clear. Your sources are identified and give proper references, including contribution from others on the newsgroup. That your audiences are identified. The quality of the report.

That the critique is no more than 1500 words and has a word count. There is an absence of typographical and spelling errors and the English is clear. The quality of the critique.

Censorship on the net – should there be any, can it be applied?   Censorship is a sign of the nanny state, trying to determine what people think and how they should spend their time. Censorship on the net is impossible anyway as it is a global phenomenon and what is allowed in one society is not accepted in another. Policing the net is not possible so laws which cannot be enforced are bad laws.

```
http://www.yahoo.co.uk/Society_and_Culture/
Civil_Rights/Censorship/Censorship_and_the_Net/
```

might be a good starting point for information.

The information haves and have-nots and the social problems this can cause   As we enter the so-called information age, those with access to information will be socially and economically rich, those without will suffer. As information is likely to be the basis of the future economy, this separation into information rich and information poor will lead to a greater economic division that at present. Such a sharp division could easily lead to greater social conflict. Left unchecked, society could easily fall apart. However, the emergent attempts to blend together the commercial, governmental and not-for-profit sectors so as to ensure that information is made available to all sectors of society has the potential to not only avert the problems but to minimize the differences in society.

```
http://www2.echo.lu/bonn/userdeclar.html
```

has a declaration of intent from Europe.

Electronic commerce – will it take off and what is required to make it happen?   On-line bookshops and CD shops are making money after a considerable investment but few other companies are making money out of electronic commerce.

However, the banks are going on-line and this will force the pace of change and ensure secure financial transaction over the net.

Companies are creating a presence on the net so as not to miss out if it takes off, but will it?

Customers like to touch and browse before buying and no matter how good virtual reality becomes it will always be virtual and will not replace strolling through a store looking at goods before buying. Whilst things like on-line book stores may succeed, not many products are bought in this way and electronic commerce will always be a fringe activity.

The following web sites might be useful to you:

```
http://www.sainsburys.co.uk/
http://www.tesco.co.uk/
http://www.yahoo.co.uk/Business_and_Economy/Companies/
Computers/Internet/
```

Distance learning using the net – they way of the future? This course is not as good as those with face-to-face teaching. It leaves one feeling isolated and unloved. We will all flounder and not learn much. It's a cop-out by the lecturing staff!

This course is much better delivered this way than by the traditional method because I can schedule my time as I see fit. I can explore the areas I am interested in rather than have things spoon-fed and pre-digested by a lecturer.

```
http://www2.echo.lu/telematics/education/en/
http://www.forbes.com/97/0616/5912084a.html
```

Electronic libraries – does the future lay this way? Who needs to go to a physical library any more? All the information one could possibly want is on the net. Librarians as we know them are a dying breed.

```
http://www.niss.ac.uk/education/hefc/follett/report/
index.html
```

the Follett report might prove interesting.

Security – is the release of encryption algorithms a threat to national security? The US Government is unwilling to let serious encryption algorithms/keys be exported because it sees it as a threat to its national security. Why? Because it would no longer be able to read messages sent by others. The following resources should help you get the discussion going:

```
http://www.yahoo.co.uk/Computers_and_Internet/
Security_and_Encryption/Encryption_Policy/
Clipper_Chip/
http://www.gildea.com/pgp/
http://www.crypto.com/
```

Assignment 2

The assignment, which contributes 50 per cent of the marks for the module consists of a workbook and possibly a floppy disc that must be handed in by 12 noon on the Friday of the twelfth week of the semester.

The assignment is to create and publish a series of web pages on a topic of your own choosing. These web pages are to be documented in a workbook. The workbook will contain examples of the major web pages created (not the raw HTML), together with your comments on the following issues:

1. Technologies and tools explored or used.
2. Design and navigation approaches and choices, including identifying who you think your web pages are aimed at.
3. Legal and technical limitations encountered.
4. A critique of your web pages and how they might be improved.
5. Sources of information.

You must hand in the workbook and either a floppy disc with the web site on it or the address of the web site clearly marked on the workbook.

Make sure of the following   Your web site is easy to navigate and is appropriate for its intended audience in terms of content and presentation. That you describe how you designed both the site, the individual pages and the navigational approach together with the tools and technologies you used to create your pages. The workbook contains examples of the HTML and other code produced.

The importance of design in the creation of a web site   Web sites are like any other software item, they need to be designed. Not only that, they need to be maintained over a period of time. Like any other item of software, they are designed with a purpose in mind and are often targeted at certain groups of individuals. All of which implies that creating a web site is just as complex and thought provoking as designing an accounting package or a piece of software to control a piece of electronics.

Before setting out to design a web site remember two things   Firstly, the underlying software that creates the site (written in HTML, Java or whatever), like any other piece of software, should be designed to be read by human beings first and machines second. Why? Because, like all software, it will need to be maintained and often the maintainer is not the person who wrote it (or if it is the time between writing it and needing to modify it is so long that the author has forgotten why it is the way it is). What this means is that layout, comments, use of standards and background documentation are all important.

Secondly, the software you are creating is designed to be used by others. This means that such things as the navigational strategies, appearance and content are all key issues. Add to that the need to understand some of the key human factor issues (such as the fact that 8% of the male population suffer from some kind of colour blindness, particularly the inability to differentiate between red and green) and you can see that designing good web pages is not as straightforward as it first appears. The reader's screen may not be the same as the one you use; it could be a 14-inch black and white monitor!

In designing your web site think about the design processes you go through and document them as part of your workbook. Discuss design options and explain why you rejected some options and say why you chose the one you did. Unlike other aspects of software engineering, there are few tools and techniques for you to make use of but this does not mean that you can ignore the design stages.

Jakob Neilsen of Sun Microsystems has much to say on web site design. You can find a number of his thoughts on:

`http://www.sun.com/columns/alertbox.html`

There is a general web site devoted to these issues at:

`http://www.cs.vt.edu/~abrams/JavaCourse/`
`References.html`

If you want to know more about using HTML direct see an introduction to HTML and CGI scripts.

Ethical, legal and copyright issues Remember:

• That the material on the web is held in many different countries and generated by many millions of people whose laws/cultures/values may not be the same as yours.
• The university rules for use of computer equipment and resources.
• The laws of the UK.
• That material on the web is copyright unless otherwise stated. Just because you can download it does not mean that you can use it.

Created by Gordon Bull/Mike Smith September 1997 Modified October 1998 Version 2.01
Comments, suggestions, etc. M.A.Smith@brighton.ac.uk [Home page]
Printed/Displayed June 8 11:45:59 1999

8

Distance Learning and the International Dimension

ROLE DEVELOPMENT FOR CLINICAL EDUCATORS BY DISTANCE LEARNING

Lynne Caladine, Ann Moore and Jane Morris

> The future of any health profession is largely dependent on the quality of the education that it provides for its future generation. Recognising the fact that clinical education is a crucial course component, we must strive to ensure that those senior practitioners who are responsible for clinical education are encouraged continually to develop their role as clinical educators.
>
> (Moore *et al.* 1996: ix)

Introduction

Clinical education in this context may be defined as: 'the essential and extensive course component of all healthcare professional courses, which "provides the focus for the integration of academic and practice based learning" in a work based setting' (Chartered Society of Physiotherapy 1991: 29).

The majority of students in the healthcare professions are required, in preparation for their role in the healthcare system, to complete a considerable number of assessed hours of education in the clinical setting. For the student, clinical placements are a testing time as they are required to demonstrate ability in the cognitive, psychomotor and affective domains whilst coping with the three-way interaction that has to occur between themselves, the patient and the clinical educator. The clinical element of healthcare professionals' undergraduate education is facilitated and then assessed by senior practitioners, fulfilling their role as educators in the clinical field. On most courses, the clinical educator's summative clinical assessment contributes towards the student's final degree classification and, ultimately, to the award of licence to practice. As this role is pivotal in providing the next generation of competent practitioners, it is crucial that clinical educators are supported by their colleagues in higher education though the provision of learning opportunities that will enable them to function confidently and effectively.

Course types

Recognizing the need to ensure that educational courses were provided for clinical educators, the Clinical Education Working Party established by the Education Committee of the Chartered Society of Physiotherapy (CSP), published *Guidelines for Good Practice for the Education of Clinical Educators* (CSP 1994). These guidelines proposed that two types of clinical education programme should be provided, if they were not already, by higher education institutions:

- Type A programmes are those that deal with the broad educational issues needed in workplace teaching and supervision.
- Type B programmes are those that deal directly with specific course issues and the relationship between the education provider and the placement providers.

The purpose of these guidelines was to provide a framework aimed at increasing collaboration and strengthening the partnership between the course teams and the placement providers, enabling dialogue between academics and clinical educators about clinical education issues and supporting senior clinicians to fulfil their role as clinical educators.

Clinicians in context

In order to appreciate the educational role of physiotherapy clinicians in context, it is necessary to briefly explain the evolution of physiotherapy education generally and at a local level in the South East of England.

Course history

Prior to 1976 all physiotherapy pre-registration courses were based in NHS schools, with a diploma being awarded on successful completion by the CSP. In the 1970s, schools began to move into higher education institutions and the first BSc (Hons) degree course was introduced in 1976. It was not until 1992 that physiotherapy became an all graduate profession with all students successfully completing physiotherapy courses being awarded a BSc (Hons) degree along with a licence to practise.

In the transition of courses to higher education there was a shift in the ethos of clinical placements. Placements began to be drawn from a much

wider geographical area and roles of clinicians and lecturing staff in relation to students on placement changed markedly. Clinicians were expected
to take on more of an educational role and visiting lecturers were expected
to use visits for liaison and pastoral purposes and to assist the clinician in
their facilitation of learning and assessment roles rather than to teach students in the clinical setting. In addition, for the first time, students were
seen as supernumerary to the workforce during their minimum of 1000
hours of clinical experience (as stipulated by the CSP).

The late 1980s witnessed the emergence of two new BSc (Hons) Physiotherapy courses in the South Thames region. The region chose to rational-
ize physiotherapy education in order to influence recruitment of qualified
staff in what was then South East Thames (Health) region and move from
having three NHS schools of physiotherapy (Guys, St Thomas' and King's
College Hospital) to the situation of commissioning physiotherapy education from two centres of higher education at the University of Brighton
and King's College London. The BSc (Hons) in Physiotherapy course at the
University of Brighton took its first cohort in 1990.

Clinical placement provision

Historically in the South Thames region, clinical placement provision, as in
most regional health authority areas throughout the UK, had been firmly
established at hospital sites attached to or in close proximity to schools of
physiotherapy. However, with the establishment of the two new physiotherapy
courses, students undertook their clinical education for the first time in
NHS trusts throughout the South Thames area. As a result of the above
changes, some senior clinicians who had historically never received students for clinical education experience before were required to take on
additional responsibility in their new role as educators in the clinical field.

To ensure that the transition period was a smooth one, the South Thames
Health Authority had the foresight to appoint a regional clinical coordinator, whose main functions were to coordinate the clinical education programmes for the two new courses, to establish new placements throughout
the region and to work together with the clinical education tutors from
King's College London and the University of Brighton to address the role
development of new clinical educators.

During their clinical experience, pre-registration physiotherapy students
had previously formed part of the workforce with students undertaking a
form of apprenticeship. Senior clinicians had acted as clinical instructors and,
more latterly, as supervisors in the clinical field. However, with the move to
higher education, clinical educators were required to take on responsibility
for both the facilitation and, in most instances, assessment of student clinical
education. These fairly major changes in the clinicians' role in student clinical
learning were highlighted by Cross in 1994, who contrasted the changes in
the clinician's role in clinical education to the more gradual and deliberate

changes that had occurred in physiotherapy practice: 'the world of the clinician involved in student learning seems to have stumbled through a variety of roles each teetering precariously on the one before' (Cross 1994: 609).

In certain health professions, there has been an assumption over the years that highly qualified practitioners will inevitably possess the ability to teach. Personal experience and that of others indicates that this is not the case.

Higher education provision

In line with guidelines issued by the CSP, both the University of Brighton and King's College London Physiotherapy Schools already provided study days for clinicians in order to familiarize them with their educational role in relation to students from their own institutions (Type B course). The aims of these sessions were mainly to ensure that clinicians were acquainted with the course structure, understood their part in the assessment process and were able to assess student performance effectively. As there was no funding for the educational role development of clinicians, these sessions were usually of one-day duration and occurred once or twice a year. There was no time to consider general educational issues. Physiotherapy educators and managers recognized the urgent need to address the omissions.

In 1993 a group of physiotherapy managers met with two lecturers from each university and the regional placement coordinator and became the South East Thames clinical education planning group. This committee had several meetings over the period of a year and identified the needs of clinicians in terms of their role-development as educators. It also identified problems that would impact on clinicians being able to participate in role development events. From these discussions, three major limitations were identified:

- source of funding for participation;
- time availability of physiotherapy clinicians; and
- motivation of clinicians to pursue study in this area.

Study day

With these limitations in mind, the need for a variety of options offering the opportunity for study of educational issues was identified. In response, staff from the two schools began to work together to develop a spectrum of opportunities for role development in this area. The collaboration initially resulted in a one-day event jointly facilitated by the original four staff members (two from each institution) and the clinical coordinator. The study day overviewed general educational (role of the clinical educator, facilitating learning, assessment and evaluation) rather than course-specific issues. There was a heavy demand for these study days and, in the first year, it was necessary to repeat the day, catering for approximately 80 clinicians on each occasion.

Table 8.1   Extract from evaluation of 1996 regional study day for clinical educators in the South Thames NHS region

---

Aims of the day
  67% 'most appropriate'
  33% 'appropriate'

Fulfilment of aims
  64% 'all aims fulfilled'
  36% 'aims fulfilled to acceptable level'

Session content
  18% 'most appropriate'
  77.5% 'very appropriate'
  4.5% 'appropriate'

Preparedness for receiving students
  65% 'much better prepared'
  30% 'would appreciate additional training'
  5% 'unprepared to receive students'

The study days were well evaluated by participants (Table 8.1) but the team facilitating the days were aware of its limitations because of the short duration.

The team began to explore how the content could be made available to greater numbers of clinicians whilst bearing in mind some of the original problems of time availability and funding. There were a number of constraints impacting on the short one-day course. The target audience was unidisciplinary and didactic input predominated, with minimal time for active learning. In addition, the course served only to raise the participant's awareness of the process of education in the clinical field, allowing little opportunity for the development of the educational skills required for the facilitation, assessment and evaluation of clinical learning.

Self-directed learning pack

The team began to work on converting the content of the study day into a format that could be used independently by clinicians and contact was made with publishers Churchill Livingstone, who expressed an interest in publishing an expanded version of the self-directed learning material. A decision was made that learning would be facilitated by including in the package a reader containing copies of key journal articles referred to in the text. The package was published in 1996 and took approximately 15 months to produce from the time of negotiations with the publisher.

The successful development of the open learning package was a consequence of the unique and collaborative structure and functioning of the project team. The team's ability to meet the project demands was enhanced by the following factors:

- The committed, positive, enthusiastic and at times ebullient approach demonstrated by all team members to meet project deadlines, despite substantial and ongoing work commitments.
- The regular peer review from all members of the project team, which provided individual authors (who were responsible for acting as 'key' authors for at least two chapters) with support and constructive feedback.
- The skills of the project leader who, in the final review and editing, ensured that parity of style and focus on key messages were evident throughout the package.

The above factors are in accordance with the principles of effective team functioning identified by Guzzo and Shea (1992), cited in West and Poulton (1997): 'Individual contributions should be identifiable and the subject of evaluation' in addition to recognizing the need for: 'clear team goals with built-in performance feedback' (Guzzo and Shea 1992: 209).

Once the package had been published, staff at the two universities began to plan stand-alone Masters level modules and courses built around the content. There had been an initial intention to plan and validate these courses jointly but this raised difficulties in terms of academic ownership and eventually both institutions developed modules and courses that suited their own needs. The University of Brighton now offers a Masters-level module – The Health Professional as an Educator – which has recently run for the third year. In 1999 it was delivered as a one-week intensive module and recruited well, with 14 participants from a range of healthcare professions (nurses and podiatrists as well as physiotherapists). The intensive nature works well for this type of interactive module. Evaluations by students rate the module very highly and many students comment on the way in which it will or has changed their practice.

Shortly after the module ran for the first time, talks began with lecturing staff from other healthcare areas in the university with a view to offering a modified and expanded version as a postgraduate certificate. There was interest from occupational therapy, nursing and clinical pharmacy, whose professions all run similar models of clinical education to that in physiotherapy. This collaboration culminated in the validation of a postgraduate certificate in 1997, with a resource pack of journal articles adapted for each profession.

The Postgraduate certificate

The postgraduate certificate was originally entitled 'Postgraduate Certificate in Work Based Learning'. The title was chosen because it seemed to reflect the concept of the course, without being tied to specific wording such as 'fieldwork education' or 'clinical education', which is profession-specific nomenclature and might discourage some professional groups from applying. The course is offered on a one-year part-time basis and requires completion of four modules (three educational modules based on the learning package and one option module) and necessitates only 13 days attendance at the university, as it draws heavily on the distance learning package and reader. The fees for the course were reduced by half for any students who were involved in the clinical education of University of Brighton students.

Despite the low fees, the course failed to recruit in the first year. After a series of consultations, the course team decided that there were several reasons for this:

* The title was deemed to be so generic that potential applicants could not identify with it.
* Funding was still an issue – although money is available to nursing staff for CPD, there is little funding available for Professions Allied to Medicine (PAMs), which includes physiotherapists and occupational therapists.
* In addition, PAMs do not have any study day entitlement in the NHS.
* There is greater incentive and motivation for clinicians to enrol on courses that develop clinical skills.

The course title was subsequently changed to PG Certificate in Clinical Education but has failed to recruit sufficient students for a second year. The course team are confident that the course has been developed ahead of its time and that, when and if funding is more readily available for PAMs' CPD, this course will be ready to meet a need. Within the next few years, it is also anticipated that changes will be made to the Act of Parliament relating to registration of these professional groups and that evidence of CPD will be necessary to maintain licence to practice. In addition, there is a national move towards formal accreditation of clinical educators. This type of course will help clinicians to meet both requirements.

Despite the failure to recruit to the postgraduate certificate, the distance learning package has been very well received and the authors are aware that many physiotherapy course teams use the distance learning material when doing their own local role development courses for clinical educators.

Conclusion

The package received good reviews. Pitt-Brooke (1997: 600) stated:

> This text comes in the form of a two-part learning package and its stated intention is to 'address the concept of education in the clinical environment in its broadest sense'. As such it offers a both innovative and pragmatic approach using an open, self-directed learning strategy ... This self-directed learning package will be a valuable resource, not just for clinical educators, at both undergraduate and post-graduate levels, but also for clinical education tutors in physiotherapy schools who have the responsibility for providing courses for clinical educators.

Rationale

In summary, the rationale for the development of the package was as follows:

1. To address the role development of clinical educators – as highlighted previously, changes had occurred in physiotherapy education and these changes impacted not only on the college-based learning but also on student learning in the work-based setting.
2. To respond to the need for a flexible mode of course delivery – changes in health service provision, as a result of the establishment of local NHS trusts in both the acute and community sectors, placed further demands on the role of the senior clinicians. Senior physiotherapists were responsible not only for treating patients and educating physiotherapy students but also for fulfilling contractual obligations. These additional demands made increasing demands on senior clinicians and, as a result, their attendance at courses tended to focus on those that developed their specialist clinical skills.
3. To meet the standards for good practice for the education of clinical educators – the Chartered Society of Physiotherapy established guidelines for good practice for the education of clinical educators in 1994, recommending that education providers develop the following programmes for supporting clinical educators in their role.

Lesson learned

The team effort involved in the production of the package was a positive experience of creative writing and mutual support. The specific dynamics of the group meant that we could all benefit from critical evaluation of our writing by a peer group we respected and by whom we did not feel threatened. Each team member showed the same level of commitment and meetings usually moved shamelessly into social events at the end of long review sessions.

Despite the obvious need for a flexible package addressing the role development of senior clinicians to that of clinical educator, changes in the political climate resulted in senior clinicians preferring to pursue clinical skill development courses, which obviously impacted on our ability to recruit.

Future plans

In the light of our experience to date, we intend to:

*   continue to lobby to access money for PAMs role development;
*   recruit widely (multi-professional), as experience of delivery to a multi-professional audience is very positive;

- involve key clinicians at postgraduate certificate level to encourage cascading of skills as educators within a trust, linked to accreditation (already being piloted);
- explore the effects of the learning experience on practice of clinical educators via a longitudinal study with possible procurement of external funding.

COURSE DELIVERY ON FOUR CONTINENTS

Ivan Birch

This case study reports the development of a course that originated in the UK and gradually metamorphosized into one offered also in North America, Africa and Australasia. Distance learning elements were added as needed to meet the requirements of course delivery across these other continents.

Background

Like many of the PAMs, podiatry had operated in a very isolated fashion; many private practitioners worked alone and there was little interdisciplinary contact. This isolation prevented the profession from developing and occupying its appropriate place in the healthcare arena. It was also a significant contributor to the lack of a substantive podiatric research base.

In 1988 the CAPAM (Credit Accumulation for the Professions Allied to Medicine) project was initiated. It was intended to encourage the development of modular courses that could be studied on a part-time basis. Each module would carry a number of credits and, by their accumulation, students could be awarded a recognized qualification. At that time, the majority of the PAMs still had a diploma course for their primary qualification, characteristically of three years duration and centred around the acquisition of practical skills and knowledge. This award was somewhat at odds with many other disciplines, which were awarding honours degrees as the primary qualification. One of the significant attractions of the CAPAM project was that it offered the opportunity for practitioners of the PAMs to acquire a degree.

In collaboration with two other schools of chiropody in the south of England, the Department of Podiatry of the University of Brighton, then known as the School of Chiropody of Brighton Polytechnic, developed a two-year, part-time course of study, leading to the award of an honours degree in podiatric studies. As the prospect of a degree-level qualification becoming the norm for state registration was already being mooted in some quarters at this time, it was recognized that such a top-up degree would inevitably have a limited life span. The course team believed that five years, with cohorts of 20 students, was a reasonable prospect. Validation took place in November of 1988 and the course commenced the following January. Since then, some 300 students have graduated, the course having been run in the UK, Canada, South Africa and New Zealand. It was drawn to a close in 1999.

Attendance pattern and content

At the time the usual pattern of attendance for such a course was one day a week. This had a number of drawbacks for podiatrists. The staffing implications for service managers and the monetary implications for those in private practice prevented many practitioners from accessing such courses. This attendance pattern also excluded practitioners from further afield in the UK. The course team felt that much could be gained from having as wide a geographical spread of students as possible, so as to both broaden the spread of professional experience and encourage intraprofessional liaison. The pattern chosen was a series of six two-day study blocks and a five-day summer school during the first year, followed by six one-day research seminars during the second. The impact of the study blocks on work commitments was reduced by running them on Friday and Saturday, with the second year research seminars on the Saturday. An advantage of this model was that there quickly developed a strong social element to the course, which contributed greatly to the development of a far stronger cohesion between the students than could have been hoped for on a part-time course. This was possibly the only course in the world that had its own membership of a night club!

The nature of the course content was dictated by a strong belief that the profession lacked a sound research base. Initial debate identified the obvious need to pick up where the diploma course left off in terms of specific content, while at the same time facilitating the development of an approach to healthcare that would ultimately lead to an improvement in patient outcomes. While the final design consisted of a first year composed of six discrete modules, the intention was to use these subject areas as vehicles to deliver a wide ranging consideration of the research process. The first year was to provide a solid foundation on which the second year could be constructed. The second year was entirely given over to the execution of a research project.

During the course of the next four years, the course evolved and developed. It became apparent that while the notion of a modular structure made sense in terms of the original CAPAM project, it made little sense from an educational standpoint, proving to be an obstacle to the integration of the course content into clinical practice and the development of a holistic approach to research. Gradually the discrete modules were overlapped and then merged completely.

The attendance pattern remained unchanged until the notion of running the course overseas emerged. There was a growing feeling amongst the course team that the thorough integration of course content could best be achieved by having fewer but longer study blocks. The combination of a strong desire to allow the course to evolve from an educational standpoint and pragmatism saw the change to a format of two three-day and one six-day blocks in the first year and four two-day research seminars in the second. This attendance pattern was subsequently further improved with a move to three four-day blocks, thus reducing the stress on both staff and students of six days of intensive work. This final version has proved to be a much more satisfactory arrangement for all concerned. The practitioners and employers have reported that this arrangement has greatly eased the problem of rearranging patient case loads. Coupled with the developments that had taken place in the learning and teaching strategies being employed, it allowed much more productive use of the hours available.

Learning and teaching

The prospective students were mature professionals and one of the objectives of the course was to encourage practitioners to become lifelong learners. Clearly the onus of responsibility had to rest with the student, particularly as contact time was at a premium. In 1989 the course team were still in the early stages of getting to grips with student-centred learning and, as a result, what developed was a mix of student-centred and didactic techniques. The study blocks consisted largely of teaching sessions, while activity between blocks was based on a number of assessment exercises.

The students were divided into support groups of five or six and encouraged to keep in frequent contact between study blocks. In this way tasks such as collecting references could be shared and motivation maintained. These informal groups worked remarkably well, although the concept of sharing information did not come easily to some of the students who, for the whole of their working lives, had toiled in isolation. The intention was for these groups to meet physically between study blocks for informal support sessions. Although the early groups were confined to the relatively small geographical constraints of the UK, it soon became apparent that the combination of geographical distance (the first cohort recruited from England, Scotland and Northern Ireland) and work and home commitments was not going to make these meetings easy. While a number of these physical meetings did take place between study blocks the majority were confined to the blocks themselves. With six study blocks and the summer school the groups were meeting fairly frequently. However, by 1993 the course team was preparing to run the course in Canada, and with the subsequent reduction of the number of study blocks, the issue of support and motivation between blocks became much more pressing.

During the preparation to run the course in Canada, there was a fundamental shift in the learning and teaching strategy. The importance of facilitating the development of the skills and attitudes that encourage lifelong learning had become increasingly apparent. As a result, the amount of didactic teaching had progressively reduced but in 1993 there was a significant and intentional shift to a wholly student-centred approach based on action learning. The importance of the groups or, as they now were, self-facilitated action learning sets, was therefore greatly increased.

The first morning of the first study block was spent allocating students to sets and allowing the sets to identify issues and develop coping strategies. A number of team-building exercises were also undertaken. These exercises proved to be of great benefit not only because of their ability to highlight the advantages and problems of working in groups (a new experience for many podiatrists) but also because of their ability to break down barriers of hierarchy and status. As hard as some individuals try, it is difficult to be supercilious when lying on the floor building a bridge out of paper and paper clips.

By the end of the first study block, each set had a full understanding of what was expected of them and had constructed and signed a learning agreement. Each of the first-year study blocks and each of the four two-day second-year research seminars concluded with a set meeting and the production of individual action points, copies of which were given to each of the set and the course team.

Communication

As physical meetings of the groups between study blocks had proved to be largely impossible even within the geographical confines of the UK, there was no possibility of them taking place overseas, where the geographical spread of students in the same action set was in some cases in excess of 2000 miles. The UK students had found that communication could be achieved satisfactorily using a combination of phone and fax. One of the first tasks in Canada was, in liaison with the students, to develop a more formal means of communication. Several hours of the first study block in Ottawa were given over to the execution of this task. The outcome was a sophisticated mechanism of communication by phone and fax and the production by each of the sets of a schedule of communication. At that time the Internet was a relatively new concept to most of the students and, although available to some of the staff, it was not viewed as being a major support mechanism.

Communication with the department proved to be more problematic. The cost of the intra-group communication paled into insignificance once the students started to submit draft work to the department. Towards assessment submission deadlines, the department's fax machine would, on Monday mornings, be buried under hundreds of pages of draft documents. At this point one student from Manitoba started using the Internet on a regular basis. The advantages soon became apparent to other students and within six months some ten students were using the Internet as their prime means of communication with the department. However, at that stage not all students had Internet access and therefore intra-set communication remained phone and fax based. Even in 1994, when the course was delivered in New Zealand, only two or three of the students used the Internet to any substantial extent. The substantive shift to the Internet took another year and a move of the course to South Africa.

Post-apartheid, South Africans were desperate for communication with the rest of the world and, as a result, by the time the course started in

Johannesburg, all the students had Internet access and were not afraid to use it. There followed a very steep learning curve for the staff but, with the increase in staff expertise, came an encouragement for the students in all locations to start using the Internet as their prime means of communication. Within six months, set meetings across the world were taking place on the Internet. Interestingly the South African students have remained in the vanguard of technological usage, with UK students more reticent. One issue should be noted: the South African students had the latest versions of all software. The university was consistently one or two versions behind, making the deciphering of enclosed communications on the Internet very difficult and sometimes impossible. Future projects of this type should budget for the constant updating of software.

The staff

The success of this course has been largely due to the dedication of the course team. Saturday working in support of the course was never a problem for the course team and it was this level of commitment that paved the way for the even more radical twists that were to take place later in the course's development. Because this was a new venture for the students, requiring considerable commitment and sacrifice, the course team believed that similar levels of dedication should be forthcoming from themselves. The students were part-time, fitting the course work and background reading around heavy patient case loads and family commitments, and many had not taken part in organized education for some years. Much of the student activity took place in the evenings and at the weekends and these were the times when the students needed the help and support. With this in mind, on day one of the course, all the students were given a list of the course team members' home phone numbers, which were used extensively. This has continued to be the accepted practice. The only time this proved to be a problem was with one or two of the antipodean students. The time difference seemed to be a complete mystery to them and for a period of two years it was not unusual to receive phone calls about literature references at 2.0 a.m.

The students

To embark on a course like this requires considerable student commitment financially, academically and spiritually. Many of the students in the early cohorts were private practitioners and therefore the cost implications of several days away from the practice were substantial. For most, this course marked a return to education after several years in practice. The first students to enrol were the risk takers and, as a result, were wonderful to work with. This was a lesson that was to be learnt the world over. When the course was taken to New Zealand the intention was to run it in Australia at the same time. However, having encountered some strong opposition from within the profession in Australia, the course team decided to take a diplomatic path and abandon Australia. The prospective Australian students had other ideas. They flew from Australia to New Zealand to join in with the New Zealand cohort. The mix of Australians and New Zealanders was a good one. The friendly rivalry was wonderful, as was the accompanying banter.

One of the most interesting challenges posed by the course was the throwing together of people as fellow students whose relationships outside were vastly different. Some had previously been student and teacher, some were fellow workers and some were employer and employee. The implications of this complexity of relationships were enormous although, at the outset, the full implications were not fully recognized. In the UK, several cohorts have included managers and staff from the same department. When the course was taken to South Africa in 1995, the entire full-time staff of the only School of Podiatry in South Africa enrolled, including the Head of Department. While the informal approach taken by the course team during the first study block did much to establish a new set of relationships as fellow students, problems did arise, particularly with assessment.

Assessment

The working relationships between the students were always excellent. However, the complexity of the relationships placed additional stress on some individuals when it came to assessment. The hierarchical relationships at work placed heavy pressure on those in managerial positions to achieve high marks in assessment. The potential benefits of the assessment were vastly diminished, the assessment losing its potential as a positive learning experience and becoming a hurdle of ever increasing height. With the pressures already being experienced by mature students, some of whom had been out of the educational system for some considerable time, this state of affairs was far from desirable.

In the early days the course suffered from what were, in hindsight, obvious faults. There were far too many pieces of assessment in the first year, each of which contributed a very small percentage to the final mark. The result was a compression of the first year marks into a narrow mid-range band. The differences between student achievement were more apparent in the project marks.

A major assessment issue that was totally unforeseen arose in Canada. When the first pieces of assessment were returned the Canadians were horrified to find that they were getting a full spread of marks from 0 to 100. The assessment strategies and methods employed within the Canadian pre-registration training had a tendency to produce very high marks. These students were used to scoring over 80%. The course team's marking has now passed into local folklore and there is no longer a problem, but it took some time to smooth ruffled feathers the first time around. This cultural difference in assessment norms across countries is a significant issue for the globalization of higher education.

On the basis of these lessons the assessment strategy adopted for the latest version of this course has been drastically overhauled. All first year work is graded as pass or fail; without marks. It is also hoped that this will help to reduce the competitive stress placed on the students. The final degree classification is determined entirely by the mark awarded to the project.

The course team were keen to ensure absolute parity between cohorts, no matter where their geographical location. To this end the same combination of staff was used to deliver the same study blocks in every location and the same external examiner was used for the whole course. When course work was reviewed by the external examiner no indication was given as to the country of origin. Piles of course-work would include submissions from the UK, Canada, South Africa and New Zealand all mixed together. The only evident disparity was that the first cohort in every location achieved substantially higher degree classifications than in subsequent years.

The institutions and equipment

During the course of the last five years, the course team has worked in collaboration with three educational establishments and two hospitals overseas. In all cases the relationship has been very successful and has in most cases provided an excellent opportunity for the institutions involved to gain some good press. The University of Brighton was clear from the outset that the relationship with any overseas institutions should be on a very limited basis, the other institution providing little more than teaching accommodation. This approach was fully endorsed by the course team to ensure that full control could be maintained. All members of the course team went prepared to be wheeled out to meet the local hierarchy. Tedious though these events may seem, they are extremely valuable.

From the outset the course team worked with the maxim 'assume nothing'. Consequently, team members always travelled with flip chart paper and pens (to get these things in some of the institutions requires requisitions signed by the Head of School and the Dean) and Blu-Tack (not available in some countries), reference books and a selection of research papers. On only one occasion was an attempt made to take electrical equipment. Having been subjected to some extensive interrogation and narrowly avoided arrest at Canadian customs, and after four hours spent rewiring it to make it work at 110 volts, it was decided never again.

Conclusion

The success of the course has manifested itself in several very rewarding ways: many of the students have publications based on their projects; many have gone on to higher degrees; but perhaps the most rewarding of all has been the oft repeated words 'this course has changed the way I treat my patients'. What the course has facilitated for these practitioners is an understanding of, and ability to apply, research principles to healthcare through evidence-based practice.

THE EUROPEAN INTENSIVE COURSE EXPERIENCE

Martin Daniels, Lyn Pemberton, Richard Griffiths, Thierry Nodenot and Endika Bengoetxea

The organization

The authors of this chapter represent a group of staff in European universities (Universities of Brighton and Coventry, Universidad del Pais Vasco in Spain, Universidad de Salamanca in Spain, IUT Bayonne/Pays Basque in France and Instituto Politecnico da Guarda in Portugal) who have been collaborating on a number of projects over the last decade. We report our experiences of one of these projects, an annual intensive course for students in our discipline areas, which mainly covers information technology and computing with some overlaps into language and business studies.

We started running international courses (known in Erasmus-speak as IPs or Intensive Programmes) in 1988 when the European Union began its Erasmus programme for higher education. The participating universities had had early discussions on cooperation in general but were particularly keen on developing a multi-national Masters course. The ideas behind this development were pioneering and it was felt that they could be tested out by using the IP courses. The original IP format was to provide a less ambitious two-week course for four students from each of the participating institutions and this was to be held at, and organized domestically by, one of these universities. There were various constraints imposed because of the nature of the courses and subjects represented. For instance, the IUT Bayonne had a two-year course, while courses at the other institutions were longer and, while most partners were IT specialists, the Universidad de Salamanca was represented by their Business School. Consequently, the course was targeted at second year students in an area of analysis that was seen as not being too technical. The first course took place in Bayonne in 1989 and the topic chosen was a comparison of systems analysis methodologies. The academic side of the course was organized by colleagues from three of the universities.

Since this first course, the group has been successful in bidding for Erasmus funds each year and has operated a course annually, during the Easter period, with the location cycling around all the institutions.

In the first few years the chosen topics changed for each course and this meant that the academic staff teaching on the courses also changed. This occurred for a number of reasons, one being the need to experiment with new subjects, which were not necessarily within the current curricula of the group. The change in academic staff each year meant that each course had to be designed almost from scratch.

In the last few years we have taken a slightly different approach. The broad subject area for the course has been similar each year while the specific content is allowed to evolve. This allows the teaching team to have some stability, which in turn makes course design easier. This is important as funding from the Erasmus programme, and latterly the Socrates programme, has been reduced, with the consequent effect of reducing the possibilities for holding planning meetings. A stable teaching team has promoted the development of other areas of collaboration, one of which is described elsewhere in this book (pages 105–11). The theme of the courses has developed over recent years from computer-assisted collaborative working to multimedia systems and web-based collaboration.

Funding in the early days was more generous and there was a possibility of vireing within other budget headings. The level of funding now available has meant that the length of the courses has had to be reduced (to roughly eight working days) and only three students per institution can be funded to attend. As far as planning meetings are concerned, some synergy with related projects has meant that one meeting is possible for each course. The courses remain completely free to the students with travel, lodging and subsistence costs covered. In the UK the students are chosen mainly on the basis of some evidence of language ability and it is interesting to note that it is predominately mature students in their mid-twenties who apply, rather than those who have progressed straight from A levels to university. This does not apply to the continental universities as there are not many mature students in their systems. There, students are selected on academic ability and on their perceived ability to benefit from and contribute to the course. The majority of the students are male and this probably reflects the balance of male/female students on IT courses across the institutions.

Conditions are not luxurious. By dint of necessity the accommodation has had to be cheap, but only on one occasion have students had to be rehoused because of completely unacceptable rooms. Food is usually served in university refectories and travel means wherever possible cramming into university mini-buses or hitching lifts in staff cars.

The student side

Students' motivation for attending the IP is varied. For UK students it has counted as a one module credit, so some students have sought to do it to make up a failed module, or as an extra module 'insurance policy'. Other students are mainly interested in the international experience, which appeals to them, or which has been recommended by previous students. For most it is a mixture of both.

The students are presented with an immediate set of challenges when the course begins. British students have reported initial anxieties about being with strangers, unaccustomed formality and their own language abilities. They are required to work in multinational groups, that is, not in groups with students from their own institutions or countries. The first activity is normally a group-building exercise. Additionally they will have presentations from academic staff in languages other than their own. They are thus forced to use the resources of their group to overcome any difficulties in understanding. This lack of immediate understanding of course extends to the academic material too – it is not just a matter of not understanding the language. Although, logically, the students might be faced with all five languages spoken in the group – Basque, French, Spanish, Portuguese and English – we have found that a mixture of English, French and Spanish tends to be used. Language and group working often tend to interact. Group work experience is novel to mainland European students and sometimes they lack confidence because of this. This creates a vicious circle as an English student will generally emerge as leader of each group (because English is probably the only common language, they are generally more mature, experienced in public speaking and have group work skills).

The courses centre around competing interpretations of design briefs, for instance, each group must create a business web site for a particular company. These mini-projects last for the complete period of the IP, the normal pattern consisting of lectures in the mornings and practicals in the afternoons. The courses end with group presentations of their work and finally an evaluation session.

We have found that a tremendous team spirit develops, especially when the competing groups approach is used. A single collaborating group has been tried but was unwieldy and lacked motivation. The presentation at the end, which is conducted relatively formally, usually culminates in the giving of a token prize to the winners where much emotion is displayed, group photos taken and addresses swapped. A multilingual certificate is presented to participating staff and students and is also highly prized.

Observations on the student experience

Often the friendships made during a course are maintained afterwards with exchange of e-mail and visits. In addition, participating in an IP seems to inspire students to continue their studies in another country. The UK in particular has received many students in this way. The students at the subsequent year's site often volunteer to help with the course for the following year. Usually students are left to organize the social side of the course, although normally there is one official collective event held at the weekend. The hosts typically take pride in their own region and delight in showing it off.

Of course, there are downsides. The IP is emotionally as well as academically intense and conflicts can occasionally occur. For instance, some UK students have tended to drink to excess and have not understood European attitudes to alcohol, which often challenge accepted myths. Hangovers have occasionally interfered with a group's work and this is resented by other group members, who are often shocked by it. Other cultural attitudes are challenged. Most students can manage to be flexible but insistence on exporting national attitudes causes bad feeling. One example was a UK-based vegetarian on an IP in Salamanca, who interpreted a sprinkling of tuna over a salad as a deliberate slight when it was a genuine attempt to add flavour (tuna not being regarded as flesh in this context). Staff spent much time calming emotions on both sides of the dispute. Spanish students have to get used to eating dinner too early and staying in the same bar all evening when outside Spain. Spanish Basques have to tolerate what they see as the naive opinions of other Spaniards on the Basque question: culture shock can occur between students of a single country too. Linguistic communication is not as big a problem as might be imagined but many UK students are forced to reflect on their relatively poor language skills when they see other students operating skilfully in three or even four languages. There is a feeling, however, that this situation is slowly improving.

There has traditionally been an informal evaluation at the end of each course. With very few exceptions the students have found it a valuable academic experience. Recent British participants have commented: 'An opportunity of a lifetime', 'A good opportunity to meet and work with students from other European countries whilst developing your own social and academic skills', 'If you get the chance – take it', 'Valuable experience of education in a foreign country working with foreign counterparts'. British students' attitudes towards Europe and Europeans have been changed dramatically: 'I never really encountered Europeans before and a lot of preconceptions were replaced with a feeling of warmth towards them', 'Reminder that we are part of Europe and got out of the "island" mentality for a few weeks'. Clearly they appreciate the very powerful experience of interacting in simulated work groups, which they find forces real interaction and communication. From a social point of view it is an experience that most claim they will remember for a lifetime (. . . read into this what you will!).

The teaching staff experience

In this section we explore these intensive courses from a staff perspective and examine why we have continued to run them. At the outset the idea of collaborating internationally was based very firmly in the belief that it was important and, indeed, going to be vital in the future, to be involved in European projects. It was felt that European activities would form part of our mainstream business and be a major source of funding so that we could not afford to miss the opportunities newly available. In the intervening period there have been changes in the perception of what European-ness means and a general dilution of funds and activities, but perhaps this feeling is concentrated most in the UK. Although there seems to be a ready stream of students wishing to come to the UK, international courses that involve an inverse movement have not, in general, flourished. With this somewhat gloomy background we have continued to persist in supporting the operation of IPs, for a number of reasons.

The courses have a tremendous impact, certainly culturally, on the students who attend and it is unfortunate that the numbers who are able to benefit are so small. From a pedagogic viewpoint an IP provides a lot of opportunities. In terms of subject matter there are possibilities for experimenting with new subjects on a relatively small scale without going through a web of bureaucratic procedures, and also to experiment with novel teaching methods without too much risk. For instance, in Salamanca we were able to simulate a distributed organization by locating teams in separate laboratories, which is difficult to do in many home institutions. With new subjects there is a possibility of pooling experience and knowledge that may be lacking in home institutions. In a wider context there are opportunities to see how other universities undertake their teaching and research in their particular circumstances for their disciplines and resources. And, just as with the experience of students, for staff there are many social aspects that make the IP attractive. Having built a team that is seen to be successful, there is a desire to continue, and generally the team members like each other. These are important factors. The opportunity to travel and practice language skills are further contributory factors to making a satisfactory course experience.

For staff there are also less attractive aspects. The most important, from which others stem, is probably the perceived lack of recognition within the home institutions. This means that a course depends on individual enthusiasm, energy and goodwill. This personal investment by staff has to be considerable as the courses usually take place during vacation time and require a heavy investment in time and arduous tasks such as driving/escorting students across large distances. The IPs are often not valued by one's own colleagues (in the UK anyway) who see them as a holiday or at the least marginal and oddball. Sometimes organizers are given little help from the hosting institution for setting up a course (although this is not always the case – San Sebastián, for example, has been generous in providing additional financial support). In addition, the cultural differences between countries, for example the closure of France during August or delays in answering e-mail, can be frustrating. Other differences have already been mentioned, such as the provenance of students: these can enrich a course but can be difficult to handle for a short, intensive course.

What have we learned?

This section is a summary of the main points that have been gleaned from operating the IPs over ten years. The starting point is a successful bid to the Socrates programme. Without this finance the course would not continue.

Naturally there never seems to be sufficient money but so far we have managed to run an IP each year. However, if we were not active in other areas of collaboration it is unlikely that we could maintain sufficient momentum to have sufficient contact between the staff; OLE is an example of a spin-off activity of the personal relationships built up while doing IPs. Staff have attended conferences organized by other IP staff, planned research projects with them and collaborated on a more informal level by exchanging references and papers.

As far as content and structure are concerned, we intend to allow the courses to evolve gradually without forcing large step changes. Competing multilingual groups have proved to be a successful mechanism as a learning tool and also to aiding rapid integration socially and linguistically. Certain other 'rules' have been learnt about starting off a course. It is important for the staff at this point in particular to mix socially with the students and to introduce the various building blocks that facilitate understanding a new culture, for example, how to greet and address people, how and when to buy a round of drinks, how to invite someone out and other vital niceties. Terminating a course with presentations, simple certificates and mementoes, costs very little but is appreciated by participants.

For the future

The IPs need to develop in order to maintain their freshness and vigour. We have a number of resolutions to implement which we believe will help. In particular, we will use the IP as a platform for our own professional staff development; for example by targeting subject areas in which we want to deepen our own knowledge and by being prepared to move on from material with which we are already familiar. We will provide continuity and a sense of community for current and ex-students by building up the IP's web site: photographs of each year's IP are particularly powerful souvenirs. We will also actively attempt to challenge the cultural hegemony of the English language. We suspect this requires only modest changes: for instance, making sure the staff member who speaks first in the course and describes the project speaks in another language. This should boost the confidence of the speakers of other languages. There are other possibilities too: for the students, giving presentations in a language other than the mother tongue, and for the staff, attempting to give bilingual lectures. We shall try to improve our own language competence. Although all staff know at least one other language to some (albeit basic) level, there are some with considerable fluency in four and this gives us all an incentive to improve.

9

Preparation for Professional Practice

PREPARING STUDENTS FOR PROFESSIONAL PRACTICE IN OCCUPATIONAL THERAPY USING PROBLEM-BASED LEARNING

Marion Martin

Changes in the context of healthcare

In the past few years the amount of government legislation concerning health has accelerated. The main changes impacting on occupational therapists and other healthcare professionals are as follows:

- There has been an enormous emphasis on customer satisfaction since the White Paper *Working for Patients* (DHSS 1989b) and with *The Patient's Charter* (DoH 1992a). From 1990 to 1994 formal complaints to Community Health Councils doubled, probably reflecting greater consumer awareness and higher expectations rather than a drop in the quality of the services (Øvretviet 1998). Healthcare workers now have to be more accountable to customer demands and responsive to local needs.
- The purchaser–provider split following the 1989 legislation forced providers of healthcare, such as occupational therapists, to examine their methods of working for cost and efficiency. They now have to compete with other service providers and market what they are offering in order to survive.
- A demand for quality service provision has led to a need for evidence-based practice. Health providers now have to justify the methods and procedures they use and be up to date with the latest outcomes of research into their field.
- The transition to community care requires practitioners to take on the responsibility of organizing care packages for their clients, as patients are treated in their own homes away from the hospital environment. Instead

of medical intervention, there is a need for holistic programmes requiring more creative approaches, taking into account all aspects of the client's life.
• Since the 1989 Act and the White Paper *The New NHS: Modern, dependable* (DoH 1997), health and social care staff need to work together more in multi-professional teams, and less within their own professional group. Their managers are now less likely to be from their own professional background (Lewis and Glennerster 1996); occupational therapists therefore need to be sure of their own role but flexible enough to work with others.

With all these demands, it is not surprising that health services staff lead in the list of professional groups reporting increases in stress levels during the last few years (Spurgeon 1998). An occupational therapist practising in this environment has to be resourceful enough to seek out and find support when required.

All of these changes require different qualities from those needed when health workers were based in large institutions, largely protected from the demands for accountability and the threat of litigation. The new professional practitioner has to be responsive to the changes that have taken place and lead the way for further innovations.

Changes in education

Traditional educational methods prepared clinicians for the old model of healthcare (Watson and West 1996). This type of curriculum delivered theory first, using a didactic approach, and ended with the practical experience. Students were assessed by examinations that relied heavily on memory. However, a rapidly expanding knowledge-base means that it has become unrealistic and even inhumane to expect students to assimilate the whole gamut of medical science (Boud and Feletti 1997). Even if this were possible, much of the information acquired would almost immediately become obsolete (Sadlo *et al.* 1994).

In addition, the traditional approach to professional education has been criticized for being too reductionist, as every situation that confronts the practitioner will be unique (Schön 1983). Thus, a recipe book approach to treating patients will have limited effectiveness. Health professionals now have to use their problem-solving skills more independently and to take responsibility for their own continuing professional development in order to meet the demands of today. Chapter 3 outlines the case for a variety of approaches to satisfy these needs.

The rationale for problem-based learning

Problem-based learning (PBL) is a curriculum design that addresses these changes. It is rapidly gaining momentum, having started in the mid-1960s at McMaster University medical school in Canada and, since then, has spread to other continents and health professions, including occupational therapy, physiotherapy, orthoptics, nutrition and dietetics to date (Boud and Feletti 1997; Sadlo *et al.* 1994). Engineering, law and agriculture are amongst other groups of professionals who have used PBL in their curricula (Feletti 1993).

One of the reasons for its growing popularity is that PBL is a more natural method of learning (Sadlo 1997). People learn most effectively when they are emotionally engaged in the subject and not simply letting their studies be driven by the assessment. In PBL the problem, which is directly related to the profession being studied, acts as a trigger to motivate the students to find out for themselves. As there are no set boundaries to the investigation, PBL allows students to address questions that are of the most vital significance to human existence (Margetson 1998).

According to Engel (1997), the aim of PBL is to produce students who are able to adapt and participate in change, deal with problems in unfamiliar situations, reason critically and creatively, adopt a more holistic approach, practise empathy with others, collaborate productively in groups or teams, reflect on their own strengths and weaknesses and undertake appropriate action such as self-directed learning.

Armed with an ability to use a problem-solving approach to clinical issues, the student is a self-directed practitioner, able to cope with unfamiliar situations. Earlier studies have shown that success in the world of work depends less upon technical knowledge than on a willingness to learn (Rowntree 1992). Graduates are able to analyse the client's problems and gather information from a wide range of sources, generating a range of alternative solutions that can be tried out, reflected upon and evaluated. In this way the healthcare professional is developing his or her clinical skills and becomes a lifelong learner.

An evaluation of problem-based learning

Two meta-analyses of PBL with medical students were carried out in 1992 and 1993. Norman and Schmidt (1992) claimed that, although PBL curricula did not develop superior problem-solving abilities, the retention of knowledge over a long period of time was increased and the transfer of concepts into clinical situations was enhanced. Also, student interest and self-directed learning skills improved.

Vernon and Blake (1993) looked at 35 studies and found that PBL programmes were significantly superior to more traditional programmes in student and faculty evaluations of the courses, self-directed learning and clinical functioning. In clinical knowledge there was no significant difference, whereas traditional methods of education produced higher scores on knowledge of basic science.

This evidence seems to show that PBL courses are more popular with faculty and students than more traditional programmes and that they

enhance the students' clinical performance and self-directed learning. This
research also indicates, however, that the range of knowledge in basic science decreases as subjects are studied in more depth.

Most PBL courses are hybrid models, combining group work with interactive classroom teaching. A more recent study of occupational therapy
programmes compared students on traditional curricula with those on PBL
and hybrid courses (Sadlo 1997). It found that students on 'pure' PBL
programmes were the most positive about their courses and that those on
traditional programmes had the least positive perceptions of the effectiveness of their education.

Models of problem-based learning

PBL can be delivered in numerous different ways (Barrows 1986). There
can be variations in the size of the student group, from one to any suitable number (Ross 1997). The degree to which the tutor is involved in the
process can also vary. The most directive will decide not only on the problem but the way in which it will be investigated and the resources to be
used. Less directive tutors will act as facilitators, their role being to stimulate questioning, rather than to provide answers (Barrows 1986; Ross 1997).

A major variable is the type of problem used and the ways in which it can
be presented. 'Paper cases', or written case studies, are used in many health
courses, particularly in the education of doctors, using the medical clinical
reasoning process of hypotheses generation, inquiry, data analysis, problem
synthesis and decision making (Barrows 1986; Elstein *et al.* 1978). This
process is well suited to the role of the doctor who has to make a diagnosis
and treat accordingly. Health professionals who prefer to work in a more
holistic way can use case studies for generating wider questions, which may
include the emotional, sociological, political and spiritual implications for
the person.

Other problems used as triggers to student learning can be in the form of
topics or themes. Social workers may take a current issue, such as 'The
experiences of refugees in Australia' (Bolgan and Heycox 1997). Engineers
use mechanical failures (Cawley 1997) and lawyers a hypothetical client file
(Winsor 1997).

An occupational therapy course with hybrid
problem-based learning

This Postgraduate Diploma in Occupational Therapy, which has been running for five years, has a hybrid PBL structure. Students work independently
in PBL groups for approximately six hours a week, the remaining tutor
contact time takes place in the classroom. Initially the College of Occupational Therapists (COT), the professional body for occupational therapists,

was cautious about the PBL aspects of the programme but since the original validation more occupational therapy courses have adopted this type of curriculum and it has become more acceptable. The PBL element of the course is designed to integrate theoretical concepts with the reality of the workplace, as well as facilitating the development of self-directed, independent problem-solvers.

Occupational therapists are required to complete a minimum of 1000 hours of fieldwork practice (COT 1993) before they are eligible for state registration. These hours are divided into five placements, interspersed throughout the programme, with the first beginning only four weeks after the students have started their education. This distribution of placements has several advantages for the students' learning:

- It is motivating, because they can see real patients and appreciate their needs and the role of the occupational therapist in their recovery.
- It is easier for students to make connections and appreciate the relevance of theory to practice.
- As they receive feedback on their performance, students become more aware of their learning needs and so more able to direct their own learning.

Problem-based learning on the occupational therapy course

At the start of the course, students are made aware of the aims and process of PBL. They are then divided into groups of six or seven, with a resource tutor who can be invited to join the group when he or she is available. This tutor acts as a facilitator who listens, questions and may sometimes suggest sources of information (Wilderson and Hundert 1997).

The problems used as triggers on this course are topics that are related to the theme of the unit in which they take place. For example, the topics for the unit concerning assessment include 'independence in the home environment' and 'social interactions'. Those used for the unit on 'Health promotion in a specialist team' include 'cardiac rehabilitation' and 'community mental health'. These topics are chosen by students before they leave the university to go on their placements, so that they can gather information, such as case studies, which are related to the subject they are investigating.

On their return to the university, the students reassemble in their PBL groups to share their experiences, decide on areas that need further investigation and allocate aspects that individuals wish to cover. Students can use this as an opportunity to concentrate on areas where there are gaps in their knowledge and they feel exposed or to follow up special interests that were discovered during their fieldwork experience. For example, a group with the topic 'social interactions' may investigate research into verbal and non-verbal communication; clients with communication problems, including those with aphasia, anxiety, depression, schizophrenia, learning disabilities, old age and loneliness; assessment tools for social skills; assertiveness training; family therapy; social structures and cultural issues.

Students may, and do, use a wide range of resources from the Internet, on-line searches, journals and books, to visits and interviews with clients and specialists. This potentially vast amount of information then has to be shared with the group, edited and organized into a form that can be presented to the whole cohort by the group. This may be done as a formal presentation or students may wish to incorporate role-play, videos, posters or audience participation. Informal feedback is given to the PBL group on the quality of presentation skills and on the content by their peers and by tutors. The sessions are also videoed so that the group can use this for its own development and as a learning resource for future students.

Student feedback

As students on the occupational therapy course have already completed a traditional honours degree, they were asked to compare this with their experiences of PBL. The results were as follows:

	PBL	*First degree*
1. Requires more study time	36%	64%
2. Requires student to be more organized	75%	25%
3. Develops deeper understanding	45%	55%
4. Develops a wider range of knowledge	46%	54%
5. More related to real-life issues	100%	
6. More enjoyable	70%	30%

All of the students who responded to the survey said that the PBL component of the course was more related to real-life issues than was their first degree: 'You learn skills which are central to a practical subject such as occupational therapy – problem-solving and organization'.

In common with the medical students (Norman and Schmidt 1992; Vernon and Blake 1993), the majority also found PBL to be more enjoyable, possibly because they perceived it as being more relevant to their chosen career: 'Traditional learning can be dictatorial, boring (students switch off easily), less related to real-life issues and doesn't encourage problem-solving'.

They also felt that PBL required the student to be more organized, a transferable skill that will be useful for their future practice.

However, a small majority of the students perceived their more traditional education to have facilitated deeper understanding and a wider range of knowledge: 'My first degree ensured that full understanding was certain – PBL is more "hit and miss" as there is no target to achieve'.

There was a strong feeling that it was up to the individual student to make the experience successful: 'Success in PBL depends on how much work, time and effort is put in by the individual'; 'Most of us are motivated enough to undertake self-directed learning so we have learnt a lot'.

Feedback from the employers

A survey of the managers of graduates from the PGDip in Occupational Therapy was carried out to find out if they had any strengths that could have been attributable to their education, and if they perceived any gaps. Positive aspects mentioned included their enthusiasm, maturity, confidence, ability to work well in teams, knowledge, skills and problem-solving abilities: 'Has fitted well into the department and adapted to the professional role – has made the transition from the student status well'.

Some gaps in knowledge and skills were identified but these were diverse, consistent with the fact that students cannot cover all there is to know about a subject. In general, managers were very satisfied with the standard of therapist leaving the university: 'The Brighton course appears to produce an independent, skilled, articulate, problem-solving occupational therapist, which is very impressive'.

Lessons learned

The changing nature of healthcare requires a new approach to the education of the people who are delivering the services. It would appear from the feedback from students and managers of occupational therapists from the PGDip at the University of Brighton that these students have been helped to become independent lifelong learners in part at least from the PBL aspects of the course. Of course, many of these students brought qualities with them from their previous experiences, as many of the managers commented.

There is some anxiety that PBL courses do not give enough direction to students, as they choose the areas they will study themselves. This anxiety was manifested by the professional body, by a few managers and also by some of the students themselves. It has been demonstrated, however, that students can be trusted to identify their own learning needs, as they left the course as competent occupational therapists. Whilst on fieldwork placements they were made aware of the competencies that they needed and of their own strengths and weaknesses. This fuelled their quest for knowledge when they returned to the university and informed their choices of areas to study.

The student survey also indicates some need for more support, at least in the initial stages of the course, from tutors. When the course was designed it was considered that graduates would require less support than undergraduate students, so minimal tutor involvement was built in. Student feedback indicates, however, that at least some of them would like more tutor input.

In common with other evaluations of PBL courses (Vernon and Blake 1993) there was also a perceived weakness in students' acquisition of knowledge. Ryan (1997) suggests that this issue could be addressed through 'closed loop' or 'reiterative' PBL in which students have follow-up tutorials where the results of their findings can be fed back to them for further digestion. He also argues in favour of having a tutor who is an expert in the subject, who can provide guidance and correct student errors (Ryan 1997). However, earlier writers have suggested that tutors who lack detailed subject knowledge are more effective, as they are less directive.

This course will in future use a greater variety of triggers, including paper cases, and a different model of PBL with more tutor involvement and less classroom teaching. The wide range of PBL design allows courses to be tailor-made to suit the entry level of the students and the intended learning outcomes. Faculty need to evaluate outcomes and make changes in curriculum delivery in order to produce the healthcare professionals of the future.

A PROFESSIONAL DEVELOPMENT SCHEME IN A SANDWICH COURSE: THE CASE OF COMPUTING

Daniel Simpson and Colin Jackson

Introduction

Courses in the area of IT fall into two major types. There are those that concentrate on IT as a profession and those that introduce IT as an enabling technology within some other discipline. The courses we consider here are of the first type; they aim to produce students who will undertake a career as a professional practitioner of IT. The computing professional body, the British Computer Society (BCS), accredits many of these courses. As well as developing a suitable knowledge base and skills base within the courses, we also attempt to develop in the student the principles of professionalism. By this we mean that students will be able to work within a professional code of conduct and will update their knowledge and skills throughout their careers.

The degree course discussed here has been offered, in various guises, for over 25 years at the university. For all of this time it has had professional body accreditation. The course has always had the same basic aims of producing students who have an appropriate knowledge- and skills base to be immediately useful in industry and who leave the course with a professional attitude and knowledge of what is expected of a professional in the field. An additional aim is to equip students with the tools to keep their career up to date by continuously developing their knowledge, skills and understanding. These aims are exactly congruent with those of the BCS.

Since the course started, it has had a module on professional ethics and has tried to relate this module to all other parts of the course. It has also always been a sandwich course where the students spend the third of their four years in a professional placement. In the first two years we aim to give the student the knowledge, skills and professional attitudes that will allow them to undertake a successful professional placement. The placement allows them to practise these skills in extended projects within a commercial environment. This means that the students may use the experience of what they have learned in the first two years of their course in a 'real' environment. The placement year also allows the student to bring their newly honed skills into their final year and so enrich that year of their learning. The advantages of a 'sandwich' year are now well accepted in many courses, particularly of a professional nature, and they are well recognized by students, employers and the professional bodies. Students who graduate from a professionally recognized course should have both the ability and the motivation to work according to a professional code of conduct.

Professional development scheme

Over the past decade or so many professional bodies have introduced a formalized professional development scheme (PDS). This usually allows members of the professional body to formalize and record development activities they have undertaken. Such activities could be attending courses, developing skills on the job, updating knowledge by private study, undertaking work for the profession and similar activities. The advantages and structure of the professional development scheme for the BCS are given in Senior (1998). We have always evaluated students on their sandwich year using reports from the student, the visiting academic tutor and the workplace supervisor. Once the BCS PDS had been developed, we felt that we could take advantage of this by using it within the placement year of our courses. As our courses have always aimed to produce students who wish to update their knowledge, skills and professional approach we decided to introduce the PDS to formalize and record the progress they make on their sandwich year and to start to develop their PDS portfolio.

The PDS uses as its base reference the Industry Structure Model (ISM), a BCS product designed to raise and maintain standards in the information systems (IS) industry. The current version of the ISM has nine groups of functions, which list some 60 functions that are defined to be particular areas of IS professional activity. Each function can exist at one or more levels representing degrees of professional activity and maturity; for placement students the usual levels appropriate are 1, 2 and possibly 3. Function and level are combined into a role, so, for example, the role PROG2 is Level 2 of the Programming/Software Creation function.

Operation

At the start of the placement year, the student (in discussion with their visiting tutor) maps the student's work as planned by their workplace supervisor onto role(s) of the ISM. We have no wish to interfere with the work that the company has planned for the student so it is important that the role is fitted to the job rather than the other way round. Students are then given a printout of the relevant ISM roles that detail the tasks, training, knowledge, skills and professional development activities associated with each role. In this way the student can see some structure in the year's work and has some general objectives to strive for over and above the specific company objectives. The student can then complete some minimal documentation, known as the Career Development Plan (CDP), that, at the end of a cycle (usually six months), can be signed off as being completed. Completed sets of CDPs are collected together in a PDS log book, which is designed to cover the student's whole career in the profession. Thus, not only are the students able to practise and enhance their computing skills during the year but they also gain the experience of career planning (if only at an initial stage) before entering the job market for real, after graduation.

The PDS experience has proved useful as a further item that the student can append to his or her CV. It is unfortunate that most organizations that graduates subsequently join are not yet participants in PDS and so it is not possible to have their plans and achievements validated by the employer. While it is possible for the graduate to get the experience validated at a later time by the professional body, the process is less straightforward than that of a PDS-registered employer. If, however, growing numbers of computer graduates express an interest in such a scheme, they will act as a catalyst for the promotion of professional development schemes within the organization.

We have been using the PDS on our computer science course since 1995; our overall conclusion is that it complements and enhances the sandwich training year. The course regulations require the participation of the students in the scheme: they have to join the BCS as student members and register for the PDS, which entitles them to a PDS log book. The university pays for this but we have found that our student employers are generally happy to refund this money to the university, thus undertaking a small element of sponsorship!

Benefits

The students are the main beneficiaries of the scheme; they see the many advantages that integrating their course and their professional development can bring. An added benefit is that the placement year counts as an accredited experience year towards that required for membership of the BCS. Other people involved are the placement companies and the academics teaching on the course; their views are very similar to those of the students. The main advantages quoted are that:

- the relationships between the academic course, the placement year and the professional development activities are made more explicit and coherent;

- the relationships between the parts of the educational experience are made more explicit;
- the plan for the placement year can be made more coherent and related to the students' requirements.

Issues

All professional development schemes are designed for those in professional life, rather than for students on a placement year. Many professionals will wish to study a smaller range of topics to a greater depth: however a student on professional placement will wish to experience a wider range of topics, often moving between the different career routes within the PDS. The BCS has recognized this and one of the authors of this case study (Colin Jackson) is now chairing a group to consider how the Society can best assist undergraduates (and, in time, graduates) in their professional development.

Professional development schemes are related to National Vocational Qualifications (NVQs). In 1998, having successfully integrated the PDS into our course, we turned our attention to NVQs. Some of our visiting tutors were trained as NVQ assessors and, as part of their training, they assessed a pilot group of placement students for units of those NVQs in IT that were most relevant to their placement experience. Initial experience with this proved promising. There is undoubtedly a time resource constraint in training NVQ assessors, mainly in the paperwork involved, but the process of assessing student skills has many similarities with the methods used over the years by visiting tutors. The students were mostly happy to register for such qualifications during their placement year and our initial experiment resulted in the students gaining NVQ unit awards. This work is in its early days but we shall continue to investigate the area.

Conclusion

Many professionally based courses, such as the one examined here, must introduce students to the skill base, the knowledge base and the professional approach necessary for a lifelong career in industry. Therefore, we wish to develop within our students the recognition of the need for lifelong learning and continuing professional development. The use of professional accreditation for courses and sandwich years are ways of doing this. We suggest that introducing a professional development scheme into the sandwich year considerably enhances it. Using a PDS is a good way to structure and enrich a standard sandwich scheme. It furthers the professional aims of a course and, in our experience, is well liked by all.

We are pleased to share our work and suggest that other computing courses may wish to use a similar idea. We also suggest that this work could be appropriate for other professional bodies.

ENCOURAGING GRADUATE BUSINESS START-UP IN ART AND DESIGN

Linda Ball

Introduction

This case study, from the field of art and design, will present a model for course activities that specifically foster and encourage the personal attributes, key skills and awareness relevant to self-employment. Many of the issues and principles discussed are common to all disciplines.

Future employment patterns

Changing employment patterns in all sectors of the economy mean that full-time employment and long-term job security are no longer the certainty they once were. This is not a new experience for graduates in art and design, many of whom experience a kaleidoscopic pattern of short-term contract work, part-time employment and freelance practice in the years after leaving university. In this sector, the 'portfolio' lifestyle has been a natural mode of working for many years and now graduates and professionals working in other disciplines are experiencing this more flexible work style. Inevitably, these changes mean that, in future, responsibility for personal, career and professional development will rest with individuals rather than with employers. It has even been suggested that now career paths are no longer linear, they resemble crazy paving and no one is going to lay it for you. It is: do it yourself!

21st century graduates

In the light of these changes, what do we want for our graduates in terms of the values, characteristics and qualities that will equip them for work in the next century? Press (1997: 45) offers one vision, that the crafts graduate of the future would be:

> . . . someone who embodied a new set of values that were appropriate to working patterns and society in the 21st century: a proactive practitioner, a creative and critical thinker, informed by research, a multidisciplined communicator; empowered as a sustainable entrepreneur who saw 'making' in its wider sense.

> This description could be applied to any graduate, regardless of academic discipline. It is becoming clear that graduates will need to be in charge of their own destinies. What are the implications for graduates, and consequently for the ways in which we design and deliver our courses?

Graduates for self-employment

Self-employment is a serious destination for graduates in art and design. At present, only 1.4 per cent of all British graduates enter self-employment on graduation; the figures for art and design leavers is between five and ten times higher than this national average (Higher Education Statistics Agency (HESA) 1998b).[1]

A recent independent longitudinal survey of Brighton graduates between three and eight years after graduation revealed that 59 per cent of graduates from three-dimensional crafts and 28 per cent of graduates in fashion textiles design were self-employed at the time of the survey (Cusworth and Press 1997). The survey also shows that students would have preferred more help with their progression to work from these courses. In the overall findings, more than one-third of graduates surveyed from a number of crafts-based courses entered self-employment at some time in their careers (Press and Cusworth 1998).

There was also evidence of 'portfolio' style careers and 'multi-tracking', characterized by combinations of part-time, freelance work and further study. There are implications here for the importance of encouraging independence, autonomy, ability for self-direction and personal skills as an integral part of the higher education experience. It is clear that in art and design disciplines, graduates of the future will need to have the confidence to consider self-employment or working in a small business as a viable option – at some point in their careers.

The creative industries

The Government has identified the creative industries as an expanding sector of the economy. The art, design and crafts sector is largely focused in micro-businesses and in small and medium-sized enterprises (SMEs), a growth area of the economy. Knott (1994) suggested that the contemporary crafts sector, in particular, has more than doubled its turnover in the last ten years to some £400 million, making a substantial contribution to the national economy. The same study found that crafts enterprises are not only viable but are also sustainable. Of those receiving financial help from the Crafts Council, 95 per cent were still in business after five years – three times the national average for small businesses of all kinds.

Paradoxically, despite positive growth in this area, graduates in art, craft and design subjects report that they feel ill-prepared to consider self-employment as a viable option and, although staff felt that provision was adequate (Khan and McAlister 1992), students indicated they would like a greater focus on business awareness and entrepreneurship on their courses (London Institute 1997; Press and Cusworth 1998). The overall message from graduates surveyed by the London Institute was 'give us a realistic view of the outside world and teach us the skills which help us access opportunities after we leave' (Breakwell 1998: 18). This need is endorsed by the findings of the Dearing Inquiry (NCHIE 1997), which recognized the importance of encouraging entrepreneurship and business start-up through innovative approaches to programme design that foster creativity and innovation and: 'help[ing] students to understand the pitfalls of starting a small business and strategies for dealing with them' (NCIHE 1997, Recommendation 40).

The art and design curriculum

The art and design curriculum is an ideal area of higher education to develop as a model for other disciplines with regard to preparation for self-employment, as freelance working patterns become increasingly common for those working in this sector. It is clear that the art and design higher education curriculum has the potential to prepare graduates for self-employment and freelance practice through its problem-solving and project-based approach to learning:

> A student in higher education art and design has the opportunity to acquire a reliable work methodology . . . It also includes the ability to estimate, allocate and manage time in order to meet deadlines. The project serves as a vehicle for instruction in knowledge, skills and working method, for exploration, for discovery, for encouraging independence, for critical appraisal . . .
>
> (Council for National Academic Awards [CNAA]/Committee for Higher Education in Art and Design [CHEAD] 1990: 7)

However, this potential is not always realized because the wider learning outcomes are not always made explicit, reflection does not always take place and consequently students are unable to articulate with confidence the value of their learning and the skills they have developed.

Courses already include work placements, 'live' or collaborative projects, exhibitions, careers programmes and personal and professional development modules. Again, there is potential for active learning and reflection to take place but it seldom happens. How often do we ask students to articulate and reflect on their learning from these experiences in relation to their future aspirations?

Many art and design institutions take a 'bolt-on' approach to providing career and business education, in the form of a lecture programme on 'working freelance', which looks impressive on the timetable or in a course handbook but may not be assessed in any way or involve students putting their learning into practice. Graduates often say that they wished they had paid more attention to these elements whilst still at college. It is clear that unless students are actively engaged in putting their learning into practice, or finding out information for themselves relevant to their own needs, then it is of little value to many of them.

Training for self-employment?

It has been argued that it is not necessary to teach art and design students business studies in order to prepare them for self-employment. Many educators feel that the curriculum is already too full for these aspects to be studied in any depth. Although students need a basic awareness of these areas, they benefit most from further professional development in business aspects after graduation, when embarking on freelance practice (Trustrum *et al.* 1989). Chapter 11 discusses a developmental model for personal, professional and career development, which recommends that small business awareness is addressed but that training for self-employment is left until after graduation.

Fostering key skills and attributes in the existing curriculum

However, some basic needs in relation to preparing students for business start-up can be addressed to a greater or lesser extent in the existing curriculum to help students to:

• relate course activities to their own future interests;
• research and develop their creative practice;
• understand the characteristics of successful small businesses;
• 'rehearse' the experience of self-employment.

We need to create opportunities for students to rehearse or explore the experience of self-employment within a supportive and informed framework as an integral part of their personal, creative and professional development. This could go some way towards helping students to evaluate their own potential for setting up a small business in the future. It would also prepare them for working in small design consultancies and creative businesses as self-starting employees. Given the right learning environment, students can increase their confidence and gain some of the essential skills and attributes they need within the existing curriculum.

How can this be achieved? One approach is to:

• identify which elements in the curriculum currently foster key skills, attitudes and qualities relevant to self-employment;
• make these outcomes more explicit for students;
• then to build on these foundations with appropriate levels of knowledge, awareness and experience.

In recent years, a number of art and design institutions have begun to address these issues. At Brighton, for example, a DfEE-funded research initiative entitled 'Graduate into Business' is directly focusing on the needs of art and design graduates in relation to business start-up.

The 'Graduate into Business' project

The 'Graduate into Business' project involves university staff and students, Training and Enterprise Councils and Business Links, Brighton and Hove Council, Regional Arts Associations and designers and craftspeople working in the south of England. The project is:

- researching the needs of new graduates in craft and design;
- surveying current provision in the curriculum and training for self-employment available after graduation;
- conducting a survey of the characteristics of successful self-employed craft and design graduates and their businesses;
- using the findings to prepare learning materials and programmes for undergraduates and graduates;
- establishing a web site to improve access to business start up information in the region.

Identifying key skills for self-employment

As one of its first tasks, the 'Graduate into Business' project team set out to discover what skills, attributes and qualities students need to develop on their courses to prepare them for the realities after graduation, and in particular to prepare for working freelance or business start-up.

This question was put to: (i) academic staff; (ii) graduates working freelance or running their own crafts and design business; and (iii) training and funding providers for business start-up. Each group identified a range of desirable skills and qualities (Ball and Price 1999). The overall requirement was that graduates should be self-sufficient, independent and aware of the opportunities open to them as well as of the wider learning value of their degree studies. In summary, the following seven most important attributes were listed by all groups:

1. confidence in self and work;
2. ability to evaluate themselves and their work;
3. an understanding of their place in the market;
4. ability to cost and price work – know what they're worth;
5. ability to promote themselves and their work effectively to the right audiences;
6. ability to negotiate successfully with professionals and clients;
7. ability to use their problem-solving approach to learning as a transferable process.

Although these needs are presented in the context of art and design graduates, they could well apply to graduates of other subjects too. Graduates and training and funding providers indicated that these attributes and skills were sadly lacking, which confirms research from other sources

(Breakwell 1998; Press and Cusworth 1998). This view is encapsulated by one graduate interviewee who remarked: 'We do not feel confident enough to say what our professional skills are'. Staff, on the other hand, felt there were opportunities on their courses for students to develop the attributes identified but were unable to say how students knew they were developing them. This implies that outcomes are not made explicit and reflection is not taking place.

Cultural differences

The results of these interviews also pointed to some serious cultural problems in relation to business start-up: 'A lot of people when they go into business do not think what it is going to be that makes them successful. They are trying to measure their success on how they feel because they have never done market research' (crafts graduate).

One could assume from this that art and design graduates are relying on intuition rather than utilizing business thinking to help them to succeed. Graduates are not making connections between the 'creative' and the 'business' – utilizing one to make the other happen. They are: 'not thinking about what they are making as a business' (crafts graduate). This is confirmed by other studies: 'Students don't make the connection between the desire to practice and the need to prepare for getting started' (Breakwell 1997: 19).

The cultural and language barriers between art/design and business have long been debated (Trustrum *et al.* 1990). One represents a 'kaleidoscopic' or lateral approach to thinking, the other a 'linear' logical approach. This is typified by fundamental communication problems to do with the language of business and the language of artists and makers: 'There is little point in producing fabulous designs if you cannot cost them, sell them, market them, promote them or raise the money to develop them' (fashion textiles graduate). To address this problem, it is therefore desirable that courses find ways of further integrating business and creative aspects.

The implications are that higher education needs to find ways of improving graduates' preparedness for work. Learning opportunities need to be provided that enable students to build confidence, operate independently as autonomous learners, take responsibility for themselves and their career development, adopt a professional attitude, network and promote themselves effectively and have a basic understanding of the requirements of the professional field in which they will work.

A holistic model for learning

As a result of research into independent learning on crafts courses (Ball 1996) and further work with the 'Graduate into Business' project at Brighton, the following model has been developed to provide a framework for course

Figure 9.1   A holistic model for learning

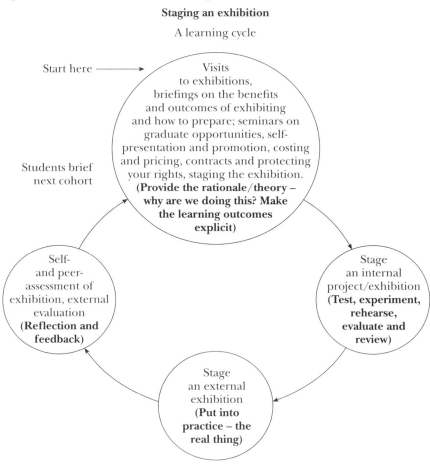

Staging an exhibition

A learning cycle

Start here ⟶ Visits to exhibitions, briefings on the benefits and outcomes of exhibiting and how to prepare; seminars on graduate opportunities, self-presentation and promotion, costing and pricing, contracts and protecting your rights, staging the exhibition. **(Provide the rationale/theory – why are we doing this? Make the learning outcomes explicit)**

Students brief next cohort

Self- and peer-assessment of exhibition, external evaluation **(Reflection and feedback)**

Stage an internal project/exhibition **(Test, experiment, rehearse, evaluate and review)**

Stage an external exhibition **(Put into practice – the real thing)**

activities based on an experiential learning cycle. This holistic model sets out to integrate personal, professional, creative, technical, contextual and business aspects of learning and can be applied to any active learning opportunity.

In Figure 9.1, the model is applied to the activity of staging an exhibition, which provides an appropriate vehicle for learning and developing the skills, qualities and attributes identified above as being important for self-employment or business start-up:

Self-evaluation, confidence, interpersonal skills, promotion of self and work, business awareness, costing and pricing, understanding the market, personal and professional skills, independence, networking, collaborating with others, operating at a professional level.

(Ball and Price 1999: 65)

The activity is supported by staff but students take responsibility for all aspects of staging the exhibition, including fund raising. In this case, what really provides additional credibility for the exercise and ensures quality of reflection is the use of past students to brief the next cohort, which they normally do positively and enthusiastically!

Course culture is the key

The thinking behind the model was influenced by the findings of the Crafts Council research study 'Helping Students to learn Independently in the Crafts' (Ball 1996). This research showed that a course culture that is open in nature, encourages student responsibility, is outward looking and involves tutors as role models and practitioners in their own right helps students to develop the kinds of characteristics needed for self-employment. In design courses that included these features and fostered these values, students aiming to set up their own businesses after graduation had already worked out that they needed to be 'self-sufficient' and possess a range of personal and professional skills and qualities that would enable them to operate independently as practitioners (Ball 1996: 88).

The same study found that students were motivated by:

- learning that explores personal interests, values and experiences;
- self-evaluation, which contributes to a sense of ownership and personal responsibility;
- having a longer term view – knowing how they can apply their learning (Ball 1996: 123).

These need to be borne in mind when designing courses and learning activities for students.

Staff development

To achieve cultural change, staff will need to be recruited for their ability to use active student learning opportunities to encourage independence, as well as for excellence in their own creative practice. Focused recruitment and continuing professional development for staff as educators and practitioners are the keys – so that staff (and students) have a shared set of values and sense of common purpose.

A whole course team approach

The following exercise has been used successfully as the basis for a day's team building and course design workshop. It needs a facilitator to keep participants on track, preferably from outside the course. Participants record their own findings on flip charts, which are typed up after the event and used for planning and reflection:

1. The whole group brainstorms the key skills, qualities and learning outcomes they want their students to have achieved by the time they graduate. They then record them on flip charts, then prioritize. (Alternatively, the group brainstorms the key skills and qualities graduates need for self-employment or business start-up. In practice, this produces broadly very similar results).
2. Divide participants into small groups of three to four and divide up the key learning outcomes between the groups, so each group is working on a different set of outcomes. Staff identify:
   • specific course activities that have the potential to develop these;
   • how students are encouraged in these activities;
   • whether these skills, qualities and outcomes are assessed, and if so how;
   • how students know that they have developed them (how does reflection take place?).
   The findings are recorded on flip charts and gaps in provision are identified.
3. Each small group presents its findings to the whole group, identifying the gaps in provision.
4. Each small group works as a team of consultants to address the gaps and to redesign a course activity to ensure that it addresses all of the criteria in (2) above.
5. The whole group reflects on what they have learned from the exercise (modelling good practice, which is then transferable to working with students in the same way). They reflect on their findings and decide on action-points for the future.

Further outcomes of this exercise for staff have been recorded: team building, building a sense of common purpose, being creative, energizing.

For the future

It is clear that staff need to improve their own awareness of current and future post-graduation opportunities, including self-employment and the needs of graduates in terms of the skills and qualities required in their future lives. This needs to be communicated to students through course activities so they can in turn:

• understand the particular strengths of graduates completing their courses;
• have the confidence to communicate and apply these in the workplace;
• understand the contribution graduates can make in terms of their own knowledge, skills and experiences in a wider context – the transferability of their learning processes and intellectual skills;
• develop the confidence to consider self-employment or working in a small business as a viable option.

The models and examples presented in this case study have a much wider application than for the preparation of craft and design graduates for self-employment. In the future, graduates of all subjects will need to be self-starting, independent, lifelong learners and problem-solvers.

As one student said: 'At the end of the day, it's very important to have those skills: to be able to negotiate your position in the business world and stand on your own two feet is paramount. You're not going to have a member of staff there for you afterwards . . .' (Ball 1996: 125).

Note

1. The five institutions with the highest rates for self-employment were art and design institutions, ranging from 5 to 13 per cent.

10

Assessment and Standards

ASSESSMENT AND STANDARDS IN IMPLEMENTING ACCREDITATION OF UNIVERSITY TEACHERS: A CASE STUDY

Maggie Blake and Stuart Laing

Introduction

University teachers, long involved in design, delivery and assessment of programmes for the professional education of others, now have the opportunity to demonstrate their own professional capability. The newly created Institute for Learning and Teaching in Higher Education (ILT) is responsible for identifying particular areas of professional academic practice that teachers will be required to address in order to establish their credentials for ILT membership.

Membership may be achieved in two ways. Firstly, individuals can take responsibility themselves for compiling and presenting documentation to justify membership of the ILT. Secondly, institutions can offer courses and programmes for staff, to support them in compiling evidence of professional development and capability for the ILT. These courses/programmes will be scrutinized by the ILT and, if appropriate, will be accredited. Institutions will have responsibility for quality assurance of the programmes, which will be subject to review by the ILT. Successful participants of accredited courses will gain an automatic stage of ILT membership.

It is difficult to argue against the case for this national development in terms of professional accountability, credibility and comparability with other professions. But how is it to be done?

This case study explores some of the critical issues which have arisen at the University of Brighton as systems and programmes to support academic staff to gain ILT membership are put in place. These can be grouped into three main areas:

1. The management of change, including: effective consultation processes, gaining consensus and who 'teaches the teachers' or 'facilitates' the accreditation process.
2. The nature of the programmes that meet the needs of a wide variety of academic staff at different stages of professional development whilst achieving an effective yet acceptable approach to teacher observation. Of concern is the role of APEL, particularly in relation to existing staff teaching qualifications and the use of APEL in the context of the stated ILT aims. The role of the professional portfolio is also important.
3. Assessment issues concern the academic level of programmes and systems acceptable to both the ILT any ensuing academic awards as well as the process of assessment.

The management of change

Mindful of the heterogeneity of staff who now have the opportunity to gain membership of the ILT, consultation processes took place within the university during 1997–8. There was a genuine desire to glean the views of staff, given that any curriculum development is a complex process and there is no point in developing something that nobody wants. The consultation process included giving information about current practice at Brighton and national policy as it developed. The main aim was to gather staff views about the way forward for Brighton. It was an open process in that no final decisions about future teacher accreditation had been predetermined.

The current situation

To date, accreditation provision for academic staff in learning and teaching at Brighton has focused on new or developing teachers in higher education. There are two established programmes, the Postgraduate Certificate in Teaching and Learning in Higher Education and a short course, 'Facilitating Learning in Higher Education', both of which are based in the Centre for Learning and Teaching (CLT). The CLT has two full-time teaching staff supported by a selected group of staff from a range of subject disciplines across the university who contribute to delivery of the programmes.

The first course leads to an academic award and is targeted at mostly new full-time members of academic staff. The second programme, the short course, gives successful participants Masters level credit points and is for part-time and research staff with responsibility for some teaching. Both courses are at Masters level and have been 'recognized' by, and lead to a stage of membership of, the Staff and Educational Development Association (SEDA). SEDA is an association run by a network of staff from the national higher education community who are involved in academic staff development. The SEDA network, operating on a peer assessment basis, recognizes some 50 courses in the UK, the vast majority of which are at Masters level. Both the Brighton courses provide 'scaffolding' for staff to build up a professional portfolio that addresses the stated values and meets the objectives required by SEDA.

The consultation process

This included:

- meetings between CLT staff and all six Faculty Management Groups in the university;
- a CLT news-sheet, disseminated to all academic staff, which provided information about current Brighton provision as well as national developments. Views were sought about the way forward for the university;
- an in-house learning and teaching conference focusing on teacher accreditation (which included contributions from Clive Booth (Chair of the Accreditation and Teaching in Higher Education Committee, CVCP) and John Randall (Chief Executive of the Quality Assurance Agency for Higher Education));
- an e-mail survey seeking to gather views about teaching accreditation. This message elicited a response from about one in four members of the university's total 579 teaching staff.

The consultation indicated that the prevailing response to national teacher accreditation at Brighton was positive. There was, however, a significant amount of disquiet about whether the likely future provision in Brighton, or indeed nationally, would be appropriate for experienced teachers. Many of the issues that arose matched the concerns of the three main areas already outlined, but some areas of concern were arguably more surprising. They included:

- the ubiquitous use of the 'teacher' in the national accreditation context. Some felt that they were 'lecturers' and that the term 'teacher' is associated with schools (this despite the fact that the two main lecturer unions, the Association of University Teachers (AUT) and the National Association for Teachers in Further and Higher Education (NATFHE) use the term 'teacher' in their titles). Resistance to the term 'teacher' was particularly strong amongst staff in the science and technology disciplines;
- concern about the possible future mandatory nature of teacher accreditation and fears about 'failing' to get a 'licence to teach'. Some wanted to know if the process would affect appraisal and promotion;
- uncertainty about the nature of the national ILT accreditation process. For example, what about academic staff who do very little, if any, teaching?
- disquiet about the use of the professional portfolio of evidence, citing it as boring and a paper-collecting exercise;
- questions about funding: will lecturers be given explicit time to work towards ILT membership?

Gaining consensus

An examination of the data revealed that the minority of respondents who are against any form of teacher accreditation fell into three categories. These are: (i) experienced lecturers (many with teaching qualifications); (ii) active members of the teacher unions; and (iii) lecturers whose role involves little teaching. A decision was taken by the teaching team in the CLT to invite members of this equivocal minority to become involved in the development process. This was done in the belief that teacher accreditation developments would benefit from a sceptical input rather than leaving it all to the enthusiasts.

Programme deliveries

ILT policy publications have indicated that teacher accreditation programmes should not be the sole preserve of 'learning and teaching' professionals (ILT: 1998, paragraph 56). Clearly, those responsible for both development and delivery of any programmes need to have the respect of their colleagues. Moreover, there is an implicit assumption here that different academic disciplines will have different approaches and concerns and that generic learning and teaching experts have a limited, if none the less important, role to play in the future accreditation of teachers. It was therefore decided that deans and heads of schools from across the university should nominate experienced staff with a good reputation for sound professional practice, particularly in relation to teaching. These staff would be invited to join the CLT for a proportion of their working time on a secondment basis for accreditation development and (possibly) delivery of some programmes. This process is already underway. Three staff, all principal lecturers, representing three of the six faculties, are currently seconded to the CLT.

Resourcing accreditation

The issue of time and resources to undertake the accreditation process was clearly a concern for many lecturers. However, this issue is not such a problem area as anticipated. Currently, university staff have the opportunity to take part in a large number of in-house staff development events in addition to being supported to attend national conferences and, in many cases, to undertake research into direct pedagogic issues. It was therefore noted that future developments should be informed by this and that they should seek to 'harness' the staff development already taking place in order to allow these activities to contribute to the accreditation process. This perspective does not deny the likely need for some increased resources, particularly in the first few years, to be devoted to the introduction of the accreditation process, but it does seek to emphasize the need to look for continuities with existing staff development plans and for ways of validating the good teaching practice that already exists.

The initial foundations for gaining consensus were thus laid and working parties to develop pathways were set up.

The nature of the programmes, both existing and for development

The two existing programmes at Brighton are primarily focused on new teachers in higher education. Two assumptions underpin both courses. One is that the subject expertise of participants is up to date – the university is not going to appoint staff who are not up to date! The second assumption is that participants will not have much experience of reflective practice in teaching in higher education. The content of the courses is therefore heavily weighted towards introducing ideas about the nature of learning and the teaching strategies to facilitate learning effectively.

Three characteristics of the two existing Brighton programmes can be highlighted here. Firstly, both courses are dependent on the portfolio of evidence approach. Secondly, the process of APEL is not applicable and, thirdly, the observation of teaching involves peers who act as 'critical friends'. The existing courses provide a 'scaffolding' for participants to compile their portfolio.

The content of both courses includes consideration about:

- the effectiveness of different learning and teaching strategies;
- theories about the nature of learning;
- different learning styles;
- the effectiveness of various assessment approaches;
- the effectiveness of evaluation strategies.

A second important factor is that the course process requires participants to reflect on their own professional practice. Schön (1987) has written convincingly of the connection between reflection on current practice and enhancement of future practice. In addition to reflection on practice, participants undertake some form of peer observation of teaching, presently arranged by the participants themselves.

When asked about the difference the courses had made to professional practice during annual review in 1998, the Brighton participants were generally positive. Participants felt it had a lasting impact.

The professional portfolio approach

The ILT has so far indicated that its approach will follow the SEDA model for accrediting courses/pathways. Clearly, elements of the existing Brighton provision will be useful when designing programmes for experienced staff, especially in relation to the portfolio approach. For example, the content of existing programmes is designed to address the values and objectives of SEDA. So the 'mapping' process, whereby evidence about professional practice is matched against the values and objectives of SEDA, is facilitated by the programme of work. This helps in the compilation of an accessible and coherent portfolio. It does not take a huge leap of the imagination to use this experience to design guidelines for staff to compile a portfolio that will meet the objectives of the proposed ILT 'national statement'.

APEL

The future use of APEL in the accreditation process is complex. A significant percentage of staff have some form of teaching qualification, in many cases these were obtained a number of years ago. Clearly, any qualification, whenever obtained, will have informed subsequent practice. The stated function of the ILT, however, is to: 'improve the quality of teaching and learning' (ILT 1998: section 5). It follows that, whilst existing teaching qualifications are an important element, it is the continuing development of practice that predominates. It may be, then, that the term APEL is not appropriate in this context and that accreditation of experiential learning (AEL) is more relevant. This is likely to be a controversial area: data from our consultation have indicated that a number of lecturers with teaching qualifications feel they should be given automatic ILT membership.

Observation of teaching

Observation of teaching is another complex area. So far, there have been no definitive announcements emanating from the ILT about how universities should approach this. In the near future it is likely that, at Brighton, quality of teaching will continue to be judged against current review and evaluation procedures, peer observation of teaching as well as external Quality Assurance Agency (QAA) Subject Reviews, Ofsted inspections and other professional body reviews.

If the accreditation of teachers is to have real credibility, then it is likely that, in the longer term, credible guidelines about this important area will be developed by the ILT. In an age of increased distance and computer-based learning the simple concept of 'classroom observation' as a proxy for quality of staff/student interaction will need considerable refinement.

Assessment

The concept of 'assessment' provokes discussion in any sector of education. Notions of comparability, definitions of level and valid judgements about outcomes are still areas of intense national debate. In the context of teacher accreditation programmes, this is further complicated by the view that the whole process should be about 'development' and continuous improvement. So how ineffective does someone have to be before they are deemed to be incompetent so long as they continue to improve? Whilst there has been some confident discussion about subject threshold standards, there has been little discussion about threshold standards for teaching in higher education.

Standards and the ILT

There has been some reference to standards, albeit somewhat less than explicit, in the 1998 ILT *Implementing the Vision* policy paper. This states that the teacher ILT accreditation framework and the 'standards of professional practice' need to be underpinned by a solid foundation of understanding in the higher education community about the practice of teaching (ILT 1998: paragraph 12). It begs the question, however, about the nature of the standards. The Booth Report (CVCP 1998) outlines a number of areas of professional practice that university teachers need to address in the accreditation process (ILT 1998: paragraph 2.5, Table 2). Table 2 for the most part describes areas of professional practice rather than sets standards for professional practice. For example, there is a box that states simply 'Mark and give feedback to students on assignments'. In the whole table the word 'appropriate' is used six times and the word 'improve' three times. There is nothing about academic level and no explanation about what is meant by 'appropriate' or 'improvement'. The paragraphs that follow (2.6 and 2.7) are similarly coy about 'level' and prefer to describe areas of expertise rather than delineate required standards. Furthermore, Appendix A of the Booth Report purports to outline initial thinking about the outcomes, underpinning knowledge and professional values of the 'National Statement'. Again, the content of this is largely descriptive, using judgemental epithets such as 'appropriate', 'satisfying' and 'supportive'. The epithets are useful but give no indication about levels or 'standards' *per se*. The dilemma of the planners is understandable. Although the majority of courses currently recognized by SEDA are at Masters level, there are some that are not, including two from prestigious old civic universities. What does this mean?

It cannot, surely, mean that the evidence presented by the staff of these two great universities is lower in level and therefore by implication lower in standards than other institutions? It is more likely that there is still no national consensus about academic levels. It no doubt also reflects views about the nature of 'knowledge' and about whether the content of teacher accreditation programmes embraces a corpus of knowledge that is acceptable for Masters-level study. Hence, perhaps, the caution of the ILT planners at this stage. To be fair, they have indicated that they will put in place systems to collect, analyse and disseminate information about learning and teaching and good practice to institutions (ILT 1998, paragraph 17). In the meantime, most institutions are likely to continue to develop the teacher accreditation processes that have evolved thus far, which usually means Masters-level programmes and pathways.

Masters level at the University of Brighton

The justification for the Masters level of the Brighton programmes is predicated on several factors. One is that course participants are well qualified professionals who are already functioning at postgraduate level in an intellectual context. The assumption is that reflection on practice, however new that practice is to the course member, will be reflection that reaches a postgraduate level of intellectual endeavour. Another factor is that the courses' content is based on the notion that there is a propositional knowledge base for learning and teaching. Propositional knowledge in this context is described by Eraut (1994a) as knowledge that underpins and enables professional action. This knowledge base in learning and teaching practice is, for example, informed by theory and the testing of the theory in practice.

Another factor relevant here in relation to level is that the portfolio of work, which is submitted at the end of the courses, is peer- and tutor-assessed with reference to the South of England Education Consortium (SEEC) (1997) Masters-level descriptors, giving a wider validity.

There are caveats about our current provision in relation to the courses' content and these are worth reiterating. These are that new teachers have limited knowledge of the theory and practice of teaching but will have up-to-date subject knowledge. The inclusion of a number of experienced teachers on the courses enriches learning opportunities.

The academic level of future provision

In planning for systems to help a wider range of academic staff gain ILT accreditation, it is important to distinguish between competence, academic level of work and academic awards. Whilst no definite accreditation system is yet in place at the University of Brighton, two issues are of paramount importance to the working parties as they develop programmes and pathways. One concerns choice for academic staff, whilst the other concerns the credibility of the programmes from a national as well as a local perspective.

The issue of choice is simply resolved. Programmes that lead to an academic award and membership of the ILT will continue to be developed, building on the experience of the two existing programmes. A 'basket' of modules will be available to staff and these will have particular importance in the accreditation context. For example, modules concerned with IT and assessment have already been developed. Running parallel with this, there will be the opportunity for staff to develop a professional portfolio that leads to ILT membership. This portfolio, though it will show evidence of Masters-level thinking, will not lead to an academic award. The portfolio pathway that does not entail an academic award will require clear mapping if it is to be recognized and accredited by the ILT.

One crucial issue will be the Masters-level quality of the portfolio. It will not be enough to present evidence of professional practice without some critical comment if the member of academic staff is to 'engage intellectually' with the process. On the existing two programmes, the use of the 'statement of relevance' (Bourner, O'Hara, Barlow 2000) is of importance here and it may be usefully introduced into the professional portfolio without an accompanying award pathway. A 'statement of relevance' is a short piece of writing that presents a critical reflection on professional activity, whether it be attendance at a conference or the delivery of a lecture. The rationale behind this approach resonates with the Kolb learning cycle (Kolb 1984). The professional acts, reflects on the lessons to be learned and the relevance of this new learning to future practice. The process is cyclical and ongoing. The content of the portfolio could therefore include material about professional practice, which addresses the areas outlined in the ILT 'national statement', and the material would be supplemented by 'statements of relevance'. A completed portfolio provides opportunities for participants to gain a number of credit points. The member of staff may wish to use these credit points towards an academic award at Postgraduate Certificate, Diploma or Masters level, in which case some further study (including a dissertation or equivalent for a Masters award) would be required.

Finally, after initial ILT membership has been attained, academic staff will be required to 'remain in good standing'. This is a new area for teachers in higher education. At Brighton, a working party has been set up to explore the best way forward. An initial response has been to gather information about how other professional bodies, such as in the field of law and engineering, approach this requirement. Development will take place in the light of information gained from this research.

Conclusion

The discussion and the consultation process is ongoing at Brighton and will continue into the future as the routes to ILT teacher membership are implemented and evaluated. This no doubt reflects the national situation as universities as diverse as Durham and Plymouth, Aberystwyth and Brighton deliberate on their respective responses to ILT requirements for university academic staff membership. It will be essential that the ILT prioritizes the dissemination of information about approaches to teacher accreditation in different institutions in order both to inform institutions and to work towards a coherent and comparable national system.

PROFESSIONAL ACCREDITATION IN IT PROJECT MANAGEMENT

Robert T. Hughes

Introduction

The focus of this case study is software project management (PM), which has a continuing history of disasters; see Flowers (1996) for examples. The study is based mainly on the writer's experience of the assessment of project management trainees through participation in the Information Systems Examination Board (ISEB), a wing of the BCS. The views expressed are all personal ones.

One view of 'professional' higher education perceives the disciplines within higher education as part of the wider professional communities that they serve. In this model, a key role of higher education is to prepare students to become members of that professional community. As Katharine Martyn notes in her case study in relation to healthcare professionals (see pp. 191–9), a key issue is the degree to which this preparation should be narrowly practical or should have a broader educational aspect. Some degree courses may be more formally related to their respective communities than others. This may relate to the extent to which some professional communities are 'mature' and, in consequence, cohesive and structured. The question of maturity is important to software PM, particularly as it is practised in an information systems/information technology (IS/IT) environment that is itself changing rapidly.

The professional scope

One aspect of professional maturity is the degree to which there is an agreed body of knowledge. While the development of bodies of knowledge has relevance to all disciplines, in the case of professional disciplines there is the additional dimension of dialogue with the wider professional community. How software development can be turned into a proper professional discipline has exercised academic writers such as Shaw (1990) and Basili and Musa (1991), who usually want it to be a branch of engineering.

In the case of software PM as a putative discipline, a preliminary question is whether *software* PM is really any different from other types of PM. Indeed, there is a general question as to the effect of the practice context on the nature of the discipline. It has been argued that while the management of software projects does involve the skills that other projects demand, software has particular characteristics, such as its intangibility, complexity and mutability (Brooks 1987), that require special techniques. In practice, this distinction is blurred as an increasing number of engineering projects have a software element (for example, the software-based control systems in the channel tunnel) and IT projects often involve considerable numbers of non-IT activities.

One opinion is therefore that a generic PM discipline exists that can be supported by its own professional structure as represented by such bodies as the Association for Project Management (APM) in the UK and the Project Management Institute (PMI) in the US. It is also symptomatic that one UK government-sponsored project management standard, PRINCE, that was originally envisaged as being solely applicable to IT projects has now been reissued in a version (PRINCE2) that is more generally applicable. Associated with this view is the belief that a good project manager should be able to manage any project regardless of its technical environment. In practice this seems questionable: our experience with assessment shows that candidates who are familiar with the context of a case study are clearly advantaged.

So many standards to choose from

Forming a professional body of knowledge requires some degree of agreement within the wider professional community. Duncan Cullimore's case study in relation to the teaching of business IT illustrates that this kind of agreement does not arise overnight (see pages 95–104). Usually, any consensus about best practice is eventually written into professional standards and codes of practice. Such standards may have a number of purposes. For example, with a relatively immature discipline uncertainty may exist about the precise meaning of terms: at a very basic level a standard could define terminology. At a higher level, standards may define procedural or product requirements designed to ensure consistency and compatibility, for example telecommunications protocols that allow different types of equipment to operate together. At a yet higher level they may attempt to define the scope of the professional discipline itself.

With PM there exists a range of often conflicting standards. In the UK, the government, through the Central Computing and Telecommunications Agency (CCTA), has been a major sponsor of PRINCE, which has claims to be the *de facto* UK project management standard (CCTA 1996). At the same time, the British Standards Institute (BSI) has published its own *Guide to project management* (BSI 1996). The creators of these standards are at pains to state that these two standards are not to be regarded as competitors but the differences in terminologies and in the definition of core concepts cause confusion. In addition to these two standards, the PMI in the US has published a 150-page Project Management Body of Knowledge, while in the UK the APM has published its own version of a 'body of knowledge'. Account needs also to be taken of international standards, such as International Organization for Standardization (ISO)-10006 and of the NVQ Project Management competencies, in the development of which the Institute of Management has played a leading role.

Institutional influence

Focusing on specifically IT-related PM, examination of the role of the BCS is instructive. The BCS has had only partial success in shaping the body of IT practitioners into a structured professional community. BCS membership is practically never a requirement for any role in IT development. On the other hand, the BCS has a system of professional examinations and most computing degree courses in the UK conform to the requirements of the BCS so that their graduates may qualify for BCS membership.

Our experience as course providers preparing IT practitioners for BCS examinations was that people actively involved in IT development found the content of the BCS professional examination syllabus often remote from their day-to-day work and felt it was unduly influenced by academic hobby-horses. Does this experience resonate with that of people in other professions in their perceptions of their professional examinations?

The BCS has had relatively little influence on actual information systems development practice in industry compared with the CCTA. While the CCTA has little direct power outside government departments, it wields considerable influence as the government is one of the largest users of IT in the UK and, consequently, a large purchaser of products and services related to IS and IT.

Among CCTA activities has been the production of a number of guides to various aspects of IT management. In 1990, the CCTA encouraged the creation of ISEB, under the wing of the BCS, to conduct examinations and issue certificates of competence on IT-related topics, many of which had been originally defined by CCTA guidelines. ISEB was set up to be completely separate from the existing BCS professional examinations. The clear message was that these new qualifications were to have industrial credibility and not be influenced by irrelevant academic preoccupations. In part this may have reflected the poor reputation that early computer science degree courses had among many 'commercial data processing' practitioners – in the 1970s an IT manager that I worked for saw a computer science degree as a positive disqualification from employment as a computer programmer. The preparation of candidates for ISEB examinations was to be carried out by accredited training organizations. Although academic institutions could gain such accreditation (for example, the University of Brighton became an accredited provider of courses in the SSADM systems analysis method) the system was primarily geared to commercial training organizations.

ISEB assessment

In the case of PM, the problem of the range of different approaches was tackled by ISEB attempting to define a generic framework for PM. Different course providers could then teach different methodologies within that framework. Although the same examination papers were sat by all candidates, examination scripts were initially marked by course providers and then moderated centrally. The main reason for this would appear to have been to reduce central costs but it also allowed a degree of local interpretation of candidates' scripts to take account of different methods.

I have been involved with the administration of this examination as a paper setter and moderator: none of the other people involved have to my knowledge been academics. The reasons for this lack of academic involvement have been touched upon above. A noticeable consequence has been an apparent blindness to the idea of a 'professional' approach to assessment, particularly to the idea that there might be an existing body of recognized good assessment practice. One aspect of this has been that little effort has been made to explicitly link assessment to a set of competencies expected in the candidate.

Difficulties

A major problem with the ISEB approach has been ensuring that candidates who have been taught different methods are assessed consistently. In setting questions, care has to be taken to use a terminology that is commonly understood and to avoid the inadvertent use of the jargon of any one particular PM approach, such as PRINCE. For example, in PM, the term 'project' may mean different things to different people: in some cases (for example in BS 6079 and in Net Present Value calculations) a 'project' covers the whole life of a product from the original idea, through its construction and operation until its final decommissioning. However, IT developers tend to follow PRINCE2 in seeing a 'project' as the process that leads to delivery of a product and which does not include operation. The term 'project manager' also provides problems. In the past IS/IT development has typically used in-house staff as software developers over whom the project manager has had technical control. More recently there has been a move to 'out-sourcing' software development, which has often meant that a 'project manager' manages a contract on behalf of their employer but has not had direct technical control over development.

There are also often disputes about what constitutes a reasonable scenario for a case study. A scenario concerned with a project to write a software package may seem very appropriate but an increasing number of IT practitioners are not involved with software development but with activities such as network management. One proposal has been to avoid the use of IS/IT scenarios but this is not attractive, as it would fail to distinguish the IS/IT-related ISEB qualification from other general PM qualifications, such as those of the APM.

In answering questions, candidates from different course providers could give different answers that could be regarded as correct. This makes the setting of appropriate marking schemes to obtain consistent assessment very difficult.

The way forward

A way to reduce these problems is to start from a set of competencies that project managers require. The NVQ scheme has provided a model for this but does not fit our exact requirements. For example, one of its units is 'specify requirements for projects'. In IS/IT, requirements analysis is a discipline in its own right and is invariably taught separately from project management. In fact, requirements analysis is a good example of where context has a major impact on the techniques used.

Competencies can then be associated with generic processes or functions, for example 'allocate appropriate resources to activities'. This idea of generic PM functions or processes is one upon which the PMI in the US has put heavy reliance. In some cases, specific techniques, such as the use of critical path network analysis or earned value analysis, may be suggested but a course provider would be free to teach an alternative method that was technically equivalent. Each function or process has a defined assessment method for evaluating competence.

While the problem of deciding what constitutes a valid scenario cannot be solved completely, the laying down of prerequisites – the areas of knowledge that the candidate may be expected to have before embarking on specific PM training – may be helpful. This would identify the background knowledge that candidates need to have in order to understand the project scenarios. A final need is for the adoption of a glossary of PM terms that the examiners are going to use in the examination papers.

Academic idiosyncracy

Some comments now follow on how the teaching and assessment of PM within a university compares to that in the wider community. One immediate point is that the different shades of meaning in the term 'project' are again important – but in a slightly different way. For many students, the word 'project' conjures up the final-year project. In fact, the final-year project is very untypical of projects in general because, for a start, it usually has only one person involved and there are no problems of delegation and co-ordination. The research nature of many final year projects, where the final outcomes are uncertain, also makes conventional planning inappropriate. In spite of this, a BCS accreditation panel at one point recommended that PM was a compulsory final-year module in order to prepare students for their individual projects.

Mostly, however, terminology is less of a problem for internal courses as we have more control over our environment and can impose our own 'standard' terminology.

A major difference between the teaching of PM inside the university and outside is that internally we put a lot of emphasis on teaching planning using techniques such as critical path analysis (CPA). One does wonder whether a major influence on the syllabus is what is easy to assess – CPA is a natural examination question topic! In industry, much more emphasis is based on the control aspects of PM: a relatively small part of the job is planning and, in reality, planning is rarely a purely management activity but often needs considerable technical and operational input. Some ISEB candidates from industry have even expressed surprise that they needed to know anything about planning techniques.

One problem that is common to both spheres is that of the relevant scenarios. Modularity within universities has encouraged the idea that topics that appear in more than one degree programme may be taught as common modules. PM appears to be a good example of this but, when it comes to assessment, having students from different backgrounds can be problematic. One may talk to them bravely about tackling 'multi-disciplinary' problems but computing students tend to take a focused view of what is relevant to their needs and specifically IT-related scenarios help to demonstrate the need for PM in their own area of interest.

Although modularity demands that modules are independent, this also leads to isolation. It is accepted as good practice that each module's assessment should be completely independent. With PM, while it would be ideal for a PM module to involve the planning and control of a project that is to be done as part of the work for another module, this seems to be contrary to a very narrow view of modularity. The concept of modularity needs to be enriched to embrace the idea of a collection of modules together constituting an effective educational system – in engineering practice, some of the most important attributes of 'modules' concern the way that they interface with one another.

It is illuminating to compare the approach of commercial course providers with that typically used in a university. Staff in industry clearly believe in the efficacy of small group teaching – course providers typically limit class sizes to 15. Although there are moves to distance learning, residential courses still appear to be the favoured mode of delivery. Staff who work in demanding and fast-moving environments feel they need to 'get away' if they are to take on board new techniques and knowledge. Another difference in environments that is striking to the academic is how little even trainers and course providers read the literature on their subject area: many have not even heard of what might be regarded as the classics in the field.

Conclusions

This case study has examined the concept of the 'professional community' in one particular context at one particular stage in its development. A major lesson is that academics developing vocational subjects may have difficulties in understanding and communicating with the community they are attempting to serve, particularly where the field is a rapidly developing, technological one. Academics have to be aware of the wider environment, otherwise their graduates may be at a disadvantage when they pass into the professional community. Given the confusion that can exist in emerging professions, institutions of higher education have a proactive role to play. Despite the criticisms that some have made about the differences in the standing of degrees from different institutions, the meaning of university-based first and postgraduate qualifications is often better understood by the general public, including employers, than the qualifications of some emergent professional bodies. While higher education institutions can exploit opportunities to run the kind of short course that commercial training organizations do, a more valuable and strategic role may be to run more 'academic' courses that reflect on, and look at the wider implications of, current work practices. Typically, these would be at Masters level using models such as the Masters in Business Administration (MBA). One implication of this would be that a research regime that gave more support to research into work practices would need to be promoted.

DYSLEXIA IN THE PROFESSIONS – THE CASE OF NURSE EDUCATION

Katharine Martyn

Introduction

This is a case study of dyslexia in education for the 'new' profession of nursing. Some of the issues raised apply only to nursing education and practice; others also apply to many other professions.

The impact of dyslexia on nursing practice is, in the author's experience, rarely discussed except in the context of exam boards. The concerns raised seem to reflect the tutors' viewpoint that nursing takes place in complex settings and of the need to ensure the protection of the vulnerable patient. The discussions imply that dyslexia will be a handicap. They doubt the competence of the student and believe that dyslexia will inhibit effective communication not only between nurse and patient but also between the nurse and other healthcare professionals. The almost invariable response to questions raised is to refer to the need for the formal identification of the level of disability through an educational psychologist's report and the subsequent provision of educational support throughout the period of the course. It would appear that an assumption is made that the support provided through the academic mechanism will be effective and appropriate within clinical practice. This case study looks at the experience of two students to explore the understanding that nurse lecturers have of dyslexia, the issues of competence and disability, the perceptions of the student about the practical nature of nursing, the expectations of the clinical setting and the nature of the support required by the student in practice.

The nature of dyslexia

It has been estimated that as many as one in ten adults suffer from some form of dyslexia (British Dyslexia Association [BDA] 1998). Coupled with the increased demand for registered nurses (DoH 1998), it is reasonable to suggest that many nursing students will be identified as having this form of disability. Whilst dyslexia is itself not a measure of intelligence (BDA 1998), definitions of dyslexia refer to learning and include concepts such as phonological difficulties (Snowling 1995), visual processing deficits (Willows and Terepocki 1993) and visual perceptional deficits (Garzia 1993). These factors are associated with difficulties in learning to read but can also impede on the development of mathematical skills and the individual may have poor working short-term memory function (McLoughlin, Fitzgibbon and Young 1994).

Within a three-year nursing programme, 2300 hours are spent in the clinical setting (English National Board [ENB] Regulations 1993), where students apply their knowledge and skills in the care of patients. The students are supported in practice by registered nurses. In clinical practice, an individual will be required to process text and assimilate meaning in an environment that is often not conducive to effective communication (Lelean 1973).

The students interviewed in this case study were identified as having dyslexia. Their inclusion clarifies some of the issues raised and highlights potential difficulties within the management of a nursing course. Comments from colleagues and preceptors provide insight as to belief systems about disability and competency and the purpose of the preregistration programme in nursing.

All groups were informed as to the purpose of the paper and permission was gained for their inclusion within the text.

The students' experience

Student 1

This student was not initially identified as having an educational need until her preceptor, concerned about her lack of participation, contacted a tutor and remarked: '. . . she does not like to write in the care plan and is always finding other things to do . . . her spelling is so bad that when she does write I cannot understand what she is trying to say . . . I don't think she is safe [in the clinical area]'. On being interviewed, the student remarked: 'On entering the ward I saw all those people . . . they all seemed to know what they were doing. I picked up a care plan . . . and panicked'. The student had identified that care was not 'just given' but was planned and documented, which would require both reading and writing. Her subsequent anxiety, avoidance of writing and the negative response she received from the preceptor reinforced her opinion that she 'really wasn't very clever'.

The views voiced by this student highlighted her perception of her abilities. She stated that she had received support throughout her school life but had hoped it would not be necessary on her nursing course. In discussion, she had stated that she felt there was no need to mention her 'needs' as she felt that in 'nursing there wouldn't be any problems'. Following an assessment and the provision of tutorial support this student later remarked:

> . . . now I go to a tutor at Brighton, he helps me with writing and essays . . . they [the tutors] don't seem to know much about hospitals so it doesn't help in nursing . . . It's better now on the wards, I tell the staff that I have dyslexia . . . they seem to understand and help me with my spelling. I try to work really hard . . . that way they [the staff] seem very pleased with me. I don't get involved with the drugs and things . . . I just do what I did as a HCA [healthcare assistant].

Student 2

This student nurse volunteered, at the beginning of his course, that he had dyslexia. He was referred for an educational psychologist's report and is now in receipt of a computer and tutorial support. He said: 'I've always had difficulties with spelling and maths. I have to read things several times before it means anything . . . I know there is coursework and I will need some support . . .'. This student was very confident and appeared to be coping well with all the components of his course. As his personal tutor, and in the writing of this paper, I asked him whether he had problems in practice. His response was as follows:

> . . . It's blind panic . . . it's very difficult to do things slowly, reading and the like . . . I need to spend a long time . . . There was one occasion when I had to read the theatre list and check that the right notes were ready with the right patient. I just froze . . . they must have thought I was thick. They [the staff] don't like that; they want us to be in there quickly, so now I watch what they are doing and copy. If I don't hear clearly what they have said then it takes me a while to sort it out in my head . . . Once I've learnt the routine, it's fine. I haven't had to use the computer or do many assessments but that will be OK . . . they are mostly tick boxes.

I then asked the student whether the support he was receiving was helping in clinical practice:

> Not really . . . they are very good with writing and essays . . . and the computer . . . keeps telling me that I've repeated myself . . . or underlines sentences . . . but that isn't the same when on the wards . . . I've stopped going to the tutorials at Brighton . . . it didn't help . . . the computer is great for all those things.

When asked whether he thought there would be difficulties in practice he said:

... I don't tell them, it makes it more of a problem ... like a disability you know ... when I did my learning disabilities it made me think ... the criteria is often linked with IQ ... I don't think I'm stupid but other people may think so ... it's only a problem if I'm stressed ... once I know the routine it is all right ... I'll just have to get round it. Like take away ... in maths ... When I did my school placement I was with these children and I was helping with their sums ... if they had asked me something direct I would have been scared ... you know ... then I thought ... It's not just words ... it's more in your head where things are muddled you do know things but you can't see your mistakes.

Student support

Each student has a range of support provided and for all students this support is designed to assist them in the development of their skills in practice, to achieve the academic requirements of the course and to become a professional registered nurse. In practice, each student has an identified preceptor. Also, associated with that area of clinical practice is a link tutor who supports both the preceptor and, indirectly, the student. The student has an identified personal tutor and can be referred to student support services through the usual university mechanism.

Discussions with individuals from each group have highlighted the lack of awareness, knowledge or understanding about dyslexia and how this may affect the student's progress. All of those questioned thought that dyslexia was merely a difficulty in 'spelling and reading'. This view is common, the term dyslexia being synonymous with a range of learning disabilities predominantly recognized in childhood (Riddick 1996). A review of the literature has shown that there is little written about the impact dyslexia has on adulthood and in the workplace.

The students have identified some of the problems facing them in practice yet there appears to be a gulf between the learning support provided and the support that they felt was needed in the clinical setting. One factor that emerged from both students was their unwillingness to declare their need, as in the case of Student 2, who was concerned about being labelled as 'stupid'. In many cases, dyslexia appears to be identified only when coursework seems not to reflect student's ability. A number of students are being referred for an 'assessment' only after failing assignments. Webster (1994) suggests that tutors may not identify that there is a learning need and assume that the student is either less able or has been less conscientious with their course work.

Comments from various tutors about students with dyslexia have included the following: 'I just thought the student was not very bright ... the written work was all over the place. She seemed to be able to discuss the care but in reality she was unable to write down what she said'. Another tutor assumed in practice that the students 'sink or swim' and, while she recognized there might be a need, did not consider it her role to provide additional support. The lecturer who supported Student 1 commented:

> She is a very nice girl . . . but I am not sure whether she will make it. I have gone over her coursework several times but even after explaining things and showing her how to put things down it doesn't change. She can't seem to see what I am saying although she nods her head when I am with her but then goes and does something different. Even when I write things down . . . She has taken up hours of my time, now that she is doing it again [the student failed her coursework] I get her to write, then cut up her work into paragraphs and sentences, stick them down in a better order and then get her to write again. It is better – only just.

Other tutor's comments include: 'the support I give the student is far more than any other', 'I write down specific instructions and discuss issues in practice', 'there is not much I can do (in practice), as there is no time available', 'I am never sure if the student will be safe and I question my stance in supporting her, knowing she will never progress very far'. The preceptor of Student 1 voiced her concerns about the safety of the student in practice. These concerns stemmed from the fact that the student took a long time to read, had difficulty reading aloud at hand-over and could not recall the names of specific drugs and their dosages. She qualified her concerns by saying: 'I don't want you to think I'm being horrible . . . she is a good worker . . . and the patients like her . . . I just don't think she is safe'. The preceptor in this instance identified concerns over safety, which echo the concerns raised within the exam board setting. Other concerns raised by tutors also refer to clinical practice: 'It takes her a long time to settle into a ward, she can't change quickly and gets fixed on doing things in one way . . . if a patient questions her she panics . . . when she's unsure she smiles and nods but you know she isn't clear'. Another tutor remarked: 'I can't have someone like that in my area (coronary care unit) I need people who can think quickly, can make decisions and respond to every changing situation'. These comments, whilst reflecting concern over reading and writing, alluded to concerns over 'slower thought processes'. The preceptor for Student 2 remarked:

> He's very caring . . . and always checks things . . . sometimes he's slow but he is well liked by the patients and staff. He notices things and is always giving information . . . I think his slowness is because he is thinking . . . not making quick judgement . . . which is good here . . . He doesn't spend time writing . . . or on the computer.

This preceptor clearly valued the student's approach and considered him safe.

Following their educational psychology report both students were eligible for additional support ranging from computer equipment, extended time in examinations, group tutorials and sessions on study skills. What is apparent from the students is that, whilst they valued the offer of support, they could see its relevance only in the context of 'writing essays'. There is an obvious need to ensure that these skills are made relevant to the clinical setting. In starting this process, updates for nurse educators on the nature of dyslexia and strategies that can be used to overcome difficulties would be appropriate. A recent study-day by the learning support team on the nature of dyslexia and the support that could be offered was well received. Afterwards, many lecturers commented that the session had made them think about how they were supporting students and to reflect on what difficulties the students may face in practice.

Discussion and conclusions

The experiences of these students raise issues for the profession of nursing. As nursing has moved from the occupational to the professional arena, so there has been a shift in the preparation of nurses from the purely apprentice-led courses to courses supported by education from within the higher education framework.

It could be argued that the move into higher education had disadvantaged the nursing student with dyslexia, their difficulties being highlighted by the academic requirements of the course. Alternatively, it could be argued that by highlighting difficulties and providing support, we, as a professional group, have been forced to consider the impact of dyslexia on students' development and the level of 'reasoning' that we believe is required in nursing practice by the registered nurse. The students questioned had articulated that they could 'cope' in practice. Even the student whose needs were identified by the preceptor in practice was ultimately successful in the component of her programme. This suggests that much of the delivery of care, at this early stage, is not impeded by the apparent difficulties that were experienced by the students. These students coped, one by avoiding difficult and complex situations the other by learning the routine. What is not clear from all these views is whether they were functioning as developing professional nurses or merely as competent carers, if indeed it is possible to separate the two.

The United Kingdom Central Council (UKCC) clearly considers that the registered nurse is a practitioner who is capable of not only assimilating data but also of processing, analysing and making clinical judgements (UKCC 1992). Indeed, the NHS Executive, in its 1998 consultation document *A Strategy for Nursing, Midwifery and Health Visiting* (NHS 1998), clearly sees the registered nurse as fulfilling a complex role. It describes the nurse as being someone who values 'the essential aspects of caring', that 'restates the values which underpin nursing' whilst playing a key role in tackling 'health inequalities' and developing 'clinical and professional leadership'. The wording within the document implies that registered nurses will be assuming an intellectual role within which far-reaching decisions about nursing practice will be made. As a professional group we must ask whether dyslexia will inhibit a student's ability to attain such a level by restricting access to learning opportunities and the subsequent development of the qualities and skills that appear to be embodied in the professionalism of nursing.

One tutor clearly believed that, in an acute setting, dyslexia would compromise safety. This raises an issue as to the purpose of the preregistration course: is it to become competent in 'general nursing' or to equip students to function in all settings? The ENB (1993) clearly believes that the preregistration programme is a general qualification and that 'specialist' nurse education occurs at the post-registration level'. In this case, can a student with dyslexia become competent in general nursing? There is currently no evidence that the nursing student with dyslexia is unsafe (Cobley Parry 1997). In my own experience, students with dyslexia either acquire skills to overcome their disability or, as identified, function at a limited level within the practice area. Review of the guidance for students with 'special educational needs' provided by the ENB refers only to support within the context of examinations (ENB Circular 1990). No specific disabilities are identified to preclude a student from embarking on a nursing programme, the decision to accept a student remaining with individual institutions.

The assessment of practice documentation is designed to provide a comprehensive assessment of students' abilities. Yet the areas pertaining to using the skills, which an individual with dyslexia may find difficult, remain non-specific and couched in broad terms such as 'documenting data' and 'recognizing learning needs'. Indeed, Student 1 passed her assessment of practice even though the student herself identified that the focus of her activities were restricted to areas in which she felt safe – activities she had participated in as a healthcare assistant. Both students had identified that they restricted their activities, choosing situations in which they could function without reference to their disability. Such choices could be considered appropriate at this stage of their training. As they progress and are expected to take on greater responsibilities, these restrictions may inhibit their development unless they have developed the skills and confidence to overcome their disability.

Specific skills need to be identified and incorporated into the documentation and assessed at an early stage of the course. This strategy has been recommended by some institutions in the US (Magilvy and Mitchell 1995; Watson 1995) as disability became highlighted through the Americans with Disability Act (1990) (cited in Watson 1995). The specific skills could include 'safely taking verbal instructions', 'understanding of terminology used', 'accurate verbal and written reports on patient's condition and outcomes, including the making of clinical judgements' and 'accurate and safe administration of medications'. This could then provide a measure of the student's abilities and difficulties. When coupled with the educational report, this could form the basis upon which support is provided. The students voiced the need to have tutorial support within the environment

198   *Katharine Martyn*

in which they practised, using medical terminology and real situations. They both felt that to overcome the fears associated with 'giving verbal reports', 'taking notes during reports', 'completing drug calculations' and 'writing down data' these needed to be practised in the clinical setting. This support could encompass the recommendations of the educational report within the context of 'real work' situations.

The psychological report on each of the students clearly identified areas of difficulty. The recommendations for each student, however, focused on support within the context of teaching/learning and assessment, with no recognition or identification as to their needs in clinical practice. As the learning support team is not composed of nurses it is unrealistic to expect them to take the educational assessment and apply it to the context of nursing. The nurse lecturers could provide a valuable link between the formal support recommended by the educational assessment and the clinical setting. The lack of discussion within the university may reflect our uncertainty as to how dyslexia affects students in a clinical setting and our failure to identify specific areas to be considered or pose questions for which we, as a professional group, have no answers. It also reflects how little is known about the impact of dyslexia for adults in the workplace setting.

It has emerged from discussions with lecturers who are supporting students with dyslexia just how time-consuming the process is. Students are currently having one-to-one support that is both *ad hoc* and is not effectively linking the learning need to the clinical programme. An informed mechanism for linking the educational assessment, learning support and course requirements is required.

One common feature from both students was the 'fear' and 'panic' they experienced within the clinical setting. Thus, an approach that gradually builds confidence from one-to-one interactions to group participation may be an essential step in ensuring they overcome difficulties. The question is then raised about the students whose difficulties appear to be so great that the level of achievement they could reasonably expect, even with specific support, would still limit their ability to function in a clinical setting. How moral or ethical is it, as nurse educators, to support students through a process knowing that their career opportunities may be limited? With the changing role of the registered nurse it may be appropriate for us to reconsider who should be eligible for registration. With the increased demand for trained nurses there is inevitable pressure on recruitment of students. The answer may lie in becoming confident in identifying students at an early stage of their programme, offering appropriate support and assessing the outcome. Those students who fail to achieve the level of competency required could then be counselled to consider an alternative pathway. Within healthcare there is an emerging group of carers who complete a competency-based training through the NVQ route. Whilst they are ineligible for the professional registration they still fulfil a valuable role. Student 1 clearly articulated that she felt it unnecessary to inform us of the support she required, her belief that nursing is a 'non-academic' pursuit being reinforced by the very nature of nursing. In the hospital setting it is possible to be very involved in patient care and, as this student identified, avoid becoming involved in complex skills. By following an NVQ-based programme Student 1 could fulfil her desire to give care and could be rewarded by the achievement of a qualification.

As professionals, we must clearly establish the level at which we expect students to function. If they are unable to meet that standard then we must advise them that the professional route is not appropriate. This applies to all students and if at exam boards we continue to debate the issue of dyslexia then we must ask: 'what is our concern?'. A qualified nurse is a student who has met our criteria. At the end of each programme the student must demonstrate competence in the areas defined by Rule 18A (Nurses, Midwives and Health Visitors Act (DoH 1992b)). If we are saying that the student with severe dyslexia, having achieved our criteria, is not competent then we must review our course and assessment strategies.

Part 3

New Directions

11

A Framework for Personal and Professional Development

Linda Ball

Introduction

This chapter provides a rationale and a model for viewing personal and professional development as an integral part of students' higher education experience and preparation for their professional lives. For the future, graduates need to be self-starting, independent, critical thinkers, able to engage with the challenges of the changing workplace in the twenty-first century. As career progression and development in all sectors of the economy becomes less predictable, the responsibility increasingly falls on the individual, rather than on employing organizations, to manage their personal development and career progression (Ball 1997). Consequently, the skills and attributes of autonomy and lifelong learning become vital for the survival and continuing personal development of the individual. Therefore, personal and professional development needs to be embedded within the student experience to encourage lifelong learning habits for the future. How can this be achieved?

A model for personal and professional development (PPD)

The proposed model offers a rationale and framework for embedding these elements within the higher education experience. It has been developed progressively as a result of recent research into personal, professional and career development at the University of Brighton and experience with various curriculum innovations in design courses. Crafts Council funded research into students' learning experiences in the art, craft and design curriculum at the University of Brighton revealed that there is much potential through course delivery methods to produce 'self-sufficient' and independent learners. In particular, courses that make links with external projects or clients, exhibitions or work experience are found to help students to develop a range of important personal and professional skills and increased confidence in themselves and their work (Ball 1996).

Since 1994, personal and professional development (PPD) has been core study in the academic programmes in design and communication. Some of the learning activities have also been evaluated and the findings have helped to refine the learning activities with which students are engaging. Further work is continuing (Ball and Price 1999) as a result of a regionally funded DfEE development project, which aims to develop the curriculum to prepare graduates more effectively for business start-up and self-employment.

What are the wider implications of the model?

Many of the principles on which the PPD model is based have a potentially wider application beyond the art and design curriculum. These principles foster autonomy and the development of self-starting individuals who can manage their own personal and professional lives effectively, now and in the future – something to which all disciplines might aspire, certainly all the disciplines closely related to professional practice.

Prerequisites to the PPD model

Common approaches in the art and design curriculum

Before considering the proposed model, it is worth taking a look at some common approaches to including PPD in the art and design curriculum. These fall into four categories:

1. *ad-hoc* or bolt-on;
2. optional;
3. core study;
4. integrated/holistic.

A typical *ad hoc* or bolt-on activity is a one-off slide lecture by a practitioner talking about their practice, with the intention that students learn by example. Despite the obvious advantages of bringing the experience of a practitioner into the course, learning outcomes in relation to professional development may not have been made explicit. Students may not have discussed the significance of this as a learning opportunity beforehand and tend to focus on the visual work/artefacts shown by the speaker, rather than on the personal and professional aspects. These kinds of activities raise issues for students about their own creative practice but don't provide an opportunity for active learning.

Some institutions offer an optional programme or module covering aspects of professional practice. Attendance is not compulsory. The provision is not part of studio practice and it may or may not be assessed in any way. These programmes are sometimes delivered by careers staff or part-time lecturers and are not seen as part of mainstream study. Although, at best, these programmes offer students the opportunity for developing self-awareness and awareness of career opportunities, they rarely involve active learning and students are not able to relate their learning to their own creative practice.

Core study activities may involve work experience and industrial placement, sometimes with an opportunity for reflection on the learning outcomes achieved, or an assessed and compulsory programme involving students in examining issues relating to their personal, career and professional development, as well as aspects of design practice. Active learning may or may not take place.

Finally, an integrated or holistic approach involves all course activities and projects integrating PPD within them. The outcomes are made explicit and this approach communicates to the student that personal and professional development are integral to their degree studies. Students intuitively address and reflect on personal and professional matters throughout their studies. The practice of self-evaluation is an integral part of the assessment process. Learning agreements, learning reviews, self-assessment and reflection feature predominantly. These aspects are accredited, assessed, holistic and take account of a developmental process. The fully integrated and holistic approach needs a whole course team approach with a cohesive and explicit set of educational values. Examples of courses that demonstrate a holistic approach can be seen as full case studies in the Crafts Council research study (Ball 1996).

There is more potential for PPD learning outcomes to be recognized, valued and assessed in the last two categories (3. and 4.) than in the first two (1. and 2.). For this reason, PPD needs to be core study or integrated.

Principles for ensuring PPD provides a quality learning experience for students

So, how can institutions design their degree programmes to include PPD? Evidence from previous research (Ball 1996) and experience at Brighton suggests that five principles or requirements need to be met if PPD is to be included successfully. Students need:

1. to develop the skill of self-evaluation as a key personal and professional skill, providing the foundation for developing independent critical judgement;
2. a rationale for engaging in personal and professional development at all levels;
3. to build on experience, therefore a progressive, developmental model is proposed;

4. opportunities to rehearse and test their personal and professional development in the curriculum;
5. opportunities to reflect on their learning, so that they can articulate the
   outcomes in these areas.

Model for PPD

The model and framework in Figure 11.1 is based on the concept of a
continuum of learning, which integrates skill development and stages of
development. Each level, or stage, embraces knowledge, understanding and
personal and professional attributes. The value of the model is that it provides a rationale for staff to develop appropriate learning activities and for
students to use it as a framework to chart their own progress at each level.
The model is therefore presented to students as part of the learning materials and helps form the rationale for engaging with PPD programmes.

The model provides an entry/exit continuum. On entry, students are
normally in a state of dependence and seeking direction. Their critical
abilities and ability for self-evaluation are usually undeveloped and they
have a limited and untested working method. They are often inclined to
engage in a surface approach to learning and: '. . . focus their attention on
the details and information in a lecture or text. They are trying to memor-
ise these individual details in the form they appear or to list the features of
the situation' (Gibbs 1992: 182). Their immediate concerns are to acquire

Figure 11.1 Model and framework for PPD in the art and design curriculum

A continuum of learning

	Level 1	Level 2	Level 3	Post-graduation	
On entry					*On exit*
Dependence				Independence	
Seeking direction				Self-directed	
Surface learning				Deep learning	
Focus on product of learning				Focus on process of learning	
Abilities for self-evaluation undeveloped				Abilities for self-evaluation developing	
Critical abilities undeveloped				Critical abilities developing	
Unskilled				Skills used intuitively	
Working method undeveloped				Working method used intuitively	

Student – Researcher – Investigator – Practitioner – Consultant

Figure 11.2 Skill development continuum

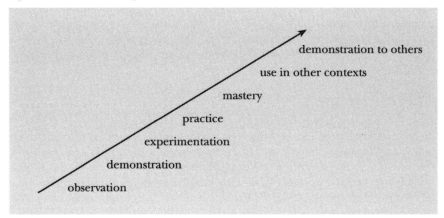

knowledge and skill so that they can produce a tangible result or product for evaluation by tutors – a body of studio work, an essay. On graduation, it is the intangible learning process that will have the longer life, not the degree-show portfolio of art work, which will have a limited life expectancy and value.

By the time they graduate, we intend and anticipate that our students are working and learning independently, with a well developed range of working methodologies, which they use intuitively. They are finding their own direction and able to direct and plan their own work. They recognize the value of their learning processes and are less focused on the end result. Their skills are well developed and often used without thinking (intuitively). The nature and direction of the work is bound up with personal meaning, leading to self-actualization or 'deep learning', in which 'they attempt to relate ideas together and construct their own meaning, possibly in relation to their own experience' (Gibbs 1992: 182).

The stages of development and skill development

Student, researcher, investigator, practitioner, consultant, represent the phases to be passed through, each stage building on the previous one. The levels of study are placed on the model to provide an indication of how students progress through the stages of development in their degree programmes. The consultant phase is more likely to occur after graduation, although recent work in progress (Ball and Price 1999) has indicated that if all 'stages of development' are included in one course activity, students experience a great sense of achievement.

The stages of development link closely with the skill development continuum in Figure 11.2, which provides a framework for the encouragement of skills of all kinds, from personal skills and attributes to technical skills in the studio or workshop. The case study 'Encouraging Graduate Business Start-up in Art and Design' (pp. 166–75) demonstrates one example of how the skill development continuum is applied in practice. Again, students need to understand their own skill development as part of the rationale.

PPD as core study

As already discussed, ideally PPD is embedded and integrated into all course activities. However, there is an argument for developing PPD as a core – but discrete – activity running parallel to all other course activities, although it must be accredited and assessed. This enables students to take an overview of all course elements and provides a forum for reflection, gives credibility to the learning processes themselves as learning outcomes and provides a framework with which students can continue their personal and professional development after graduation. As far as possible, practitioners, or staff skilled in facilitating student-centred learning activities in a professional development context will be involved in course delivery.

The following core study programme demonstrates the application of the model for PPD in art and design. The programme is designed, within a limited resource-base, around a series of workshops and seminars, with active-learning projects centred on students' own interests. A rationale runs throughout, involving labour market education and practitioners' experiences. This forms a compulsory part of study, running through all levels of degree programmes in design and communication at the University of Brighton. It is worth 12 credits at each level of study. All five of the principles discussed above are present in the course design and delivery methods at all levels that are set within the model for PPD above, and a learning outcomes approach to course design is used.

Professional practice Level 1 – approaches to study and learning

Entering the continuum of learning: student–researcher   A series of workshops and seminars run parallel with both contextual studies and studio work. Students are provided with 'Learning by Design,' a set of study guides written specifically for their needs. In participative workshops, students are introduced to a theoretical model for learning, based on a problem-solving learning cycle, and the wider learning value of art and design education and practice. The relationship between these and the world of work is made clear. Students discuss their own learning approaches and compare with others. They attend workshops on self-management skills, study skills and research skills. They put these into practice via individual and group research projects. To reinforce the importance of self-evaluation, they reflect on their experiences in an assessed reflective essay.

Learning outcomes   The students will gain:

- an understanding of the skills, qualities and attitudes they develop through the design process;
- an understanding of their own personal approaches to learning;
- the ability to articulate the above;
- a range of basic study and learning skills and will identify those that they need to develop further;
- an awareness of how to work in a group;
- experience of presenting themselves and their work to others;
- reflection on what they have learned;
- an awareness of their strengths and future interests.

Professional practice Level 2 – PPD

The transition period: researcher–investigator   This unit is concerned with the further development of students' working methodologies, study and learning patterns and professional development in support of the activities they are already undertaking in their chosen individual programme. It is delivered through a series of workshops involving staff and careers counsellors, who work with students to recognize transferable skills and learn about opportunities after graduation (labour market education). As in Level 1, students focus on their progress in all aspects of their course, identify strengths and possible future directions, thereby reinforcing their awareness of the value of reflection as part of the learning process. Students develop their personal, professional and transferable skills by identifying professional practice issues for investigation, making professional contacts and networking, individually carrying out an interview with a practitioner, writing up the findings in a professional practice assignment report and evaluating the result on a range of dimensions, including reviewing the personal and professional skills they have developed. They also evaluate the assignments of their peers.

Learning outcomes   Here the students are expected to achieve:

- an understanding of their own personal development and working methodologies as a continuous process;
- an understanding of the importance of transferable skills in relation to future career choice;
- an ability to make contacts with working designers in a business-like way;
- an awareness of the working lives and aspirations of practising designers;
- an ability to present themselves and their work;
- an opportunity to reflect on their learning, identify strengths and future areas for development;
- an awareness of a wide range of career paths open to them after graduation;
- the ability to assess their own and others' written professional practice assignments.

The learning can be great and each is a unique individual experience. Students are actively engaged in an investigative assignment, researching and eliciting information from practitioners. These are some examples of comments from students about the experience:

Understanding the person behind the work we are presented with as students adds great weight to the lessons we are being taught. To have the honour to *discuss* this first hand cannot be equalled.

I have found this interview a real eye-opener because being in a freelance practice is what I really want to do but I had concerns about it. This interview has answered many of my queries and worries, for example how easy it was to set up and what things have to be done to become successful.

An evaluation of the learning outcomes from this unit of study and, in particular, the professional practice investigative assignment, is shown in Figure 11.3.

When reflecting on their learning, students have identified a range of valuable professional, research, analytical and report-writing skills and important personal and self-management skills. Overall, students reported an improvement in self-confidence in dealing with professionals:

I found that finding someone to interview and all the processes of going through it had built up my confidence in approaching the real world. It has helped me to realize what it is going to be like starting up as a new designer and there are plenty of opportunities out there apart from design.

(3D crafts student)

Other valuable outcomes have also been achieved through this assignment. For example, work experience, further contacts and freelance commissions have resulted and sometimes students have received valuable feedback about their portfolios from practitioners. The importance of this assignment is that it involves practitioners.

Professional practice Level 3 – professional and business awareness

Preparing for graduation: investigator–practitioner   This unit is designed to introduce students to the basic aspects of design practice and to widen their appreciation of career opportunities after graduation. In Levels 1 and 2 students will have developed professional attitudes and approaches to their design studies. They will have acquired a range of personal and transferable skills through their working methodologies and they will have a basic understanding of the demands of design practice through completion of an investigative assignment. In this unit they will develop an awareness of the wider personal, professional and career opportunities where intellectual and personal skills, qualities and attitudes might be appropriate. Students

Figure 11.3   3D crafts and 3D design for production – Level 2 evaluation

	$n = 39$
	No. of times
What is the most valuable thing you have learned?	mentioned
To be able to relate comfortably to professionals	19
Learning directly from practitioners	15
Useful tips and information that can help them start up in business	14
Self-employment after graduation is a realistic option	12
Setting up and carrying out an interview	12
Networking and understanding the importance of business contacts	12
Self-confidence	12
Diversity and flexibility are necessary to survive as a craftsperson	7
Approachability of craftspeople and willingness to give information to students	7
The need for absolute commitment to your work	6
The importance of being direct with people	3
What personal and professional skills have you developed?	
Communication skills	28
Confidence in dealing with professionals	21
Organization and self-management	8
Analytical and writing skills	5
What have you enjoyed most?	
Relating to professionals	30
Carrying out an interview	20
A 'real life' case study	17
Researching and gathering the information	8
What was the most difficult thing you encountered?	
Organizing and setting up the interview	16
Recording the information gathered in the interview	7
Overcoming nerves about interviewing a professional	6
Writing up the report	6
Relating to a professional	5
Getting published information about their subject/interviewee	2

put their learning into practice through engaging in live projects and staging exhibitions (see the case study on pages 166–75). Finally, students work on their career development action plan, which is the assessed work.

Learning outcomes   On successful completion of this unit, the students will have:

- a further understanding of the importance of transferable skills in relation to future career choice;
- an awareness of the wider personal, professional and career opportunities where their intellectual and personal skills, qualities and attitudes might be appropriate;

- further experience of presenting themselves and their work to others;
- reflected on their learning, identifying strengths and future areas for development;
- an understanding of how to plan and carry out self-directed strategies to achieve personal and career objectives;
- an awareness of basic aspects of business organization and design practice.

Post-graduation – continuing professional development

Consolidating learning and finding a direction: practitioner–consultant   On exit from the university, graduates begin to engage with the world of work. Recent evidence (Press and Cusworth 1998) shows that our graduates are well equipped in a range of personal and professional skills and that they enter a wide range of activities, both related and unrelated to art and design. New developments at Brighton provide continuing professional development in the form of two modules at Masters level, which combine professional development with creative practice. Graduates enter a programme of business training alongside professional practice involving mentors. They also progress to the practitioner–consultant phase through appraising small design businesses and peer evaluation of career development and business plans.

Conclusions

The implications for academic staff and course delivery

The value of this model is that is provides a framework for PPD for both staff and students. In applying the model, the five principles and requirements need to be met within the course activities devised for the students to meet their learning outcomes. There are many issues to do with the ability of staff to design and deliver such programmes and, ideally, they will be delivered by academic staff who are also practitioners. However, unless the staff themselves are addressing their own PPD, they may be unable to help students to address theirs.

The implications are that staff can begin the process of course design by using the model as framework for their own PPD. For the future, with the move towards accreditation for teachers in higher education and the formation of the Institute for Learning and Teaching (see the case study 'Assessment and Standards in Implementing Accreditation of University Teachers' (pp. 176–84)), it is important that accredited programmes take a similar holistic approach to fostering PPD, so that academic staff value themselves both as education professionals and practitioners in their own fields.

As far back as 1989, art and design educators were debating the change in their role in response to heightened expectations of student capability

(CNAA/CHEAD 1989). They proposed a reappraisal of the tutor–student relationship and a: '. . . shift to facilitating the development of transferable skills and capabilities, a shift demanding changed teaching and learning approaches'. They recommended the emergence of a new tutorial role as facilitator, consultant and monitor of student performance; the student of the future will learn more as an individual, choosing to draw on the services offered rather than receiving a prescribed body of knowledge and technical expertise. The emergence of a new breed of practitioner–consultant in the academic environment in art and design is already taking place and initiatives that foster students' personal and professional development as independent lifelong learners are developing across many higher education institutions.

Professional skills for lifelong learning

Learning processes that involve self-evaluation, practice, reflection and setting future goals are the underpinning professional skills for lifelong learning. This was one of the most important findings of the Crafts Council study (Ball 1996) in which students described independent learning as:

> . . . 'self-sufficiency in learning' meaning the ability to assess one's work and progress, to make sound critical judgements, to reflect and set future goals. Furthermore, they regarded these processes as vital for survival beyond graduation and highly transferable to other situations.
>
> (Ball 1996: 4)

12

Professional Doctorates: The Development of Researching Professionals

Tom Bourner, Rachel Bowden and Stuart Laing

Introduction

Doctoral degrees have been part of higher education since the first was conferred in Paris in the twelfth century (Noble 1994). For six centuries professional doctorates in theology, law and medicine were pre-eminent until the modern Doctor of Philosophy (PhD) originated in Berlin in the early part of the nineteenth century and then spread across the German universities, attracting students from other countries, notably the United States.

In the US, the first PhD was conferred in 1861 at Yale. About 60 years later, and after significant resistance (Simpson 1983; Winfield 1987), the PhD degree finally arrived in the UK, the first being awarded by an English university (Oxford) in 1920. Almost simultaneously, the first Doctor of Education (EdD) appeared in the US, being awarded at Harvard in 1921. Again, it was more than 60 years later when the first British EdD finally emerged, launched in 1992 by the University of Bristol (Westcott 1997).

The Engineering Doctorate (EngD/DEng) also arrived in the UK in 1992. It was developed in response to the Parnaby Report (Science and Engineering Research Council (SERC) 1990, which highlighted concerns that PhDs were not providing industry with the skills for high level careers for engineers). The EngD was introduced at three centres, Warwick, UMIST and Manchester, and Wales. The four-year doctorate, incorporating a taught component as well as an industrial research project, was designed to: '. . . provide engineers with business and technical competencies by applying new knowledge to industrially relevant doctoral research, employing the skills gained from an intensive programme of taught coursework' (Engineering and Physical Sciences Research Council (EPSRC) 1997: 1).

The position today

How widespread is the professional doctorate today?

In 1998 we surveyed the position of professional doctorates in 70 universities in England, this included 35 'old' universities and 35 'new' universities.[1] We found 109 professional doctorates 'on offer' in English universities in 1998, many recently introduced.

This growth in professional doctorates has been accompanied by a sharp rise in research degree enrolments. In 1994 less than 55,000 students registered for research degrees (including professional doctorates), of whom less than 37 per cent were enrolled part-time. By 1997 there were over 100,000 research degree students, the majority part-time. These figures are particularly significant as most professional doctorate programmes are designed to be studied part time.

As part of the *Review of the EPSRC Engineering Doctorate Pilot Scheme* (EPSRC 1997) students were asked why they chose an EngD programme:

> The main reasons REs [research engineers, that is, those enrolled on EngD programmes] gave for enrolling on the EngD were the industrial relevance of the programme and the opportunity to improve their career progression. Several REs commented that they would not have done doctoral research if the EngD had not been available.
>
> (EPSRC 1997: 3)

A study (not yet published at the time of writing) by David Scott at the London University's Institute of Education reports no reduction of students wanting to do traditional doctorates since the introduction of the Institute's EdD. The development of professional doctorates appears then to be tapping into a previously unsatisfied market.

Which universities are offering professional doctorates and in which subjects?

In 1998, 38 of the 70 universities offered at least one professional doctorate, with (as shown by Table 12.1) much greater prevalence in 'old' (pre-1992) universities.

Twenty-six of the 35 'old' universities offered at least one professional doctorate as against only twelve of the 35 'new' universities. Of the 109 professional doctorates, only 23 were in 'new' universities.

This relative lack of development of professional doctorates in the 'new' universities is perhaps surprising, as studies directly related to professional practice (for example, education, engineering, business studies and health)

Table 12.1   Incidence of professional doctorates by age of university, 1998

	Universities with at least one professional doctorate	Universities with no professional doctorates	
Very old universities (pre-1900)	Durham London* Oxford	Cambridge	
Old universities (1900–50)	Birmingham Bristol Leeds Leicester Liverpool Manchester Newcastle Nottingham Sheffield UMIST	Reading	
'Oldish' universities (1951–91)	Bath Brunel City East Anglia Exeter Hull Keele Kent Open Southampton Surrey Sussex Warwick	Aston Bradford Essex Lancaster Loughborough Salford York	
New universities (1992)	Anglia Bournemouth Central Lancashire East London Kingston Leeds Metropolitan Lincolnshire & Humberside Manchester Metropolitan Middlesex Oxford Brookes Plymouth Teesside	Brighton Coventry De Montfort Derby Greenwich Hertfordshire Huddersfield Liverpool John Moores London Guildhall Luton North London Northumbria	Nottingham Trent Portsmouth Sheffield Hallam South Bank Staffordshire Sunderland Thames Valley UCE UWE Westminster Wolverhampton

* Each of the following colleges offered at least one professional doctorate: Imperial College, Institute of Education, London School of Hygiene and Tropical Medicine, King's College, Birkbeck, UCL and Royal Holloway.

Table 12.2 Incidence of professional doctorates across subjects, 1998

Subject/title of award	Short form of title most often used	Number of programmes
Doctor of Education	EdD	29
Doctor of Medicine	MD	20
Doctor of Clinical Psychology	DClinPsy	18
Doctor of Business Administration	DBA	9
Doctor of Engineering	EngD/DEng	8
Doctor of Psychology	DPsych	4
Doctor of Educational Psychology	DEdPsy	4
Doctor of Musical Arts	DMA/AMusD	2
Doctor of Architecture	DArch	2
Doctor of Veterinary Science	DVet Med/DVSc	2
Doctor of Dental Science	DDSc/DDS	2
Doctor of Public Health	DrPH	1
Doctor of Counselling Psychology	DCounsPsy	1
Doctor of Occupational Psychology	DOccPsych	1
Doctor of Clinical Science–Psychotherapy	DClinSci–Psychotherapy	1
Doctor of Psychoanalytic Psychotherapy	DPsychPsych	1
Doctor of Theology	ThD	1
Doctor of Fine Art	DArt	1
Doctor of Surveying	DSurv	1

have always figured significantly in the historic mission of the former poly-technics. One possible explanation is that until 1992 they were constrained in the awards they could offer by the CNAA, whose regulations allowed only for a Doctor of Philosophy. It is, however, difficult to regard this as the sole explanation, as most of the development of professional doctorates in the 'old' universities has taken place since 1992.

An alternative hypothesis is that 'old' universities have been more con-cerned to protect the 'gold standard' of the PhD by allowing develop-ment of alternative titles for professional doctorates, while perhaps being less concerned at possible reputational damage by the creation of entirely new forms of award. By contrast, the 'new' universities have appeared concerned to avoid proliferation of new doctoral titles (Frayling 1997) so that variants may have been squeezed into the Doctor of Philosophy category.

The range of subjects within the 109 awards is shown in Table 12.2.

Professional doctorates are as yet found in a relatively narrow range of subjects. In 1998 only five subjects had more than five institutions con-fering doctorates with the name of a profession in the title: education, psychology, medicine, engineering and business administration. These five subjects accounted for almost 80 per cent of the 109 programmes available.

The professional doctorate

Rationale for the development of professional doctorates in England

In 1993, an Office of Science and Technology (OST) White Paper (OST 1993: 3) expressed concern about the traditional PhD: 'The Government . . . is concerned, however, that the traditional PhD is not well-matched to the needs of careers outside research in academia or an industrial research laboratory'.

There was dissatisfaction that the highest university award was restricted to those interested in careers in 'research in academia or an industrial research laboratory'.

The basic rationale for professional doctorates is the desire to develop a doctoral level award to meet a broader range of career needs than those met by the traditional PhD. The subject that accounts for most professional doctorates is education, in the form of the EdD (see Figure 12.2). We analysed the documentation produced by universities offering professional doctorate programmes to identify what career needs are aimed at. We found that they are designed to provide research-based career development for experienced and senior professionals in education. For example:

> The degree [EdD] is aimed at experienced professionals in education who wish to extend their professional expertise and training, while not intending to become career researchers.
>
> (Brunel University)

> Increasingly the School of Education received applications from senior professionals who, while wishing to undertake advanced research, did not necessarily see this as an apprenticeship for a career in a university research department.
>
> (University of Leicester)

Rather than perceiving research as an end in itself, the new EdDs have placed research at the service of professional development, that is, the development of professional practice and of professional practitioners. This stance affects the nature of the research undertaken. Whereas the PhD student can, at least in theory, research any subject at all, candidates for professional doctorates are expected to undertake research aimed at making a contribution to professional knowledge and/or practice:

> [Professional doctorates] . . . are designed for candidates who wish to focus their research towards professional or industrial practice.
>
> (Leeds Metropolitan University)

> The professional doctorate is a rigorous research-based and research-driven qualification focused on the improvement of professional practice.
>
> (University of Lincolnshire and Humberside)

In many cases, the research is on a topic relating closely to the candidate's own professional practice:

The degree of EdD will provide the opportunity for experienced professionals in education and other public services, to work at doctoral level on problems that are of direct relevance to their own professional interests and institutional concerns.

(University of Sussex)

The EdD meets the professional research needs and develops the practical ability of educational professionals, particularly in terms of collaboration, reflexivity and responsibility: to enable them to meet the challenge of developing new and responsive practices and mediating new knowledge in their work environment.

(Leeds Metropolitan University)

If the traditional PhD is intended to develop professional researchers then the professional doctorate appears to be designed to develop researching professionals.

Intended learning outcomes of the professional doctorate

We then analysed the documents produced by universities offering the EdD with the aim of identifying intended learning outcomes. We found two major themes and a minor theme. The two major themes are: (i) contemporary educational issues and theory; and (ii) practitioner-centred research; the minor theme is professionalization and the nature of professional practice.

The following statements from the documentation show variations around the theme of 'contemporary education issues and theory':

... to extend and deepen ... knowledge and understanding of contemporary education issues and (develop) a high level of research and enquiry skills.

(Open University)

... develop a critical awareness of the implications of policies for practice.

(King's College)

... achieve a critical and conceptual understanding of the most recent developments in your field, based on a rigorous examination of current research and applied theoretical perspectives.

(University of Newcastle upon Tyne)

Two intended learning outcomes are discernible in these statements: (i) knowledge and understanding of theory; and (ii) knowledge and understanding of contemporary issues in the field. Each implies different curriculum perspectives and syllabus consequences. The intention to deliver knowledge and understanding of theory results in a syllabus focused on what is known within a subject. By contrast, the intention to convey knowledge and understanding of contemporary issues in a field is likely to result in a syllabus focused on what is not known, that is, current problems in the field.

There were also variations on the 'research' theme:

Undertake a research project or thesis which will contribute to professional knowledge and practice.

(University of Hull)

... develop high level skills of inquiry which will be applied to individual research studies of relevance to participants' professional work.

(King's College)

Overall we were able to discern three different intended learning outcomes related to research: the capacity to: (i) use research methods to resolve problems in professional practice; (ii) contribute to professional knowledge and practice in the field; and (iii) apply research findings to professional practice.

The final theme, less often present, is 'professionalism':

... develops both enquiry skills and an understanding of the nature of professionalism.

(London University's Institute of Education)

... an understanding of the issues involved in professionalisation.

(King's College)

The intended learning outcomes of the professional doctorate identified here can be compared with those of the traditional PhD, namely the knowledge and skills needed to design and carry out a research project resulting in a contribution to knowledge in the chosen field of study. This may be appropriate for an initial training in research for the professional researcher but is not broad enough to meet the development needs of experienced/senior professionals. Consequently, the espoused learning outcomes of the EdD programmes are broader, with implications for the form of professional doctorates.

Other distinctive features of the professional doctorate

All 70 universities offered the PhD degree and there appears to be a broad consensus about its definition as a programme of study requiring a significant contribution to original knowledge through an independent investigation, exhibited typically through a single extended body of work and recorded in a written dissertation.

How does a professional doctorate differ from this? While there is less consensus about what a professional doctorate involves, the following features are frequently present:

1. Modular structures. The extension of modularity to the doctoral level is a major curriculum development of the new professional doctorates. For example:

> The degree has a modular structure comprising 24 units – 12 taught units and 12 represented by the dissertation. The 12 taught units include four compulsory research methods units.
> (University of Bristol)

> Taught modules are designated either Research or Subject modules. Students have a choice about the balance of the two but the following framework applies:
> Overall rating of 540 credits comprised the following:
> • subject focused courses and assessment of 60 or 80 credits;
> • research training and assessment of 100 or 120 credits; and a
> • thesis of 360 credits.
> (University of Birmingham)

2. A taught component usually accounts for a minority of the programmes, often around 30 per cent, with some evidence of systematic variation across subjects. EngDs tend towards the lower end of the range, with the taught component comprising 20–30 per cent, while EdDs have 35–50 per cent.

   The taught component is often divided into two parts: (i) that focused on the subject; and (ii) research training.

   Subject-focused coursework is often shared with Masters courses. The EPSRC (1997) EngD review commented favourably on this: 'The training . . . is usually taken from Masters training at the host institution . . . In this way, it is externally accredited as high quality and at postgraduate level' (EPSRC 1997: 4).

   The research-focused taught component is sometimes shared with PhD students:

> The taught element of the programme is the equivalent of seven modules – a tailored Postgraduate Certificate in Research Methodology (three modules), Advanced Research Methods in Education, two further assessed level M modules drawn from an approved list, and one Dissertation module.
> (Leeds Metropolitan University)

3. There is considerable variation in the research component of professional doctorates. In some cases comparability with the PhD is emphasized:

> Overall, written work in the PhD and EdD degrees are of the same length, 100,000 words. They share a common insistence upon students undertaking work of publishable quality.
> (University of Leicester)

The research thesis of between 25,000 and 40,000 words must, in the same way as do all University . . . doctoral theses, make a distinct contribution to knowledge of the subject, and afford evidence of originality by discovery of new facts and/or exercise of independent critical powers.

(London University's Institute of Education)

In other cases the candidates carry out two or more research projects. For example: 'The research element of the programme consists of two substantive research outcomes, each of 30,000 words or equivalent' (Leeds Metropolitan University).

Sometimes, there is choice: 'Your research enquiry will lead to either a thesis of 40,000 words or will comprise a major and minor study which will lead to two theses of 25,000 words and 15,000 words respectively' (University of Bath).

4. The minimum qualification for admission was the same as for a PhD: a 'good', that is, first or upper second class, degree in a relevant subject. For those without this, a 'conversion' Masters degree is normally required.

    In addition, however, admission to a professional doctorate usually requires experience of professional practice. This is usually specified in terms of minimum years of relevant employment, varying between one and five years, with three years as the median figure.

5. Typically for a PhD, assessment is by written dissertation of approximately 40,000 words (science) to 80,000 words and an oral examination. On professional doctorate programmes, the subject-focused coursework units are usually assessed separately and sometimes, though less often, the research-focused coursework taught units are also separately assessed. Often assessment of the latter is through their contribution to the research component; which is usually assessed in the same way as the PhD, involving internal and external examiners and a viva.

6. Most professional doctorates are available for part-time attendance. Many can only be studied part-time. The rest of the time the student is expected to spend in industry or a professional organization. In some cases, candidates are registered full-time with the understanding that most of their time will be spent working in an industrial or professional organization. This is the case with the EPSRC EngD:

Students will be sponsored by an industrial partner who in return will benefit from having a research engineer working on a major project in-house.

(Brunel University)

The full EngD programme runs for four years and is based on a project or series of projects, normally carried out in a company . . . the work has to make a significant contribution to the performance of the company and thus has to be in the mainstream of operations.

(University of Warwick)

7. With most PhD programmes students may individually enrol at any time of the year. By contrast most professional doctorates recruit on the basis of cohorts:

> The cohort experience is introduced at the very beginning and is intended to enhance the collaboration and responsibility expected of high level professional practice.
> (Leeds Metropolitan University)

> Structured support is provided to the cohort and to the individual student through weekend and summer schools, in meetings with supervisors, by engagement with, and contribution to, the University's research culture through networking of peers and through the articulation of research findings in a culminating conference.
> (Leeds Metropolitan University)

Cohort enrolment enables provision of structured support often missing for part-time doctoral students, thus addressing the 'social and intellectual isolation' long recognized (Advisory Board for Research Councils [ABRC] 1982) as a problem facing doctoral students.

8. The duration of study for PhDs usually has been specified as a variable. For example, the following words appear in the degree regulations of several universities: '. . . for a full-time student, minimum of 24 months and a maximum of 60 months: for a part-time student, minimum of 36 months and maximum of 72 months'.

By contrast, professional doctorates usually have a fixed period as the normal duration of study:

> The professional doctorate is a part-time degree programme to be completed over 12 terms . . .
> (University of Sussex)

> . . . possible to study for the EdD on a part-time or mixed full-time/ part-time basis. This will normally require registration for two years on a full-time basis or four years on a part-time basis.
> (University of Exeter)

Specifying a normal period of registration clearly resonates with the cohort orientation of professional doctorates.

9. Starting point for research. The PhD candidate normally undertakes a preliminary literature search and review to identify a gap in the literature. The research proposal then aims to make a contribution to knowledge by filling the identified gap. For professional doctorate research the candidate is normally expected to start with a problem in professional practice needing investigation and resolution. The research within a professional doctorate starts from a perceived need in professional practice rather than a perceived need to add to the knowledge map of a particular subject discipline.

Conclusions

The development of the professional doctorate in England has been a phenomenon of the 1990s. Most development has taken place in the older (pre-1992) universities and in the fields of education, psychology, medicine, business administration and engineering. By 1998 about half of the English universities offered professional doctorates. We confidently predict that, in the light of the rate of development during the 1990s and informal indications of further developments currently in train, by the end of the 1990s professional doctorates will be offered by a substantial majority of universities nationally.

The basic rationale for professional doctorates is the need to develop an award at the highest level to meet a broader range of career needs than those being met by the traditional PhD. There are indications that the early development of professional doctorates started with the PhD concept and modified it by simply adding taught courses. As a developmental route this minimalist approach seems to have been a cul-de-sac, as there are also indications that these programmes have not recruited well. By contrast, programmes that started from a rationale derived from the educational needs of the groups for whom they are intended, moving to learning outcomes and then to programme structure and content, seem to have been more successful. An illustration of this is the EngD, where the Parnaby Report (SERC 1990) gave the early developers a clear rationale and set of learning outcomes to work from. The EPSRC initially supported three EngD developments at three (later five) centres and its 1997 review (EPSRC 1997) judged the results to be so successful that it proposed an extension to 15 centres. We conclude that universities that seek to develop professional doctorates by tinkering with PhD programmes and rebadging the result under the title of professional doctorates will have less success than those that work through their development from first principles.

The evidence we have examined also indicates a closer integration between Masters degrees and professional doctorates than between Masters degrees and the traditional PhD. It is possible to start a PhD with a good (first or upper second) undergraduate degree in a relevant subject so a Masters degree may seem superfluous. By contrast, the role of the Masters degree in the progression from undergraduate to doctoral studies is usually explicit in professional doctorates. In many cases, a Masters degree in the field of study is a requirement for admission to a professional doctorate and this is taken into account in the length of the doctoral programme. In the other cases, where entry to a professional doctorate is set at the level of a good undergraduate degree, the students are usually required to take Masters level units in the field of study. This implies more transparent progression through the Masters level of studies. This transparency is largely due to the fact that professional doctorates have extended the principle of modularity to doctoral level studies, which makes it clear what the student has achieved at Masters level and what goes beyond that to doctoral level.

A clear example of the operations of this principle is the Doctor of Business Administration (DBA); the large majority of DBA programmes require a Masters degree in the field of study (normally an MBA) and what takes the student to the DBA level itself is a programme of research-based management development (see Bourner, Bareham and Ruggeri-Stevens 1999). The needs of part-time students at senior practitioner level, combined with what modularity makes possible in terms of flexibility of combining taught and research postgraduate study, leads us to predict that this is a development of which we will see much more in the future.

Whereas the traditional PhD was designed to produce professional researchers, the new professional doctorates are designed to produce researching professionals. To date, the professional doctorates have shown their potential for putting research at the service of the development of professional practice and professional practitioners. Time will tell whether the research-based career development for which they were designed will, in reality, lead to senior practitioners in various professional fields who appreciate the potential contribution of research to professional practice and are equipped to find research-based solutions to the problems of professional practice.

Note

1. The 'old' universities: Aston, Bath, Birmingham, Bradford, Bristol, Brunel, Cambridge, City, Durham, East Anglia, Essex, Exeter, Hull, Keele, Kent, Lancaster, Leeds, Leicester, Liverpool, London, Loughborough, Manchester, UMIST, Newcastle, Nottingham, Open, Oxford, Reading, Salford, Sheffield, Southampton, Surrey, Sussex, Warwick, York.

   The 'new' universities: Anglia, Bournemouth, Brighton, Central Lancashire, Coventry, De Montfort, Derby, East London, Greenwich, Hertfordshire, Huddersfield, Kingston, Leeds Metropolitan, Liverpool John Moores, Lincolnshire and Humberside, London Guildhall, Luton, Manchester Metropolitan, Middlesex, North London, Northumbria, Nottingham Trent, Oxford Brookes, Plymouth, Portsmouth, Sheffield Hallam, South Bank, Staffordshire, Sunderland, Teesside, Thames Valley, UCE, UWE, Westminster, Wolverhampton.

13

Practitioner-centred Research

Tom Bourner, Suzanne O'Hara and Linda France

The previous chapter addressed the issue of the growth of professional doctorates. One of the outcomes of professional doctorates is a training in research.[1] In this last chapter of the book we take this theme forward by examining research for professional practice. In particular, we focus on the increasing expressions of concern about the limited contribution of research about professional practice to the practice of professional practitioners.

The problem is usually formulated in terms of the question: 'How do we raise the impact of research on professional practice?'. This is illustrated by the title of a recent conference on 'Raising the Impact of Research and Continuing Education' (June 1998). The flier for the conference stated that:

> Raising the impact of research is increasingly important for scholars in all fields. As well as engaging with practitioners and policy-makers, researchers also need to provide evidence that their work is well regarded by their peers.

This example is from the field of education but it could as easily have been from management, the other area of professional practice with which we have a professional familiarity. There seems to be recognition that education research makes too little contribution to the practice of teachers and that management research makes too little contribution to the practice of managers; we suspect that research on the practice of other professionals makes too little contribution to those professions also.

The 'impact of research on professional practice' is illustrated in Figure 13.1 as the arrow from professional research to professional practice.

Formulating the problem as: 'How do we raise the impact of research on professional practice?' suggests solutions along the lines of wider dissemination of research results and, in particular, attention to dissemination to practitioners as well as other researchers. Thus, for example, we have schemes to encourage the publication of PhD findings, we have concern expressed by the research councils that applications for research grants should include plans for dissemination of research findings beyond the research community

Figure 13.1   Relationship between research and professional practice

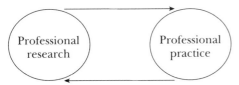

and we have statements from government ministers calling for the presentation of research results in a form that will be accessible to practitioners. In the words of Charles Clarke MP, then Minister of State at the DfEE: 'Findings must be presented in an accessible form so that a wide variety of practitioners can translate the implications into their context' (Clarke 1998).

These solutions would strengthen the arrow from research to professional practice.

The way that problems are formulated can have a critical impact on the answers that are available. Formulating the problem by the question, 'used above' focuses attention on the arrow from research to professional practice.[2]

Our intention is to reformulate the problem to: 'How can professional practice be enhanced by research?'. This is a broader formulation that shifts attention from the links *between* research and professional practice to encompass research and professional practice themselves. This formulation opens up more options. In terms of Figure 13.1, it directs attention to all three of its component parts: (i) research; (ii) professional practice; and the more common concern with (iii) the relationships between them.

In this chapter we offer a solution to the broader question: 'How can professional practice be enhanced by research?'. The following section explains why we believe that practitioner-centred research provides an answer.

Practitioner-centred research: a research process to enhance professional practice

Practitioner-centred research (PCR) aims to create improvements in professional practice by adding to the stock of usable knowledge of professional practice. It is the intentional creation of new knowledge of professional practice of a kind that can be shared by other professionals.

PCR starts from the following premises:

* research on professional practice has had too little effect on professional practice;
* professional practitioners themselves have much discretion over whether or not to adopt new professional practices;
* in deciding whether to adopt a new practice the common question: 'Does it work?' is less important than the practitioner-centred question: 'Can it work for me?'

What sort of knowledge do practitioners need to improve their practice? Consider an idea (hypothesis?) for an improvement in professional practice. What are the questions that a practitioner needs to be able to answer in order to accept and adopt the putative improvement? We suggest that there are three core questions: (i) 'Can this idea work?'; (ii) 'Can it work in the context of my own professional practice?'; and (iii) 'Can it work for me?'. Research that does not provide the knowledge to enable all three questions to be answered will have little impact on practice.

The research question that is usually asked: 'Does it work?', misses the point. That some practitioner somewhere has made a new practice work doesn't mean that it is a new practice that other practitioners in other situations are able or willing to adopt.

The concept of 'professional judgement' gives practitioners much discretion about the practices that they use. The decisions that practitioners take in the course of their practice, and the practices that they choose to adopt, are based on their skills, their professional knowledge and their values and beliefs. There are likely to be tacit aspects of their practice that are influenced by their beliefs and values, such their capabilities, and the criteria that they use to judge success or failure will be influenced by their beliefs and their values. Professional work is mediated through the beliefs and values of the professional practitioners. Practitioners will not adopt new practices if the beliefs and values that are embodied in the new practice are much different from their own.

A practitioner-centred research report will include all three of the following elements:

1. sufficient information about the emergent professional practice *per se*, to replicate it in the context(s) where it has proved successful;
2. sufficient information about the contextual factors on which the new practice depends to enable other practitioners to decide whether they can apply it in the context(s) of their own practice;
3. sufficient detail of the beliefs and values that underpin the practice to enable other practitioners to decide whether they want to adopt it in their own practice.

In practice, the second element is likely to take the form of information about the context(s) of its origin. This is the sort of contextual information that would be expected of sound, case study research. The third element is likely to take the form of information about the beliefs and values of the originators of the new practice. A practitioner considering whether to adopt a new practice needs an answer to the question: 'Am I enough like the originator(s) to be able to share their successful experience with a new practice?'.

In much the same way as scientific researchers have to be explicit about the physical context of their research results and social researchers have to be explicit about the social context of their research, so practitioner researchers have to be explicit about the personal context of their research.

In an important sense, professional people use themselves as the instruments of their work – and they themselves provide a personal context to the practices that they employ.

In the expression 'practitioner-centred research' we are using the term 'practitioner' to refer to professionals who have been educated and trained to engage in the work of professional practice and who have some discretion over how they carry out that work, that is, they are in a position to use their professional judgement in terms of their professional practice. This not only includes those who work in traditional professional areas, such as medicine, education and law, but also practitioners of many of the professions that have emerged more recently, such as: managers, engineers, counsellors, designers, consultants, social workers, and so on.

Subject knowledge and knowledge-of-practice

The distinction between 'subject knowledge' and 'knowledge-of-practice' is important for PCR. This distinction is most clearly seen in the case of lecturers working in institutions of higher education, where subject knowledge and knowledge-of-practice are very distinct. For an economics lecturer in a university, keeping up to date with subject knowledge is likely to include, for example, reading research results published in the *Economic Journal* and the *American Economic Review*, whereas keeping up to date with knowledge-of-practice would include knowledge of how to change teaching processes in response to the rising size of seminar groups. In a medical context, subject knowledge would include, for example, knowledge of the effectiveness of different kinds of drugs, whereas knowledge-of-practice would include knowledge of how to make use of new communications and information technologies within a doctor's practice. In a management context, subject knowledge would include knowledge of the impact of exchange rate changes on sales revenues, whereas knowledge-of-practice would include knowing how to modify staff appraisal practices in the light of changing career structures within organizations. PCR is about increasing the stock of 'knowledge-of-practice' rather than about increasing the stock of subject knowledge.

The researching professional

Whilst it is conceivable that professional researchers outside of professional practice could conduct PCR, in practice, we would normally expect PCR to be undertaken by professional practitioners.

Practising professionals themselves have a privileged position in engaging in this process as they are able to test out and refine their ideas through application to their own professional practice. Once they are clear that their ideas can work, they are in a position to disseminate them in a way that enables other practitioners in their field to evaluate whether the ideas will work for them too, that is, whether they will work in their own context(s) and whether they are willing to adopt them. In this way PCR is primarily located within the domain of the researching professional rather than the professional researcher.

PCR is a way of converting the personal learning from new developments in professional practice into knowledge that other practitioners can use and, by so doing, adding to the stock of knowledge available to all practitioners.

Epistemological basis of PCR

In this section we look at research in its most general sense, summarize some research traditions and then look at the implications for research designed to influence the practice of professionals.

We define research as the intentional creation of shared new knowledge. Each element of this definition is important:

- Intentional – because we recognize that knowledge can be created by accident, serendipity or as a by-product of some other process.
- Creation – is used in preference to the word 'discovery' because we want to include not only new knowledge of what already exists in the world but also knowledge of that which could exist but does not exist yet. In other words, we want a definition of research that includes not only 'discovery' but also 'invention'. That definition needs to be broad enough to encompass not only finding out about what currently exists in the world but creating new parts of the world.
- Shared – because new knowledge that is not shared does not add to the stock of knowledge from which we can all draw.
- New – because 're-inventing the wheel' doesn't add to the stock of knowledge.
- Knowledge – because research goes beyond merely providing more data.

Research in the science tradition

The ground rules of science were first systematically set out by Francis Bacon in the 1620s and were based on empiricism, induction and objectivity:

- Empiricism – that is, based on evidence drawn from the physical world (rather than, say, intuition or opinion).
- Induction – that is, basing general laws on the patterns found in the evidence.
- Objectivity – that is, independent of the influence of the values and beliefs of the researchers.

The ground rules of science are not immutable; in the last half of the twentieth century the 'induction' ground rule has been over-turned by the work of one person, Karl Popper, such that the core process has shifted from 'verification' to 'falsification'.

The modern tradition of science requires that investigators acknowledge that new scientific hypotheses can be the result of intuition or inspired guesswork, rather than the product of induction and that empiricism is more important at the stage when hypotheses are being tested than when they are being developed.

Research in the humanities tradition

Our professional backgrounds are not in the field of the humanities so we are guided by the words of the distinguished scholar, Professor Bruce Archer, former Director of Research of the Royal College of Art:

> Science still seeks ultimately to explain and Humanities still seek ultimately to evaluate . . . It is in the nature of the Humanities disciplines that their judgements are made within a framework of values. There is no such thing as 'objective' Humanities research. That is why it is so important for the investigator to declare his or her 'theoretical position'. Nevertheless, some Humanities research strives to present findings generalisable within a given context. In such a case, it is up to the reader to determine whether or not the argument and the findings remain valid in that or a different context.
>
> (Archer 1995: 9)

Several points are worth drawing out from this statement.

- The nature of research in the humanities tradition differs substantially from that of the science tradition.
- Science and the humanities seek to contribute two different kinds of knowledge: '. . . Science still seeks ultimately to explain and humanities still seek ultimately to evaluate . . .'.
- It is important for the humanities researcher to declare his or her theoretical position.
- Judgements, in the humanities research tradition, are made within a framework of values.
- It is for the reader of humanities research, rather than the researcher, to decide whether the findings remain valid in a different context from that of the original research.

We draw two key conclusions from the above.

1. The definition of research as 'the intentional creation of shared new knowledge' can contain research traditions as different as those of science and the humanities.
2. Within that definition of research different kinds of knowledge require different kinds (traditions) of research. In the examples above, contributing knowledge of explanations of physical phenomena requires research in the science tradition, whilst contributing knowledge of an evaluative kind requires research in the humanities tradition.

It is these two conclusions that lead to our contentions that:

• The kind of knowledge that professionals need for improving their professional practice is not identical with that provided by the science research tradition or the humanities research tradition.
• Just as science and the humanities require their own different research traditions so does professional practice.
• PCR offers a research tradition that is appropriate to deliver the kind of knowledge that professionals require to improve their professional practice.

A way of viewing the different kinds of knowledge of different fields of study is in terms of the kinds of questions brought by the users of the knowledge. Scientific knowledge is about explanation and people come to the stock of scientific knowledge with the question: 'Is this true?'. Humanities knowledge is about evaluation, so people ask the question: 'How good is this?'. As practitioner, knowledge is about usability, people need to ask: 'Can I use this?'.

Two examples

In this chapter, we have neither the space nor the intention to provide many detailed examples of PCR but it may help the reader to gain a clearer appreciation if we can provide a couple of examples. Accordingly, in this section, we give two examples: one drawn from our own work (O'Hara *et al.* 1999) and one drawn from the work of other researching practitioners (Brockbank and McGill 1998). Both examples are drawn from professional practice in the field of higher education, as that is the area where we have most experience.

Example 1: hi-fidelity case studies in management education

The hi-fidelity case study was developed as a way of overcoming the 'low-fidelity' of the traditional case study approach. In a 'hi-fidelity' case study, students (who are also practising managers) offer their own real, current, managerial problems to small teams of other students, who act as consultancy groups. These groups produce individual, customized solutions to the live problems and generate genuine management learning.

The low fidelity of traditional case studies results from insufficient contextual background and important questions that are left unanswered. It is not possible to delve any deeper than the written text of the traditional case: there is no-one to consult in person and interpretations of what might be the case remains exactly that.

By contrast, the hi-fidelity case study is a way of using the experience of practising managers as material from which to learn. Participants who supply the case material open themselves up to scrutiny from their peers; those in the consultancy team need to act professionally in a different environment and role. Also, all this really matters both for clients with real problems and the peers and friends acting as consultants. The role that members of the staff team take on during the exercise has elements of all of the following roles: facilitator, mentor, coach, supporter, minder and process observer.

One belief underlying this development in educational practice is that real problems in the 'here and now' offer more scope for significant learning than imaginary problems or edited descriptions of the 'there and then'. Another belief is that students learn more from those learning experiences that exercise their emotions as well as their intellects than from those that engage only their intellects. The people who developed the hi-fidelity case study value holistic learning and the emergent learning that goes beyond learning outcomes that are pre-planned by the tutor.

Example 2: practices to facilitate reflective learning

Brockbank and McGill's *Facilitating Reflective Learning in Higher Education* (1998) describes a number of practices that will be new to most professional practitioners in higher education. But a lecturer who believes that the only purpose of higher education is to convey critical understanding of a subject discipline is unlikely to be able or willing to adopt the new practices. Moreover, it would be disastrous if such a person were instructed to adopt the practices advanced in the book. It is not surprising that in this book Brockbank and McGill each provide short biographical sketches of their own experiences of education and their responses to those experiences. This helps to clarify for the reader where 'they are coming from' in terms of their beliefs and what they value in the practice of education.

What PCR is not

When we seek to convey the idea of PCR we find that people often relate it to processes and ideas with which they are already familiar. We often have the response: 'So is it then a form of X?'. The most common 'X's have been 'action research', 'reflective practice' and 'evidence-based practice'. In this section we seek to clarify the distinctions between PCR and these related ideas.

PCR is not action research

Action research is a form of social research that, typically, involves making changes to resolve a problem that exists in a social context. A commonly quoted definition is:

Action research aims to contribute both to the practical concerns of people in an immediate problematic situation and to the goals of social science by joint collaboration within a mutually acceptable ethical framework.

(Rapoport 1970)

The researchers in a programme of action research are often professional researchers from outside the 'immediate problematic situation' and it is not necessary to give explicit consideration or report their beliefs and values. By contrast, a necessary condition of PCR is that explicit attention be paid to the beliefs and values of the researcher–practitioners and that these be included within a research report. Also, PCR is eclectic in terms of research approaches and methods, so a researcher–practitioner may use processes used in action research but might equally choose to use the methods of 'appreciative enquiry', which was, in part, developed as a reaction against the problem-focused orientation of action research.

PCR is not reflective practice

Reflective practice includes individual practitioners engaging in evaluation of their own work to learn the lessons and thereby move their own practice forward. There is no necessary intention in reflective practice to create new knowledge that is available to other practitioners; the process of reflection can be an intensely personal and private one. By contrast, PCR, in aiming to create shared new knowledge of developing practice, is necessarily a public process.

PCR is not evidence-based practice

In theory, evidence-based practice means integrating individual practical expertise with the best available external evidence from systematic research (see Sackett *et al.* 1996). In practice, it often seems to mean that practitioners may not move their practice forward until there is clear evidence for a change in that practice. Evidence-based practice is largely about how and when to integrate new subject knowledge into professional practice, whereas PCR is about integrating knowledge-of-practice into the work of professional practitioners.

PCR is not 'simply talking to colleagues about experience'

'Empirical research' is not just 'anecdotal evidence' and, similarly, PCR is not just talking to colleagues. PCR requires the same attention to research rigour that is expected in other fields of research. Good PCR requires as much rigorous attention to the technical and objective aspects of an innovation in professional practice as that expected of a good scientific report; it requires as much attention to the physical and social context of the innovation as that found in good case study research. In addition, it requires that serious attention be paid to the personal context of the researcher–practitioners involved in terms of the beliefs and values that are embodied in the new practice.

Some implications of PCR

The centre of gravity of PCR lies with researching professionals rather than professional researchers. The development of PCR implies that professionals will need more training in research. They will need training in evaluating the research of others. This implication of PCR is similar to the educational implication of the more widespread adoption of evidence-based practice. But professionals will also need more training in using research methods to resolve problems of professional practice and in reporting their results. Consequently, research training is likely to play a larger role in programmes of education for professionals at both pre-service and in-service stages. In particular, the growth of professional doctorates supports, and is supported by, the rise of PCR.

A second implication of PCR for professional education is the need to address both researcher development and personal development within programmes of professional education. An awareness of the importance of beliefs and values for practitioner research implies that professionals need to pay explicit attention to their own beliefs and values, rather than allowing them to have an implicit effect on their practice. Our experience is that professionals often have difficulty articulating the values and beliefs that inform and affect their own professional decisions and practices, which sometimes lie entirely out of their conscious awareness. Clarification of those beliefs and values that have a significant effect on developing professional practice is a requirement of PCR.

A third implication is that PCR is likely to be resisted and probably dismissed by those professional researchers who feel threatened by the rise of researching professionals. At first sight, PCR does seem to pose a threat to professional researchers. However, this is an illusion. PCR is research-expanding rather than research-shifting. It creates scope for additional research within the fields of professional practice; it is not an alternative to the work of professional researchers. We expect to see more professional researchers in the future, alongside the rise of researching professionals, as the value of research to policy and practices is increasingly realized.

Professional researchers will continue to be valued in all those areas where they have been successful. The researching professional will extend the use of research methods and processes into domains that have proved relatively inaccessible to professional researchers. Professional researchers based outside the field of practice to be investigated will be preferred when 'close involvement' with the research topic is a disadvantage. For example, where it is difficult for practitioners to 'see the wood for the trees', where access to data is more accessible to outside researchers, where future problems are being investigated rather than current problems, where policy rather than practice is at issue and where the search is for universal principles.

Conclusions

PCR is concerned not only with the objective or technical component of an innovation or new development in professional practice but also with the beliefs and values that underpin it. The reason for this is that the decisions that professional practitioners take, and the practices that they adopt, are based not only on their skills and their professional knowledge but also on their beliefs and values. Consequently, professional practitioners are resistant to new practices unless they can accept that they are in accord with their own beliefs and values.

In this chapter we have looked at how research can enable new practice to be shared. We can summarize the argument in a number of propositions, some less contentious than others:

- Research has had too little impact on professional practice.
- Research can be defined as the intentional creation of shared new knowledge.
- The form of new knowledge that is sought determines the form of the research tradition.
- The new knowledge that practitioners need if they are to adopt a new practice must be sufficient to enable them to answer the following three questions: (i) 'Can it work?'; (ii) 'Can it work in the context of my own professional practice?'; and (iii) 'Can it work for me?'.
- A report of PCR requires: (i) an account of the researched practice, *per se*, and its outcome(s); (ii) an account of the context(s) in which it has been successful; and (iii) an account of the beliefs and values that underpin it.

We have sought to identify the elements of a research 'tradition' that will contribute to the kind of knowledge that would enable practitioners to decide whether or not to adopt a new practice. In doing so, we have drawn on different research traditions, including that of the humanities, where 'judgements are made within a framework of values' and where it is 'important for the investigator to share his or her theoretical position'.

We have argued that it is important for practitioners to be explicit about the beliefs and values underlying proposed new practices. If we are to practice what we preach then we should be explicit about the beliefs and values we see as most significant in terms of the practice of PCR. Key beliefs are:

- Professional practice can be significantly enhanced by research.
- Professional practice is mediated through practitioners beliefs and values.

And what are the key values? To stress that these are values we express them in the language of 'shoulds':

- We place a high value on the ideas and experience of practitioners. The ideas and experience of practitioners *should* be shared as a way of advancing professional practice.
- We value research as a means of resolving problems of professional practice. Practitioners *should* be enabled to use research processes as a way of resolving the problems of professional practice.

It is one thing to share new knowledge but another thing entirely to share new practice. It is not surprising that research that could affect professional practice has had little effect on professional practice: research reports have rarely provided practitioners with all the information that they need to enable them to decide whether or not to adopt new practice.

Notes

1. It is worth noting also that a research-based dissertation is virtually a standard requirement of Masters level courses in the subject disciplines that are closely related to professional practice.
2. We could, with profit, also look at the arrow in the other direction too; from professional practice to research. This could be strengthened by, for example, encouraging practitioners to engage researchers to investigate problems of professional practice, e.g. via professional bodies funding research into the problems of professional practice. However, even in this case we are still looking at the *relationships* between research and professional practice, which are represented in Figure 13.1 by the two arrows.

References

Advisory Board for Research Councils (ABRC) (1982) *Report of the Working Party on Postgraduate Education* (the Swinnerton-Dyer Report), Cmnd 8537. London: HMSO.

Alavi, M., Wheeler, B. and Valacich, J. (1995) Using IT to reengineer business education: an exploratory investigation of collaborative telelearning, *Management Information Systems Quarterly*, 19(3): 293–312.

Albanese, M.A. and Mitchell, S. (1993) Problem-based learning: a review of literature on its outcomes and implementation issues, *Academic Medicine*, 68(1): 52–81.

Anderson, G., Boud, D. and Sampson, J. (1996) *Learning Contracts: A Practical Guide*. London: Kogan Page.

Archer, B. (1995) The nature of research, *Co-Design Journal*, 1(2): 6–13.

Areskog, N. (1995) Multi-professional education at the undergraduate level, in K. Soothill, L. Mackay and C. Webb (eds) *Interprofessional Relations in Health Care*. London: Edward Arnold.

Argyris, C. and Schön, D. (1978) *Organisational Learning: A Theory of Action Perspective*. Reading: Addison-Wesley.

Ball, B. (1997) The career management skills required by graduates in a changing labour market, cited in Hustler, D., Ball, B., Carter, K., Halsall, R., Ward, R. and Watts, A. (1998) *Developing Career Management Skills in Higher Education*. National Institute for Careers Education and Counselling Project Report. Cambridge: Careers Research and Advisory Centre.

Ball, L. (1996) *Helping Students to Learn Independently in the Crafts*. Research study funded by the Save and Prosper Educational Trust, Crafts Council.

Ball, L. and Price, E. (1999) *Rethinking Business Start Up – A New Model for Success in Art and Design*. Graduate into Business, Research Report. School of Architecture and Design, University of Brighton/DfEE.

Barnett, R. (1994) *The Limits of Competence: Knowledge, Higher Education and Society*. Buckingham: Society for Research into Higher Education and Open University Press.

Barnett, R. (1997a) *Higher Education: A Critical Business*. Buckingham: Open University Press.

Barnett, R. (1997b) *Realizing the University* (based on an Inaugural Professorial Lecture delivered at the Institute of Education University of London). London: Institute of Education.

Barr, H. (1994) *Perspectives on Shared Learning: A Report from the Review of Shared Learning*. Nottingham: University of Nottingham, CAIPE Publications.

Barr, H. and Waterton, S. (1996) *Interprofessional Education in Health and Social Care in the United Kingdom: Summary of a CAIPE Survey*. London: Centre for Advancement of Interprofessional Education.

Barrows, H.S. (1986) A taxonomy of problem-based learning methods, *Medical Education*, 20: 481–6.

Barrows, H.S. (1996) Problem-based Learning in Medicine and Beyond: A Brief Overview. In L. Wilkerson and W.H. Gijselaers (eds) *Bringing Problem-based Learning to Higher Education: Theory and Practice*. New Directions for Teaching and Learning. San Francisco: Jossey-Bass, 68: 3–12.

Barton, L., Barrett, E., Whitty, G., Miles, S. and Furlong, J. (1994) Teacher education and teacher professionalism in England: some emerging issues, *British Journal of Sociology of Education*, 15(4): 529–43.

Basili, V.R. and Musa, J.D. (1991) The future engineering of software: a management perspective, *IEEE Computer*, 20(4): 90–6.

Bateson, G. (1973) *Steps Towards an Ecology of Mind*. London: Paladin.

Belenky, M.F., Clinchy, B.M., Goldberger, N.R. and Tarule, J.M. (1986) *Women's Ways of Knowing: The Development of Self, Voice and Mind*. New York: Basic Books.

Bengtsson, J. (1995) What is reflection? On reflection in the teaching profession and teacher education, *Teachers and Teaching: Theory and Practice*, 1(1): 23–32.

Bines, H. (1992) Issues in course design, in H. Bines and D. Watson (eds) *Developing Professional Education*. Buckingham: Society for Research into Higher Education and Open University Press.

Bines, H. and Watson, D. (eds) (1992) *Developing Professional Education*. Buckingham: Society for Research into Higher Education and Open University Press.

Bishop, M. (1998) *How to Build a Successful International Web Site*. Scottsdale, AZ: Coriolis.

Blackmore, P. (1997) The development of an intranet within a college of further and higher education, *Aslib Proceedings*, 49(3): 67.

Blake, D. and Hanley, V. (1998) The views of recently qualified primary PGCE teachers and their headteachers on effective initial teacher education, *Journal of Further and Higher Education*, 22(1): 15–24.

Bloom, B. (1956) Taxonomy of Educational Objectives – The Classification of Educational Goals (handbooks 1 and 2). London: Longman.

Blunkett, D. (1997) Parliamentary announcement, *The Lecturer*, special edition October 1997. London: NATFHE.

Bocock, J. and Watson, D. (1994) *Managing the University Curriculum: Making Common Cause*. Buckingham: Society for Research into Higher Education and Open University Press.

Bolgan, N. and Heycox, K. (1997) Use of an issue-based approach in social work, in D. Boud (ed.) *The Challenge of Problem-based Learning*. London: Kogan Page.

Booth, M., Furlong, J. and Wilkin, M. (eds) (1990) *Partnerships in Initial Teacher Training*. London: Cassell Education Ltd.

Borko, H., Livingstone, C., McCaleb, J. and Mauro, L. (1988) Student teachers' planning and post-lesson reflections: patterns and implications for teacher preparation, in J. Calderhead (ed.) *Teachers' Professional Learning*. London: Falmer Press.

Boud, D. (ed.) (1993) *Developing Student Autonomy in Learning*. New York: Nicholls Publishing Co.

Boud, D. (ed.) (1998) *Developing Student Autonomy in Learning*, 2nd edn. London: Kogan Page.

Boud, D. and Felleti, G. (eds) (1991) *The Challenge of Problem-based Learning*. New York: St Martin's Press.

Boud, D. and Feletti, G. (eds) (1997) *The Challenge of Problem-Based Learning*, 2nd edn. London: Kogan Page.

Boud, D., Cohen, R. and Walker, D. (eds) (1993) *Using Experience for Learning*. Buckingham: Society for Research into Higher Education and Open University Press.

Bourner, T. (1989) Action Learning: what's it all about? *International Foundation for Action Learning (IFAL) Newsletter*, 7(7): 5–10.

Bourner, T. and Flowers, S. (1998) Teaching and learning methods in higher education: a glimpse of the future, *Reflection On Higher Education*, 9: 77–102.

Bourner, T., Bareham, J. and Ruggeri-Stevens, G. (1999) *The Doctor of Business Administration: what is it for?* Unpublished paper, University of Brighton.

Bourner, T., Cooper, A. and France, L. (2000) Action Learning: from management development to generic university learning method, *Innovations in Education and Training International* (in press).

Bourner, T., O'Hara, S. and Barlow, J. (2000) Only Connect: Statements of Relevance, *Innovations in Education and Training International* (in press).

Bradshaw, D. (1992) Classifications and models of transferable skills, in H. Eggins (ed.) *Arts Graduates, their Skills and their Employment*. London: Falmer Press.

Brailsford, T.J. and Davies, P.M. (1997) Knowledge tree: putting discourse into computer based learning, *Association for Learning Technology Journal (ALT-J)*, 51, 19–26.

Braye, S. and Preston-Shoot, M. (1995) *Empowering Practice in Social Care*. Buckingham: Open University Press.

Breakwell, R. (1998) Along Cork Street, in L. Ball (ed.) Conference Report: 'Crafts 2000: a future in the making'. Tillington Hall, Stafford: November 1997. London: Crafts Council.

Bridges, D. (1993) Transferable skills: a philosophical perspective, *Studies in Higher Education*, 18(1): 43–51.

British Dyslexia Association (BDA) (1998) *A Guide for Lecturers and Tutors in Higher Education*. http://www/bda-dyslexia.org.uk/do2adult/a11hetut.htm.

British Standards Institution (1996) *BS 6079: 1996 Guide to Project Management*. London: British Standards Institution.

Broadbent, J., Dietrich, M., Roberts, J. (1997) *The End of the Professions? The Restructuring of Professional Work*. London: Routledge.

Brockbank, A. and McGill, I. (1998) *Facilitating Reflective Learning in Higher Education*. Buckingham: Society for Research into Higher Education and Open University Press.

Brooks, F.P. (1987) No silver bullet: essence and accidents of software engineering, *IEEE Computer*, 20(4): 10–19.

Brown, A. and Bourne, I. (1996) *The Social Work Supervisor*. Buckingham: Open University Press.

Bucher, R. and Strauss, A. (1961) Professions in progress, *American Journal of Sociology*, 66: 325–334.

Calderhead, J. (1987) The quality of reflection in student teachers' professional learning, *European Journal of Teacher Education*, 10: 269–78.

Calderhead, J. (1988) The development of knowledge structures in learning to teach, in J. Calderhead (ed.) *Teachers' Professional Learning*. London: Falmer Press.

Calderhead, J. (1989) Reflective teaching and teacher education, *Teaching and Teacher Education*, 5(1): 43–51.

Carpenter, J. and Hewstone, M. (1996) Shared learning for doctors and social workers: evaluation of a programme, *British Journal of Social Work*, 26: 239–57.

Cawley, P. (1997) A problem-based module in mechanical engineering, in D. Boud (ed.) *The Challenge of Problem-Based Learning.* London: Kogan Page.

Central Computing and Telecommunications Agency (1996) *PRINCE2.* London: The Stationery Office.

Centre for the Advancement of Inter-Professional Education (CAIPE) (1997–8). Bulletin report on a proposed systematic review of outcomes from inter-professional education. London: CAIPE.

Chadbourne, R. (1992) *The National Schools Project at Belmont Senior High School: A Formative Review of the First Nine Months.* Perth, Australia: International Institute for Policy and Administrative Studies.

Chang, C.K. and Chen, G.D. (1997) Constructing collaborative learning activities for distance CAL system, *Journal of Computer Assisted Learning,* 13(1): 2–15.

Chartered Society of Physiotherapy (CSP) (1991) *Curriculum of Study.* London: CSP.

Chartered Society of Physiotherapy (CSP) (1994) Clinical education working party guidelines for good practice for the education of clinical educators, *Physiotherapy,* (80)5: 299–300.

Chown, A. (1996) Post-16 teacher education, national standards and staff development forum: time for openness and voice? *British Journal of In-service Education,* 22(2): 133–50.

Clarke, C. (1998) Resurrecting research to raise standards, *ESRC Updates,* ESRC: Corporate News. http://www.esrc.ac.uk

Cobley Parry, R. (1997) Spell check, *Nursing Times,* April 16, 93(16): 38–41.

College of Occupational Therapists (COT) (1993) *Curriculum Framework for Occupational Therapy. SPP 161.* London: COT.

Committee of Vice-Chancellors and Principals (CVCP) (1998) *Accreditation and Teaching in Higher Education – Final Report* (Booth Report). London: CVCP.

Copeland, W.D. (1981) Clinical experiences in the education of teachers, *Journal of Education for Teaching,* 7: 3–17.

Council for National Academic Awards (CNAA)/Committee for Higher Education in Art and Design (CHEAD) (1989) 'On not sitting with Nellie,' a modest proposition on pressing issues of teaching and learning in higher education in art and design. Mimeo, CNAA/CHEAD.

Council for National Academic Awards (CNAA)/Committee for Higher Education in Art and Design (CHEAD) (1990) Teaching and learning in higher education in art and design, 2nd National Conference Report.

Council of Deans and Heads of UK University Faculties of Nursing, Midwifery and Health Visiting (1998) Breaking the Boundaries: Educating Nurses, Midwives and Health Visitors for the next millennium: a position paper. London: Council of Deans and Heads of UK University Faculties of Nursing, Midwifery and Health Visiting.

Crepaz-Keay, D., Binns, C. and Wilson, E. (1997) *Dancing with Angels: Involving Survivors in Mental Health Training.* London: Central Council for Education and Training in Social Work.

Cross, V. (1994) From clinical supervisor to clinical educator: too much to ask? *Physiotherapy,* 80(9): 609–11.

Cullimore, D. (1996) An investigation into the reporting of information technology skills in OFSTED inspections of business studies and economics in the South East and North East of England. Paper presented to the AEEE Conference, Cork.

Cullimore, D., Brumfitt, K. and Atkinson, A. (1996) An evaluation of the strategies for integrating information technology in the teaching of business education in the 14–19 curriculum, in W. Walstad (ed.) *Secondary Economics and Business*

Education New Developments in the United Kingdom, United States and Other Nations.
Sussex: Economics and Business Education Association.

Cusworth, A. and Press, M. (1997) Learning through making, working papers. Mimeo, Art and Design Research Centre, Sheffield Hallam University.

Davies, P. (1996) Effective use of information technology, in S. Hodkinson and M. Jephcote (eds) *Teaching Economics and Business.* Oxford: Heinemann.

Davies, R. and Ferguson, J. (1997) Teachers' views of the role of initial teacher education in developing their professionalism, *Journal of Education for Teaching,* 23(1): 39–56.

Department for Education (DfE) (1993) Circular 14/93: The initial training of primary school teachers: new criteria for courses. London: DfE.

Department for Education (DfE) (1994) Student numbers in higher education – Great Britain 1982/3 to 1992/93, *Statistical Bulletin,* 13/94, August.

Department for Education and Employment (DfEE) (1997) *Circular 10/97: Teaching: high status, high standards. Requirements for courses of initial teacher training.* London: DfEE.

Department for Education and Employment (DfEE) (1998a) *The Learning Age: A Renaissance for a New Britain,* Green Paper. London: HMSO.

Department for Education and Employment (DfEE) (1998b) *Higher Education for the 21st Century: A Response to the Dearing Report.* London: HMSO.

Department for Education and Employment (DfEE) (1998c) *Further Education for the New Millennium: a response to the Kennedy Report.* London: HMSO.

Department for Education and Employment (DfEE) (1998d) Circular 4/98: Teaching: high status, high standards. Requirements for courses of initial teacher training. London: DfEE.

Department for Education and Science (DES) (1989) *Circular 24/89: Initial teacher training: approval of courses.* London: HMSO.

Department for Education and Science (DES) (1991) Student numbers in higher education – Great Britain 1979 to 1989 *Statistical Bulletin,* 10/91, May.

Department for Education and Science (DES) (1992) Student numbers in higher education – Great Britain 1980 to 1990 *Statistical Bulletin,* 8/92, June.

Department for Education and Science (DES) (1984) *Circular 3/84: Initial teacher training: approval of courses.* London: HMSO.

Department of Health (DoH) (1992a) *The Patient's Charter.* London: HMSO.

Department of Health (DoH) (1992b) Nurses, Midwives and Health Visitors Act. London: HMSO.

Department of Health (DoH) (1997) *The New NHS: modern, dependable.* London: HMSO.

Department of Health (DoH) (1998) *Nursing Recruitment and Retention: Sharing Ideas.* London: HMSO.

Department of Health and Social Security (DHSS) (1989a) *Caring for People.* London: HMSO.

Department of Health and Social Security (DHSS) (1989b) *Working for Patients.* London: HMSO.

Dillon, P. (1998) A review of telematics in teaching and learning, *Journal of Information Technology for Teacher Education,* 7(1): 33–49.

Disessa, A. (1986) Artificial worlds and real experiences, *Instructional Science,* 14: 207–227.

Downie, R.S. (1990) Professions and professionalism, *Journal of the Philosophy of Education,* 24(2): 147–59.

Draper, S. and Oatley, K. (1991) Highly interactive visual interfaces. Video and tutorial notes, University of Glasgow.

Dworkin, G. (1988) *The Theory and Practice of Autonomy*. Cambridge: Cambridge University Press.

Elstein, A.S., Shulman, L.S. and Sprafka, S.S. (1978) *Medical Problem Solving: An Analysis of Clinical Reasoning*. Cambridge, Massachusetts: Harvard University Press.

Engel, C.E. (1997) Not just a method but a way of working, in D. Boud (ed.) *The Challenge of Problem-based Learning*. London: Kogan Page.

Engineering and Physical Sciences Research Council (EPSRC) (1997) *Review of the EPSRC Engineering Doctorate Pilot Scheme*. Report of the Review Panel to the Engineering and Physical Sciences Research Council. Swindon: EPSRC.

Engineering Council (1997) *Standards and Routes to Registration*, 3rd edn. London: Engineering Council.

English National Board (ENB) (1990) *Guidelines regarding provision for candidates who have handicapping condition taking examinations leading to entry to parts 1,2,3,4,5,6, 7,8,10,12,13,14,15, of the professional register*, ENB Circular 1990/17/RW. London: ENB.

English National Board (ENB) (1993) *Regulations and guidelines for the approval of institutes and courses*, Section 3, 3.83 April 93. London: ENB.

Eraut, M. (1992) Developing the knowledge base: a process perspective on professional education, in R. Barnett (ed.) *Learning to Effect*. Buckingham: Society for Research into Higher Education and Open University Press.

Eraut, M. (1994a) *Developing Professional Knowledge and Competence*. London: Falmer Press.

Eraut, M. (1994b) The acquisition and use of educational theory by beginning teachers, in G. Harvard and P. Hodkinson (eds) *Action and Reflection in Teacher Education*. Norwood, NJ: Ablex.

Eraut, M., Alderton J., Cole, G. and Senker, P. (1998) *Developing Knowledge and Skills in Employment*, Research report No. 5. Brighton: University of Sussex Institute of Education.

Erskine-Cullen, E. (1995) School–university partnerships as change agents: one success story, *School Effectiveness and School Improvement*, 6(3): 192–204.

Esselink, B. (1998) *A Practical Guide to Software Localization*. Amsterdam: John Benjamins.

Feletti, G. (1993) Inquiry based and problem based learning: how similar are these approaches to nursing and medical education? *Higher Education Research and Development*, 12(2): 143–56.

Flowers, S. (1996) *Software Failure: Amazing Stories and Cautionary Tales*. Chichester: John Wiley & Sons Ltd.

Franks, R. (1997) Practice makes perfect: an investigation into the practice component of some professional courses. Unpublished M.Ed. dissertation.

Frayling, R. (1997) *Practice-based Doctorates in Creative and Performing Arts and Design*. Warwick: UK Council for Graduate Education.

Fryer, R.H. (1997) *Learning for the Twenty-First Century*. First Report of the National Advisory Group for Continuing Education and Lifelong Learning. London: HMSO.

Galloway, S. (1998) The professional body and continuing professional development: new directions in engineering, *Innovations in Education and Training International*, 35(3): 231–40.

Garzia, R.P. (1993) cited in B. Riddick, *Living with Dyslexia* (1996) London: Routledge.

Gewirtz, S. (1997) Post-welfarism and the reconstruction of teachers' work in the UK, *Journal of Education Policy*, 12(4): 217–31.

Gibbs, G. (1992) *Improving the Quality of Student Learning.* Oxford: Oxford Centre for Staff Development, Technical and Educational Services Ltd.

Gijselaers, W.H. (1996) Connecting problem-based practices with educational theory, in L. Wilkerson and W.H. Gijselaers (eds) *Bringing Problem-based Learning to Higher Education: Theory and Practice.* New Directions for Teaching and Learning. San Francisco: Jossey-Bass, 68: 13–21.

Gillon, R. (1986) *Philosophical Medical Ethics.* Chichester: Wiley for British Medical Journal.

Glossasoft Consortium (1994) Methods and guidelines for interlinguality in software construction. Deliverables 9.1, 10.1, 11.1, LRE Project No 61003. http://www2.echo.lu/langeng/projects/glossasoft/index.html

Goffman, E. (1959) *The Presentation of Self in Everyday Life.* London: Penguin.

Guzzo, R.A. and Shea, G.P. (1992) Group performance and intergroup relations, in M.D. Dunnette and L.M. Hough (eds) *Handbook of Industrial and Organizational Psychology,* 2nd edn. 3: 269–313. Palo Alto, CA: Consulting Psychologists Press.

Halsall, R. and Hustler, D. (1996) Higher education – a clear sense of vision? in R. Halsall and M. Cockett (eds) *Education and Training 14–19: Chaos or Coherence?* London: David Fulton Publishers.

Hanson, D. (1997) *Cultivating Common Ground: Releasing the Power of Relationships at Work.* Oxford: Butterworth–Heinemann.

Harlock, L. and Knott, C. (1998) *Accrediting a Post Qualifying Year: A Model of Good Practice.* A Commissioned Report by CCETSW, London and South East Region.

Harris, M. (1996) *Report of the HEFCE, CVCP, SCOP Review of Postgraduate Education.* Bristol: HEFCE.

Harvey, L. and Bowes, L. (1998) *The Impact of Work Experience on the Employability of Graduates.* Presentation for the launch of the Centre for Work Experience, 20 October 1998, London.

Hastings, M. (1996) The importance of including mental health system survivors in approved social work training, in S. Trevillion and P. Beresford (eds) *Meeting the Challenge: Social Work Education and the Community Care Revolution.* London: NISW.

Hatton, N. and Smith, D. (1995) Reflection in teacher education: towards definition and implementation. *Teaching and Teacher Education,* 11(1): 33–49.

Henry, J. (1993) Managing experiential learning: the learner's perspective, in N. Graves (ed.) *Learner Managed Learning: Practice, Theory and Policy.* Leeds: Higher Education for Capability.

Higher Education Statistics Agency (HESA) (1996) *The Shape and Size of Higher Education in the Mid-1990s.* A Report for the National Committee of Inquiry into Higher Education. Cheltenham: HESA.

Higher Education Statistics Agency (HESA) (1997) *Students in Higher Education Institutions 1996/97,* Data Report. Cheltenham: HESA.

Higher Education Statistics Agency (HESA) (1998a) *Higher Education Statistics for the United Kingdom 1996–97.* Cheltenham: HESA.

Higher Education Statistics Agency (HESA) (1998b) *First Destinations of Students Leaving Higher Education Institutions, 1996–97.* Cheltenham: HESA

Higher Education Statistics Agency (HESA) (1999) *Student Enrolments on Higher Education Courses at Publicly Funded Higher Education Institutions in the UK for the Academic Year 1998–99,* HESA Press Release PR 29, 27 April.

Hodkinson, P. (1995) Professionalism and competence, in P. Hodkinson and M. Issitt (eds) *The Challenge of Competence: Professionalism through Vocational Education and Training.* London: Cassell.

Homer, R. (1998) *Report on the 'Alive' Videoconferencing Project – Potential Use for Mentor Support in Initial Teaching Training*. University of Brighton School of Education Occasional Paper, July 1998.

Honey, P. and Mumford, A. (1992) *The Manual of Learning Styles*. Maidenhead: Peter Honey.

Horder, J. (1991) Centre for advancement of inter-professional education: starving for collaboration, *Nursing*, 4(33): 16–18.

Hunt, M. (1979) Possibilities and problems of interdisciplinary teamwork, in M. Marshall, M. Preston-Scott and E. Winecott (eds) *Teamwork: For and Against. An Appraisal of Multi-disciplinary Practice*. London: British Association of Social Work.

Hurd, S. (1995) *3rd National Survey of Computer Use in Economics and Business*. Stafford: Staffordshire University Business School.

Institute for Employment Studies (IES) (1996) *University Challenge: Student Choices in the 21st Century*. A report to the CVCP, report number 306. Brighton: IES.

Institute for Learning and Teaching (ILT) (1998) *Implementing the Vision*. York: ILT.

Inter-Consortium Credit Agreement (InCCA) (1998) *A Common Framework for Learning*. London: DfEE.

Ives, B. and Jarvenpaa, S. (1996) Will the internet revolutionize business education and research? *Sloan Management Review*, 37(3): 33–42.

Jamieson, I. (1994) Experiential learning in the context of teacher education, in G. Harvard and P. Hodkinson (eds) *Action and Reflection in Teacher Education*. Norwood, NJ: Ablex.

Jarvis, P. (1983) *Professional Education*. Beckenham: Croom Helm.

Johnson, R.T., Johnson, D.W. and Stanne, M.B. (1986) Companion of computer assisted, cooperative and individualistic learning, *American Educational Research Journal*, 23, 3 quoted in P. Davis (1996) Effective use of information technology, in S. Hodkinson and M. Jephcote (eds) *Teaching Economics and Business*. Oxford: Heinemann.

Kano, N. (1995) *Developing International Software*. Redmond, WA: Microsoft.

Kaplan, I.P., Patton, L.R., Hamilton, R.A. (1996) Adaptation of different computerised methods of distance learning to an external PharmD degree programme, *American Journal Pharmacy Education*, 60: 422–5.

Kennedy, H. (1997) *Learning Works: Widening Participation in Further Education* (the Kennedy Report). Coventry: Further Education Funding Council.

Khan, N. and McAlister, S. (1992) *Study and Work in the Crafts – Survey of Student Perceptions*. London: Crafts Council.

Knott, C.A. (1994) *Crafts in the 90s*. London: Crafts Council.

Kolb, D. (1984) *Experiential Learning*. Englewood Cliffs: Prentice Hall.

Korthagen, F.A.J. (1988) The influence of learning orientations on the development of reflective teaching, in J. Calderhead (ed.) *Teachers' Professional Learning*. London: Falmer Press.

Larson, E.L. (1995) New rules for the game: interdisciplinary education for health professionals, *Nursing Outlook*, 43(4): 180–5.

Leggat, R. (1993) Student days on modem campus, *Computer Guardian Supplement, The Guardian*, 4 November: 17.

Leiba, T. (1993) Current developments in inter-professional education, *British Journal of Nursing*, 2(12): 631–3.

Lelean, S.R. (1973) *Ready for Report Nurse*, RCN research publication. London: RCN.

Lewis, J. and Glennerster, H. (1996) *Implementing the New Community Care*. Buckingham: Open University Press.

Lock, N. (1995) School experience in initial teacher education: management issues for headteachers of primary schools, *School Organisation*, 15(3): 313–27.

London Institute (1998) *Career Management Skills Project*. London: DfEE.

Magilvy, J. and Mitchell, A. (1995) Education of nursing students with special needs, *Journal of Nursing Education*, January 1995, 34(1): 31–6.

Maki, W.S. and Maki, R.H. (1997) Learning without lectures: a case study, *IEEE Computer*, May, 30(5): 107–8.

Margetson, D. (1998) What counts as problem-based learning? *Education for Health*, 11(2): 193–201.

Marsick V. (1990) Experience based learning: Executive learning outside the classroom, *Journal of Management Development*, 9(4): 50.

Marton, F., Beaty, E. and Dall' Alba, G. (1993) Conceptions of learning, *International Journal of Educational Research*, 19: 277–300.

Marton, F., Entwistle, N. and Hounsell, D. (1984) *The Experience of Learning*, Edinburgh: Scottish Academic Press.

McGill, I. and Beaty, E. (1995) *Action Learning*, 2nd edn. London: Kogan Page.

McGill, I., Segal-Horn, S., Bourner, T. and Frost, P. (1989) Action learning: a vehicle for personal and group experiential learning, in S.W. Weil and I. McGill (eds) *Making Sense of Experiential Learning*. Buckingham: Society for Research into Higher Education and Open University Press.

McLoughlin, D., Fitzgibbon, G. and Young, V. (1994) *Adult Dyslexia. Assessment, Counselling and Training*. London: Whurr.

McNay, I. (1995) From the collegial academy to corporate enterprise: the changing cultures of universities, in T. Schuller (ed.) *The Changing University?* Buckingham: Society for Research into Higher Education and Open University Press.

Middlehurst, R. and Kennie, T. (1997) Leading professionals towards new concepts of professionalism, in J. Broadbent, M. Dietrich and J. Roberts (eds) *The End of the Professions?* London: Routledge.

Moore, A., Hilton, R., Morris, J., Caladine, L. and Bristow, H. (1996) *The Clinical Educator – Role Development: A Self Directed Learning Text*. Edinburgh: Churchill Livingstone.

Morrell, P. (1997) Building intranet-based information systems for international companies, *Aslib Proceedings*, 49(2): 27–31.

Moss Kanter, R. (1994) Dilemmas of teamwork, in C. Mabey and P. Iles (1994) *Managing Learning*. London: Routledge.

Myhman, B. and Eriksson, B. (1997) *So You've Invested in a Videoconference System – But Why Don't People Use it?* Available: http://www.videoconference.com/feature.htm# Myhrman and Eriksson

National Advisory Council for Education and Training Targets (NACETT) (1998) *Fast Forward for Skills: NACETT's Report on Future National Targets for Education and Training*. London: NACETT, October.

National Committee of Inquiry into Higher Education (NCIHE) (1997) *Higher Education in the Learning Society* (The Dearing Report). London: NCIHE.

National Health Service (NHS) Executive (1998) *A Strategy for Nursing, Midwifery and Health Visiting*. Consultation document HSE. London: HMSO.

National Institute of Adult Continuing Education (NIACE) (1993) *An Adult Higher Education: A Vision*. Leicester: NIACE (England and Wales).

Noble, K. (1994) *Changing Doctoral Degrees: An International Perspective*. Buckingham: Society for Research into Higher Education and Open University Press.

Norman, G.R. and Schmidt, H.G. (1992) The psychological basis of problem-based learning: a review of the evidence, *Academic Medicine*, 67(9): 557–65.

Norris, D.M. and Dolence, M.G. (1996) IT leadership is the key to transformation, *Cause/Effect*, 19(1) Spring: 12–20.

Nummi, T., Ronka, A. and Sariola, J. (1998) *Virtuality and Digital Nomadism: An Introduction to the LIVE Project (1997–2000)* Helsinki: Media Education Centre, Department of Teacher Education, University of Helsinki, Media Education Publications 6 [http://www.helsinki.fi/~tella/mep6.html]

O'Hara, S., Reeve, S. and Flowers, S. (1999) Promoting autonomous learning on MBA programmes: a live consultancy case study approach. Unpublished paper, Management Development Research Unit, University of Brighton.

Office for Standards in Education (Ofsted) (1995) *Information Technology – A Review of Inspection Findings 1993/94.* London: HMSO.

Office of Science and Technology (OST) (1993) *Realising our Potential – Strategy for Science, Engineering and Technology.* London: HMSO.

Oliver, R. (1994) Information technology courses in teacher education: the need for integration, *Journal of Information Technology for Teacher Education*, 2(2): 141.

Øvretveit, J. (1998) Proving and improving the quality of national health services: past, present and future, in P. Spurgeon, *The New Face of the NHS*. London: Royal Society of Medicine Press Ltd.

Parlett, M. and Dearden, G. (eds) (1981) *Introduction to Illuminative Evaluation: Studies in Higher Education.* Guildford: Society for Research into Higher Education.

Perry, W. (1970) *Forms of Intellectual and Ethical development Through the College Years: A Scheme*, New York: Holt, Rinehart and Winston.

Pietroni, P. (1992) Towards reflective practice – the languages of health and social care, *Journal of Interprofessional Care*, 6(1): 7–16.

Pitt-Brooke, J. (1997) Review of the clinical educator: role development. A self-directed learning text, *Physiotherapy*, (83)11: 600.

Press, M. (1997) A new vision in the making, *Crafts Magazine*, 147, July–August.

Press, M. and Cusworth, A. (1998) *New Lives in the Making, The Value of Crafts Education in the Information Age.* Research commissioned by the Crafts Council, final report. Sheffield: Art and Design Research Centre, Sheffield Hallam University.

Rapoport, A. (1970) Three dilemmas in action research, *Human Relations*, 23(6): 466–513.

Rawls, J. (1971) *A Theory of Justice.* Cambridge: Cambridge/Harvard University Press.

Reeve, S. (1993) Some implications of open learning as curriculum strategy within further education, in N. Graves (ed.) *Learner Managed Learning: Practice, Theory and Policy.* Leeds: Higher Education for Capability.

Reeves, S. and Pryce, A. (1998) Emerging themes: an exploratory research project of an inter-professional education module for medical, dental and nursing students, *Nurse Education Today*, 18: 534–41.

Revans, R.W. (1982) *The Origins and Growth of Action Learning.* Bromley: Chartwell Bratt.

Riddick, B. (1996) *Living with Dyslexia.* London: Routledge.

Robertson, S.L. (1996) Teachers' work, restructuring and postfordism: constructing the new 'professionalism', in I.F. Goodson and A. Hargreaves (eds) *Teachers' Professional Lives.* London: Falmer Press.

Rogers, E.M. (1995) *Diffusion of Innovations*, 4th edn. New York: The Free Press.

Ross, R. (1997) Towards a framework for problem-based curricula, in D. Boud (ed.) *The Challenge of Problem-based Learning.* London: Kogan Page.

Rowntree, D. (1992) *Exploring Open and Distance Learning.* London: Kogan Page.

Russell, T. (1988) From pre-service teacher education to first year of teaching: a study of theory and practice, in J. Calderhead (ed.) *Teachers' Professional Learning.* London: Falmer Press.

Ryan, G. (1997) Ensuring that students develop an adequate, and well-structured, knowledge base, in D. Boud (ed.) *The Challenge of Problem-based Learning*. London: Kogan Page.

Sackett, D., Rosenberg, W., Gray, J., Haynes, R. and Richardson, W. (1996) Evidence based medicine: what it is and what it isn't, *British Medical Journal*, 312 (7023) 13 Jan: 71–2.

Sadlo, G. (1997) Problem-based learning enhances the educational experiences of occupational therapy students, *Education for Health*, 10(1): 101–14.

Sadlo, G., Warren, D. and Agnew, P. (1994) Problem-based learning in the development of an occupational therapy curriculum, part 1: The process of problem-based learning, *British Journal of Occupational Therapy*, 57(2): 49–54.

Schön, D.A. (1983) *The Reflective Practitioner: How Professionals Think in Action*. New York, NY: Basic Books.

Schön, D.A. (1987) *Educating the Reflective Practitioner*. San Fransisco, CA: Jossey-Bass.

Science and Engineering Research Council (SERC) (1990) *The Engineering Doctorate: A SERC Working Party Report* (The Parnaby Report). Swindon: SERC.

Searl, M. (1993) Campus without walls, *Times Higher Education Supplement*, 19 November.

Senior, K. (1998) Scheming out a career, *The Computer Bulletin*, March, 21–3.

Shaw, M. (1990) Prospects for an engineering discipline of software, *IEEE Software*, 7(11): 15–24.

Shulman, L.S. (1986) Those who understand: knowledge growth in teaching, *Educational Researcher*, 15(2): 4–14.

Siegel, D. (1997) *Secrets of Successful Web Sites: Project Management on the World Wide Web*. Indianapolis, IN: Hayden.

Silver, H. (1990) *A Higher Education: The Council for National Academic Awards and British Higher Education, 1964–89*. London: Falmer Press.

Simpson, R. (1983) *How the PhD Came to Britain: A Century of Struggle for Postgraduate Education*. Guildford: Society for Research into Higher Education.

Smith, J. (1997) An independent learning module: would it work for you? Sharing a Global Perspective, World Federation of Occupational Therapists Conference, Montreal, 31 May – 5 June.

Snowling, M.J. (1995) Phonological processing and development dyslexia, *Journal of Research in Reading*, 18(2): 132–8.

Sosabowski, M.H., Herson, K. and Lloyd, A.W. (1998a) Implementation and student assessment of intranet-based learning resources, *American Journal of Pharmaceutical Education*, 62(3): 302–6.

Sosabowski, M.H., Herson, K. and Lloyd, A.W. (1998b) Enhancing learning and teaching quality – integration of networked learning technologies into undergraduate modules, *Active Learning*, 8: 20–5.

Sosabowski, M.H., Herson, K. and Lloyd, A.W. (1999) Hurdles to successful implementation of 'learning trees', *British Journal of Education Technology*, 30(1): 61–4.

South East England Consortium (SEEC) (1997) SEEC Criteria Consortium for Credit Accumulation and Transfer.

Spurgeon, P. (ed.) (1998) *The New Face of the NHS*. London: Royal Society of Medicine Press Limited.

Stark, R. (1994) Supervising teachers and student teachers: roles and relationships in primary initial teacher education, *Scottish Educational Review*. 26(1): 60–70.

Statutory Instruments (1983) *Nurses, Midwives and Health Visitors Rules Approval Order*, 873, Norwich: HMSO.

Tait, J. and Knight, P. (1996) *The Management of Independent Learning*. London: Kogan Page in Association with Staff and Educational Development Association.

Taylor, I. (1997) *Developing Learning in Professional Education: Partnerships for Practice*. Buckingham: Society for Research into Higher Education and Open University Press.

Teacher Training Agency (TTA) (1996) Teachers for our future: could your school join a partnership for training new teachers? Norwich: HMSO.

Teacher Training Agency (TTA) (1998a) Circular 4/98: Teaching: high status, high standards. Norwich: HMSO.

Teacher Training Agency (TTA) (1998b) *National Standards for QTS, Subject Specialists and Head Teachers*. Norwich: HMSO.

Teaching Company Centre (TCC) (1996) *Work Based Learning for Associates: Guidelines*. Oxford: Teaching Company Centre Directorate.

Timmis, S., Brown, K.N., Gilbert, M.J. *et al.* (1998) *Student Learning Using CAL: Case Studies in the Evaluation of the PCCAL Consortium Commercial and Academic Services*. Bath: Commercial & Academic Services.

Trowler, P.R. (1998) *Academics Responding to Change: New Higher Education Frameworks and Academic Cultures*. Buckingham: Society for Research into Higher Education and Open University Press.

Trustrum, L., Grundy, R. and Bancroft, G. (1989) *The Business of Design: Professional Practice and Business Awareness in Design Degree Courses: Summary Report*. Research project funded by the Design Council/CNAA. London: Design Council.

United Kingdom Central Council (UKCC) (1992) *Code of Professional Conduct*. London: UKCC.

University of Brighton (1997) General Examination and Assessment Regulations. Brighton: University of Brighton.

Valli, P. (1992) *Reflective Teacher Education. Cases and Critiques*. Albany, NY: University of New York Press.

Van Manen, M. (1995) On the epistemology of reflective practice, *Teachers and Teaching: Theory and Practice*, 1(1): 33–50.

Vernon, D.T.A. and Blake, R.L. (1993) Does problem-based learning work? A meta-analysis of evaluative research, *Academic Medicine*, 68(7): 550–63.

Von Wright, J. (1992) Reflections on reflection, *Learning and Instruction*, 2: 59–68.

Wagner, L. (1995) A thirty-year perspective: from the sixties to the nineties, in T. Schuller (ed.) *The Changing University?* Buckingham: Society for Research into Higher Education and Open University Press.

Warnock, M. (1996) What a waste, *Times Higher Education Supplement*, 18 October, 18–19.

Watkins, C. and Whalley, C. (1993) Mentoring beginner teachers – issues for schools to anticipate and manage, *School Organisation*, 13(2): 129–38.

Watson, D. and Bowden, R. (1997) *Ends Without Means: The Conservative Stewardship of UK Higher Education 1979–97*. Education Research Centre Occasional Paper, University of Brighton.

Watson, D. and Taylor, R. (1998) *Lifelong Learning and the University: A Post-Dearing Agenda*. London: Falmer Press.

Watson, D.E. and West, D.J. (1996) Using problem-based learning to improve educational outcomes, *Occupational Therapy International*, 3: 81–93.

Watson, P. (1995) Nursing students with disabilities: a survey of Baccalaureate nursing programs, *Journal of Professional Nursing*, 11(3): 147–53.

Webster, G. (1994) A student's struggle – the problem of dyslexia, *Nursing New Zealand*, 2(3), 18–19 April.

Weinstein, J. (1994) *Sewing the Seams for a Seamless Service: A Review of Developments in Interprofessional Education and Training.* London: Central Council for Education and Training in Social Work.

West, M.A. and Poulton, B.C. (1997) A failure of function: teamwork in primary health care, *Journal of Interprofessional Care,* 11(2): 205–16.

Westcott, E. (1997) A professional in the dock, *The Times Higher Education Supplement,* 16 May, iii.

Wilderson, L. and Hundert, M. (1997) Becoming a problem-based tutor: increasing self-awareness through faculty development, in D. Boud (ed.) *The Challenge of Problem-based Learning,* London: Kogan Page.

Williams, A. (1995) School based initial teacher education: a benefit as well as a cost, *Journal of Teacher Development,* 4(3): 35–40.

Willows, D.M. and Terepocki, M. (1993) cited in B. Riddick (ed.) (1996) *Living with Dyslexia.* London: Routledge.

Winfield, G. (1987) *The Social Science PhD; The ESRC Inquiry on Submission Rates.* London: Economic and Social Research Council.

Winsor, K. (1997) Applying problem-based learning to practical legal training, in D. Boud (ed.) *The Challenge of Problem-based Learning.* London: Kogan Page.

Winter, R. and Maisch, M. (1996) *Professional Competence and Higher Education: The ASSET Programme.* London: Falmer Press.

Wright, N. and Cordeaux, C. (1996) Rethinking video-conferencing: lessons learned from initial teacher education, *Innovations in Education and Training International,* 33: 194–202.

Youll, P. and Walker, C. (1995) Great expectations? Personal, professional and institutional agendas in advanced training, in M. Yelloly and M. Henkel (1995) *Learning and Teaching in Social Work: Towards Reflective Practice.* London: Jessica Kingsley.

Zeichner, K., Tabachnik, B.R. and Densmore, K. (1987) Individual, institutional and cultural influences on the development of teachers' craft knowledge, in J. Calderhead (ed.) *Exploring Teachers' Thinking.* London: Cassell.

Zuber-Skerritt, O. (1992) *Professional Development in Higher Education.* London: Kogan Page.

Index

Page numbers in **bold** indicate whole case studies.